My Struggle for Life

JOSEPH KEATING

with an Introduction by
Paul O'Leary

UNIVERSITY COLLEGE DUBLIN PRESS
Preas Choláiste Ollscoile Bhaile Átha Cliath

First published 1916
This edition first published by
University College Dublin Press 2005

Introduction © Paul O'Leary 2005

ISBN 1-904558-44-5
ISSN 1393-6883

University College Dublin Press
Newman House, 86 St Stephen's Green
Dublin 2, Ireland
www.ucdpress.ie

Cataloguing in Publication data available
from the British Library

Introduction typeset in Ireland in Ehrhardt by
Elaine Burberry, Bantry, Co. Cork
Text design by Lyn Davies, Frome, Somerset, England
Printed in England on acid-free paper by Antony Rowe Ltd

CLASSICS OF IRISH HISTORY

General Editor: Tom Garvin

Original publication dates of reprinted titles are given in brackets

CONTENTS

MY STRUGGLE FOR LIFE

Note on the text

My Struggle for Life is printed as a facsimile of the original 1916 edition published in London by Simpkin, Marshall, Hamilton, Kent & Co.Ltd.

INTRODUCTION

Paul O'Leary

BIOGRAPHICAL NOTE

Joseph Keating (1871–1934), the son of Irish migrants, was born in the coalmining village of Mountain Ash in south Wales. His parents were of humble origins. His father, Cornelius, hailed from Cahirciveen in County Kerry, and his mother, Mary Hurley, was a native of Youghal in County Cork. They left Ireland when young with few material resources, and Cornelius remained a manual worker for the rest of his life. For reasons that are difficult to explain fully, a number of their seven children made considerable progress in life. One son, Mathew, who began life working in the mines, would become a journalist, Irish Nationalist MP for South Kilkenny (1909–18) and a director of Shell (Ireland); a daughter, Mary, married into a middle-class family and became active in the women's suffrage movement. A fascination with, and commitment to, politics is a theme that unites these children and might explain their note-worthy social mobility in the context of the period. Other siblings made new lives for themselves in other ways: John became the repre-sentative of an engineering firm, while Kate married and migrated to the United States where she and her husband farmed in Iowa.

Joseph Keating was no exception to the family trend. From unpromising beginnings as a door boy in a coalmine and a series of dead-end jobs, he obtained work in the commercial department of a newspaper and became a popular novelist. By the end of his life he had published eleven novels, a book of short stories, a translation of one of Émile Zola's novels, and had had a play of his performed in the West End of London. His autobiography, *My Struggle for Life*, was published in 1916.

One of the interesting features of *My Struggle for Life* is the light it sheds on the identity of second-generation Irish people in Britain, a group that has become the subject of some debate recently.[1] While Joseph Keating came to be seen by later commentators primarily as a Welsh working-class writer, it is clear that for him his identity was more complex and hybrid than that description implies. Here is how he describes himself in 1916:

> I was entirely Irish in every way – in blood, traditions, sympathies, training, and temperament. I regarded Ireland as my country . . .
>
> Yet this bit of Wales, where I was born and had spent my first twenty years was so rooted in my Irish heart that I neither would nor could think of any other place on earth as my home. It seemed to me that the feeling of nationality had nothing to do with the land of birth, but was inherited in the blood.[2]

This statement provides an intriguing insight into the sensibilities of second-generation Irish people, many of whom identified strongly with Ireland despite living in another country for the entirety of their lives. What is rarely discussed in the case of such people in Britain (unlike Irish Americans) is that their identities often embodied a duality, that of Irish ethnicity and an attachment to their place of birth outside Ireland. Because this tended to avoid an explicit attachment to Britain (at least among the Catholic Irish), this phenomenon has been difficult to study.

My Struggle for Life provides acute and insightful observations about how this complex identity was formed. It sheds light on the nature of social life in an Irish-Catholic community in the diaspora towards the end of the nineteenth century, sensitively evoking the texture of family life and extolling the virtues of Irish working-class 'neighbourliness'. As Joseph claimed later: 'There was no bawdy talk in the young men's conversation . . . The girls of the colony were bright-eyed and pure . . . the rate of illegitimacy would work out at, perhaps, two in a million.'[3] This dewy-eyed description was all of a piece with his development as a romantic novelist.

This Irish community exemplifies what the historian David Fitzpatrick has characterised as 'the middle place' occupied by the Irish in Britain between 1870 and 1914, a transitional stage characterised by a move away from the social exclusion and alienation of the decades surrounding migrants at the time of Great Famine in the 1840s but without yet achieving full integration in British society by the outbreak of the First World War.[4] The Irish community in which the Keating children were born and raised ('The Barracks') displays some features of the so-called 'clannishness' of the earlier period, while beginning to shake off the worst effects of that forced introspection. Joseph Keating's view of his upbringing – written from the perspective of 1916 – emphasises the direction in which Irish working-class settlements in Britain subsequently developed.

In this context, Joseph's account of his childhood is particularly engaging. At the beginning of the 1870s Mountain Ash was – as he would write when older – 'a charming pastoral village set in a wooded valley and sheltered by wonderful mountains'. For the child, therefore, life in this emerging industrial settlement was counter-balanced by the close proximity of an altogether different environment comprising fields and woodland, farming and wildlife. This provided an adventure playground in which the boy – and his imagination – could roam freely. Nevertheless, it was a rural world at one remove, in which a consciousness of the lives of those who laboured on the land was absent; for Joseph himself, rural life as a lived experience must have resided solely in the oral tradition of his family recalling their past lives in Ireland. As he discovered when he entered the world of work in his early teens, the boundaries of his own life were shaped by the demands of industrialism.

Even allowing for the mellowing perspective induced by the passage of time, his description of his birthplace in terms of pastoralism successfully captures the sense of an industrial settlement which had not yet become totally urbanised, either in terms of its size or its prevailing culture. The complete transformation of this area of the south Wales coalfield by the processes of rapid economic growth and high rates of in-migration from rural Wales and England had still not yet occurred and would only really gather pace when Keating was a young adult. Then it would become for him a darker place, marred by spoil tips, its inhabitants surrounded by a 'network of shunting trucks, with the glare of pit-lights, blacksmiths' fires, the shrieking of steam engine whistles, and the clatter of colliery machinery'. Elsewhere he would write that civilisation had advanced 'barbarously'.[5] His way of envisioning this change and writing about it owes a great deal to the genre of romantic fiction that he had embraced by the time he wrote his life story.

During the 1870s most adult inhabitants of Mountain Ash, whether they were Welsh, Irish or English, would have spent their formative experiences in rural society elsewhere. This is evident in the cultural practices they brought with them to south Wales. Joseph's vivid descriptions of folk customs, like the wake of his grandmother, provide an unrivalled historical source about the culture and social habits of the Irish in nineteenth-century Britain, and demonstrate how the rituals of private life were transported from the Irish countryside to new urban or, in this case, semi-urban settings. Consistent with his interpretation of his community as being a particularly moral one, Joseph described the wake in terms of a ritual of prayer, smoking, snuff-taking, storytelling and good-naturedness; curiously, there is no reference to the drinking of alcohol or elements of misrule that often characterised such events elsewhere in the region as well as in rural Ireland.[6] His descriptions help to take us beyond the hostile observations of the behaviour of Irish migrants provided by many outside observers in the mid-nineteenth century and reveal a determination to appear 'respectable'.

It is undoubtedly at this stage of his life that a life-long fascination with storytelling was born. Joseph was clearly fascinated by the folk tales related at home during his youth, and perhaps the outlandishness of the characters he heard described finds a distant echo in the popular novels he would write as an adult. His formal education was, in the terminology of the school system of the time, 'elementary', and it is unlikely that a grounding in the basics of literacy and numeracy did much to encourage his literary aspirations. He left the local Catholic school at the age of twelve, and worked for six years in a local colliery, initially as a door-boy earning six shillings and sixpence a week. At fourteen he went down the pit, where he progressed from collier boy to pit labourer and, finally, haulier. He left the pit at eighteen.

In the little leisure time he had during this period he studied shorthand, Euclid and French grammar and read as many novels as he could get hold of. His description of his approach to this material as reading and studying in 'unmethodical abundance' is typical of working-class autodidacts of the period. Although he spent a relatively short period of his life working at a colliery, the experience clearly made an enormous impact on him and influenced the choice of subject matter in a number of the novels he would write. Even though he moved on to a variety of jobs that included working as a fitter's labourer, a shorthand clerk, a scavenger and a travelling salesman, none of these occupations excited his imagination as much as the all-encompassing world of the colliery. Finally, he became a junior newspaper reporter in south Wales and subsequently attempted to launch a full-time career as a writer in London.

Our major source for these biographical details is the autobiography *My Struggle for Life*. As a writer who began life in the manual working class, he had broken away from the practice of his Victorian precursors, who sought to solve the problem of writing about their class mainly through autobiography, by first writing a number of novels and short stories based on that experience. But he did not succeed in fully overcoming the difficulties of structure and form posed by the novel, and in many ways his most abiding and engaging piece of writing remains *My Struggle for Life*. Despite this, the book cannot be considered separately from his fictional writing. It is more than a re-telling of 'the facts' of his life and is clearly shaped by the approach he adopted to writing stories and novels.

THE WRITER

Some of Joseph Keating's novels were little better than romantic potboilers, but several contain examples of genuine literary ability and succeeded in reflecting some of the wider social concerns of the period. The cultural critic Raymond Williams described Keating's fiction as 'one significant moment of emergence or perhaps, more strictly, pre-emergence' in the Welsh industrial novel.[7] However, an emphasis on the transitional nature of his fictional writing begs a number of important questions (a transition *from* what *to* what?) and has detracted attention from the way his writing reflected some of the concerns and debates in British society between 1900 and 1918. The remainder of this Introduction attempts to locate his writing and his ambition to become a full-time writer in the specific circumstances of late-Victorian and Edwardian Britain.

Like many other working-class writers of his time, Keating was unable to afford to buy contemporary fiction during his teenage years and early adulthood and had no access to a library from which he could borrow it. As he was only able to purchase second-hand books, he relied exclusively on established (indeed, in most cases dead) writers for his reading matter. Thus it was that he read Swift, Pope, Fielding, Richardson, Smollett, Goldsmith, Sheridan, Keats, Byron, Shelley, Dickens, Thackeray and the classical Greek philosophers. Consequently, his literary sensibilities and ambitions were shaped by the classics rather than more contemporary developments in the novel. Together with the difficulties of adapting working-class life to the conventions of the middle-class novel, the influence of this reading matter formed a formidable obstacle to him finding a distinctive voice in his fictional writing. Aware of his inadequate education and his lack of formal instruction in writing, he decided to seek assistance in the technical aspects of grammar and composition from a tutor, assisted by independent study. It was at this time that he began familiarising himself with psychology through the works of Herbert Spencer in an attempt to gain a deeper understanding of human motivations.

In 1895 he gave himself five years to secure an acceptance from a publisher. His first two attempts at fashioning a publishable novel were failures and later he attributed their deficiencies to his using material from outside his personal experience. In 1899 he began *Son of Judith: A Tale of the Welsh Mining Valleys*, which was published the following year after rejections from six publishers. This book has been identified as one of the very few examples of a novel at the turn of the century that portrayed the lives of the industrial working class.[8]

One reviewer commended the author for his fidelity in representing the working-class speech of the coalmining valleys of south Wales and praised *Son of Judith* as being 'a capital piece of workmanship'. Nevertheless, he claimed that the plot was one of 'Æschylean gloom' and that the subject matter was 'mean and sordid' because of the class of people it concerned; this was its principal weakness from 'the popular point of view'.[9] Joseph Keating would have taken this type of criticism to heart, because as well as seeking an outlet for his creativity in the novel he was intent on making a living out of writing. In this respect, there was always a tension between his rootedness in a specific culture and his ambitions as a writer. For someone from his background in the early twentieth century, attempting to become a full-time writer was an unusual ambition and a formidable challenge. As such, he was sensitive to the needs of the market, particularly as expressed to him by publishers and reviewers, and it is probably responses to his first published novel that eventually persuaded him to experiment with less familiar social contexts.

Son of Judith was not a great financial success. Like other aspiring authors of the period who attempted to become professional or semi-professional writers, Keating depended to a large extent on the publication of short stories in some of the many periodicals that came into existence during the 1890s and the first decade of the twentieth century. These publications catered for a new reading public, juxtaposing articles on self-improvement with fiction of a romantic kind. Moreover, the move away from dependence on the serial novel, which had been such an influential feature of fiction writing in the nineteenth century, meant that editors of magazines were willing to accept short pieces that could be composed and dispatched fairly quickly. This development in publishing provided an entirely new avenue into the world of full-time writing for aspiring writers. Keating took full advantage of the opportunities this innovation afforded him by publishing in various literary magazines on both sides of the Atlantic.[10] To improve his connections with publishers he moved to London briefly in 1904 and returned there in 1906.

An initial group of his stories were collected in a volume published in the year he returned to London. The contents vary from what appear to be no more than simple character sketches to more fully worked short stories and they have the air of preparatory studies, just as a painter might sketch an individual before beginning a bigger work. Part of this was determined by the demands of the magazines. It is in this slim volume that we see his imaginative engagement with the industrial society of south Wales most clearly. As the title – *Adventures in the Dark* – indicates, almost all are set below ground in the mines, probably a unique example at that time of fiction being located in an enclosed world of work that few who read the book could have known at first hand. The dominant image of the pit that emerges in these stories (and in a number of his novels) is that of a living organism, breathing, creaking and moving, requiring respect from those who enter it and specialist knowledge to navigate its dark passages safely.

The perspective from which Keating approached his subject matter was distinctively Catholic:

> In the 'Angelus', Millet's peasants are bending under a whole world of sadness, while across the fields come the sounds of the Angelus bell like the voice of their souls whispering spiritual consolation. Turning from Millet's peasants to the hills-people, I saw in the character of the collier the same monumental simplicity and heroism.

This initially unexpected identification of the peasants in Jean-François Millet's painting *The Angelus* (1857–9) with mineworkers in industrial south Wales is revealing. Keating's writing tried to keep in creative tension a romantic view of working-class life and the reality of manual labour in the colliery below ground as he had experienced it. It was, at root, an attempt to equate the complexity of social relations in industrial society with the perceived simplicity of peasant life in the countryside. This effect is achieved as a result of the essentially closed nature of social relations in mining communities, where physical community often coincides with class, and because of the possibility of seeing the miner's life as entwined with nature much as the peasant's existence is. Although Keating was aware of, and admired, the classic French novel of coalmining life, Émile Zola's *Germinal* (1885), and wrote in a compelling way about the world of work, his attachment to a view of the miner as virtuous hero prevented him from fully developing this aspect of his writing. But it is also the case that his desire to exploit his personal experience of manual work was curbed by his need to make a living from his writing and the perception of what his audience would buy.

Joseph Keating's romantic novels have usually been viewed in opposition to his industrial novels, whereas for him the two categories were inextricably intertwined. He made this clear in a prefatory note to the novel that achieved greatest commercial success, *Maurice: A Romance of Light and Darkness* (1905), in which he defined 'romance' as 'a painted portrait of reality':

> The painter of a portrait and the writer of romance are bound by the same principle. The painter must not put in colours and features that are not in his subject. On the other hand, he must be able to see all the real tones and characteristics of his subject, pass them through his brain to the end of his pencil, and reproduce them in their essential, not accidental, relationship. Then his picture will shine with meaning, and will light the world to a new truth. This, of course, calls for an eye that sees in life more than is visible, a mind that reads more than is written in nature's lines. It is like seeing the idea in the conception, before it has left the brain to be imperfectly set down in writing.

The apparent confusion between 'romance' and 'reality' identified by some later commentators is, in fact, at the heart of popular romantic writing. According to one critic, the appeal of romance as a genre lies precisely in its capacity for dissolving the boundaries between the actual and the potential.[11]

Keating continued his explanation of the melding of romance and reality in his writing by injecting a religious sensibility in the discussion. He describes the way in which 'the value of bringing to the world some fragment of a new truth' resides in its ability to bring us to a more complete understanding of 'the Almighty's design, and nearer to that ideal of perfection, which, despite our worldly malpractices, is the secret and eternal desire of the soul'. His imagination was rooted as much in visual culture as it was in a literary sensibility:

> My desire was to construct huge pictures of life, with real details of what I had seen, felt, and thought, all moulded into wonderful harmonies of story, truth and characterization. I saw each of my books as if it were a human heart telling its story.[12]

Ultimately, however, his commitment to the conventions of romantic writing ensures that his novels are imprisoned in a Manichean view of the world, expressed in terms of a series of contrasting dualities: light/dark, good/evil, beauty/ugliness. Arguably, it was this mindset that prevented him from fully exploring through his fiction the more fluid and complex nature of the identity he inhabited throughout his life, one that was rooted in a distinctive Irish migrant community but which was also entailed negotiating between that heritage and the society around him. It is only in his autobiography that he dealt with this issue successfully.

In 1910, the year he returned from London to Mountain Ash, *Maurice* (1905) was reprinted in a cheap sixpenny series, this time with a different subtitle: *The Romance of a Welsh Coalmine*. This was a clear attempt by his London publisher to take advantage of the interest sparked by industrial unrest in the British coalfields at that time, and especially because of the controversy created by the infamous riots at Tonypandy in the Rhondda Valleys. It was this, rather than the renewed interest in Wales sparked by the peasant novels of Caradoc Evans (as Stephen Knight has claimed[13]), that prompted Keating to engage once more with authentically Welsh material. The controversial use of troops at the mining township of Tonypandy – sanctioned by the then Liberal Home Secretary Winston Churchill – ensured that the incident became rooted in the history and traditions of the British labour movement.[14] *Maurice* was one of the few fictional interpretations from inside a mining community to explain the hidden working world of the coalminer to a wider public. However, it is almost as though the explicit assertion of romance in the book's subtitle in 1910 was an attempt to gloss over the naked class conflict that had emerged in the region, thus making his story more palatable to an audience outside mining communities. An article by Keating in the Conservative *Western Mail* a little later demonstrates his determination to save the good name of the Welsh miner from accusations of lawlessness.[15] Significantly, the reprint of *Maurice* carried an endorsement on the flyleaf from the Liberal government minister David Lloyd George, who hailed it as being 'true to life' and an accurate depiction of the character of the people who lived in the coalfield and the conditions under which they lived and worked.

Keating's complete identification with the myth of the virtuous miner, which had been part of the dominant culture in south Wales since his childhood, was demonstrated most clearly by his attitude to 'foreigners'. At first sight, this is one of the most paradoxical aspects of his writing. The plot of *Maurice* turns around the presence of 'foreigners', shady continentals who are immediately identifiable by the way they dress and by their secretive and suspicious behaviour. Although the novel also features an Irishman,

Grig, from Kerry, he is clearly not 'foreign' in the same way and acts as the eponymous hero's guardian. This lack of foreignness is not achieved by playing down Grig's ethnicity; in fact, Grig acts as the personification of Ireland:

> Grig's eyes and features told of the more particular fact of nationality. His great forehead, square, with its high corners of most pronounced ideality, bespoke the imaginative Celt. But it was not the Cymric Celt. There were peculiar lines in his face. Humour and sadness were written in them so plainly – yet so subtly that they defied reproduction. But if in desperation you wanted to put his nationality beyond all question, you would say, 'The map of Ireland was in his face'.[16]

The clear distinction made here between the Irish and 'foreigners' is symptomatic of an imperial mentality that drew boundaries between the peoples of the United Kingdom and those considered to be 'un-British'. Blaming outsiders for criminal or otherwise morally reprehensible behaviour was a feature of the defence of the heroic and virtuous miner, and it was a theme Keating returned to in his newspaper piece of 1911.[17] It is a telling fact that he felt able to re-position Irish migrants as 'insiders' by establishing a contrast with characters of dubious morals from other countries.

While the years of industrial unrest ensured that fiction located in a coalmining environment retained a certain topicality, there was a limit to the appetite of London publishers for material of this kind. Even so, branching out into other areas was not easy. A novel set in London high society, *The Great Appeal* (1909) had received unexpected publicity from the magazine *London Opinion*, which placarded the Strand proclaiming 'Novelist Insults the King', but it was still a commercial failure. In 1910 he published short stories in the *Pall Mall Magazine* and the *Red Magazine*, but by Easter 1911 he was experiencing difficulties selling his stories. Furthermore, he could not find publishers for two new novels he had written, in spite of the fact that their subject matter chimed with fashionable topics of debate. He concluded disconsolately that his 'attempts at writing to please the public were failures'.

This situation was exemplified by developments in 1912. During that year he courted bitter public controversy over the manuscript of a novel called *The Marriage Contract*. Comparisons between this work and a novel by H. G. Wells called *Marriage* published that year ignited a debate in *T. P.'s Weekly* (the newspaper founded by T. P. O'Connor, the Irish Nationalist MP and journalist) about the then controversial and emotive subject of divorce. During the nineteenth century the law had increasingly intervened to regulate private relationships within the family, while demands for women's suffrage chipped away at the paternalistic ideology of family life. In 1912–13 a Royal Commission sat to discuss divorce. Many novelists addressed issues of this kind during these years, with authors of the so-called 'marriage novels' rejecting the formula of a plot ending with a redeeming marriage of contentment for the key protagonists.[18]

Joseph Keating's contribution to this genre was castigated by a number of commentators who had been invited by *T. P.'s Weekly* to give their judgement on whether the book should be published. One of the weaknesses they identified was his lack of sure touch in describing unfamiliar social situations. By locating the plot in the social environment of the upper classes, he allowed his characters to commit a series of social faux pas in fictional settings that he would undoubtedly have committed in person had he found himself in similar social situations to those he portrayed. This was, after all, a class society that policed social difference by a myriad of tiny habits and unwritten rules of behaviour that were designed to identify and confound social outsiders. Consequently, Maud Churton Braby, the author of conservative marriage manuals, was able to declare the novel's plot and characters too far from real life to pose a serious moral dilemma.[19] Because of the treatment of adultery in the book, the writer and critic C. E. Lawrence concluded that it was 'possibly a novel that would appeal to that (presumably) large section of the public which requires in its fiction, not life, reality or art, but the frankly erotic'.[20] He rejected comparisons with H. G. Wells's novel on the grounds that Keating's treatment of adultery was too flippant. Although in retrospect the subject matter and the fictional treatment of it appear to be innocuous, the issue was a major problem for contemporary sensibilities: another critic castigated Keating for inviting sympathy with a female character who had 'dishonoured her husband'.[21] In total, it took five years to find a publisher for this manuscript, but once it was accepted in 1914 it reached a second edition within five weeks of publication. In the meantime, he was saved financially by another novel, *The Perfect Wife* (1913).

One aspect of the difficulty Keating experienced in navigating between the vividly realised world of manual work that characterises some of his literary output and the conventions of the romantic novel is his inability to create convincing and realistic depictions of women. The difficulty might have stemmed in part from the close relationship he had with his mother in what was clearly a matrifocal Irish household.[22] His autobiography is revealing on this point and demonstrates the way he idolised – and idealised – those women he apparently knew best. Significantly, a concern with women and marriage dominates the titles of much of his literary output. Even so, Keating appears to have experienced considerable difficulty in imagining female characters, to the extent that at one stage in his writing career he required a female friend to 'model' the characters he wished to depict. One critic of *The Marriage Contract* summed up his lack of understanding of female psychology as being 'limited by his masculine bluntness'.[23] His depictions of the physicality of the kind of masculinity found in industrial society are always more convincing and authentic than his portrayals of women. Perhaps significantly, it was not until 1926, when he was in his mid-fifties, and when most of his fiction had been published, that he experienced marriage at first hand.

Joseph Keating's difficulty in coming to terms with the changing role of women in society is demonstrated by his relationship with his sister Mary, who was active in the women's suffrage movement. In spite of his close family connection with a suffragette, he could make dismissively patronising comments in his autobiography about female office workers at the *Western Mail*, where he was employed for a time. Intriguingly, while *My Struggle for Life* refers in glowing terms to the MP Matthew Keating on a number of occasions, there is no reference to his sister's activity in the cause of women's political rights. This is a revealing omission. When discussing Matthew Keating's parliamentary candidature in 1909 a newspaper referred to Mary as the 'equally well-known suffragette lecturer'.[24] She was also secretary of the Cardiff branch of the Women's Freedom League. It is possible that Joseph's silence on the matter stemmed from his difficulty in coming to terms with his sister's radicalism and extra-parliamentary activism. Mrs Keating Hill (as Mary became known once married) took part in a protest outside parliament in 1906 and was arrested on charges of disorderly behaviour and obstruction twice in the same week with a group of other women. On the first occasion an unnamed relative paid her fine of 20 shillings, but on the second she was imprisoned and spent Christmas 1906 in Holloway.[25]

It is tempting to speculate about whether Joseph would have praised his sister's political activity – or at least referred to it – in his autobiography had he written *My Struggle for Life* only five years later. By then he had been radicalised by the war and women over thirty years of age had been granted the vote. Mary's pre-war radicalism would have seemed less threatening to him. As it is, his silence on the matter is a reminder of a defining feature of autobiographical writing in general: its subjectivity. It is also an indicator that his treatment of women in the autobiography is of a piece with the romantic depictions of women in his novels.

POLITICS

Joseph Keating's politics reflect those of the Irish in Britain more generally in this period. Even though he was aware of the existence of Fenian sympathies in his community during the 1870s, that movement had largely run its course by the end of his childhood, and in adulthood Joseph became a supporter of the constitutional Home Rule movement, which sought to achieve a form of devolved power to a parliament in Dublin by peaceful means. Following the schism in the ranks of the Irish Parliamentary Party over Parnell's divorce in the 1890s he became, like his brother, a Redmondite Nationalist who supported the First World War in the belief that Ireland's loyal participation would hasten the granting of Home Rule by Britain. His willingness to be identified with this strand of nationalist opinion can be judged by his novel *Tipperary Tommy: A Novel of the War* (1915) and his contribution of a vividly written chapter on the recruitment of Irish brigades on Tyneside in the north-east of England to a collection of essays called *Irish Heroes of the War* (1917). The theme of another novel, *The Flower of the Dark* (1917), also turns around support for the war effort.

Through his brother Mathew, who held the constituency of South Kilkenny from 1909 until the Irish Parliamentary Party's rout at the hands of Sinn Féin in 1918, Joseph Keating was well connected in nationalist circles and met speakers from the ranks of constitutional nationalism as well as other nationalists who visited the Irish communities of south Wales before the war. Most notably, he was introduced to the ageing Fenian revolutionary O'Donovan

Rossa when the latter visited Cardiff and he provides a vivid vignette of this broken man towards the end of his life: 'He had just come out of Portland Prison where he had served a sentence of fourteen or fifteen years in horrible torture . . . His small body was shrivelled, his hair white, his pale cheeks withered and heavily lined, and every dark hollow hid a darker pain.'[26]

It would have been surprising had Keating not come into contact with socialism before 1914. His home village fell within the boundaries of the constituency won by the Independent Labour Party leader, Keir Hardie, in 1900. However, there is evidence that his contacts with socialists were more personal than his public political stance would indicate. When Hardie died in 1915 his seat was contested by the socialist and pacifist candidate T. E. Nicholas; in spite of the fact that Joseph Keating was at that stage an enthusiastic supporter of the war effort, he inscribed a copy of *My Struggle for Life* to Nicholas with the comment: 'With the author's compliments and the best of all good wishes'.[27] In the febrile political atmosphere of 1916 this was an uncommonly generous gesture from someone who took a diametrically opposed position on the war, and it was a portent of the direction Joseph's political development would take once the war came to an end.

LIFE AFTER THE AUTOBIOGRAPHY

Joseph Keating's career as an author was effectively over by the end of the war. His only play, *Peggy and Her Husband*, had been performed in the West End in March 1914, but after this he seems not to have pursued writing for the theatre any further. It is true that he published *The Exploited Woman* (1923), while another two novels appeared posthumously, *The Fairfax Mystery* (1935) and *A Woman Fascinates* (1935). But these are little more than a coda to his pre-war romantic output and have little literary merit or broader social significance. The context of economic depression and impending international conflict make the last two seem particularly marginal. His version of Zola's *Nana* (1926) was not well received. New interpreters of the industrial society in which he lived were now taking the field, providing an uncompromising picture of industrial society. On the whole, they rejected the high romantic strain that features so strongly in Keating's work. This generation broke decisively with the romantic tradition that had shaped Keating's output and were dedicated to social realism and depicting class conflict in an uncompromising manner.

Consequently, it is tempting to see the years from 1916 to 1934 in Joseph Keating's life as a perfunctory coda to the events described in *My Struggle for Life*. This would be a mistake. His life-story does not end with the publication of his autobiography. There is, however, a disjunction not long after 1916 that is more than the product of the artificial foreshortening perspective created by the appearance of his autobiography at that time. Like many others of his generation, ultimately he was radicalised by the war. He moved away from the Redmondite position on Home Rule in the light of political change in Ireland after 1918 and he quickly embraced the more radical position of republicanism represented by Sinn Féin. This shift in political allegiance was made easier by his brother's loss of his seat in the rout of the Irish Parliamentary Party in the general election of 1918. What is significant is that Joseph's embrace of the new dispensation in Irish politics was accompanied by a conversion to independent Labour politics in south Wales.

That political change in Ireland was matched by equally seismic political change in south Wales can be seen from events surrounding the founding and progress of the left-leaning Irish Self-Determination League (ISDL) in 1919. The name of this organisation reflects the historical moment of its conception, being a self-conscious adoption of the language used by President Woodrow Wilson in the post-war settlement at Versailles when re-drawing the map of Europe. In south Wales the ISDL became more or less an adjunct of the labour movement.[28]

In 1918 Joseph Keating made a bid for the Labour parliamentary candidacy in the new constituency of Aberdare. Although unsuc-cessful in his bid, he received the support of Hardie's old newspaper, *The Pioneer*. His speeches during this campaign demonstrate how far he had moved from the standpoint on politics he had espoused in his autobiography only a few years earlier. He had been radical-ised in part by his familiarity with developments in post-war Irish politics, and his views can be seen to be influenced by James Connolly's vision of a self-determined socialist future for both Ireland and Britain. This analysis is significant: for Keating it was not a case of Ireland being an entirely separate problem that needed resolving on its own terms, it was one that was intricately and inextricably related to a broader agenda of social justice in the British Isles.

These were years of personal hardship for Joseph Keating, when his ambitions as an author receded into the background and he channelled his energies into local politics. Undaunted by the setback of failing to win a parliamentary candidacy, he was elected a Labour councillor in 1923 and played a prominent part in local government until his death, becoming chairman of the local edu-cation committee and then chairman of the council in 1931. It was during these years that he married Annie Herbert. Domestic hap-piness contrasted with discord in the wider society. The south Wales coalfield was a storm centre of class conflict in the 1920s, as demonstrated most clearly by the General Strike of 1926. During these years he was a staunch defender of working people and their children and became known as the 'stormy petrel' of the council chamber. As elsewhere in the region, Irish membership of the labour movement provided an avenue of integration in society without compromising a distinctive ethnic identity.

The transformation in Joseph Keating's life, and that of many other children of Irish communities in places like the south Wales coalfield by the 1930s, was demonstrated by the way he was remembered in the obituary published in his local newspaper. While the fact of his Irish origins was noted, it was his record as a socialist and a local councillor that dominated the eulogy. He was, the newspaper intoned, 'a well-known Labour leader, and a fighter in every sense of the word'.[29] Consciously or otherwise, these words echo the sentiments that informed the choice of a title for his autobiography, published eighteen years earlier: life as struggle against the odds in a harsh and unremittingly difficult environment. As his battle for social justice in the 1920s and 1930s indicates, 'struggle' was more than a literary device chosen for dramatic effect.

Notes to Introduction

1   Sean Campbell, 'Beyond "Plastic Paddy": a re-examination of the second-generation Irish in England' in Donald M. MacRaild (ed.), *The Great Famine and Beyond: Irish Migrants in Britain in the Nineteenth and Twentieth Centuries* (Dublin, 2000), pp. 266–88.

2   *My Struggle for Life*, pp. 268–9. Keating is described as a 'Welshman' in Sandra Kemp, Charlotte Mitchell and David Trotter (eds), *The Oxford Companion to Edwardian Fiction* (Oxford, 1997), p. 219.

3   *My Struggle for Life*, pp. 13–14.

4   David Fitzpatrick, 'A curious middle place: The Irish in Britain, 1871–1921' in Roger Swift and Sheridan Gilley (eds), *The Irish in Britain, 1815–1939* (London, 1989), pp. 10–59.

5   Joseph Keating, *Maurice: A Romance of Light and Darkness* (London, 1905), pp. 168–9. On developments in south Wales at this time, see K. O. Morgan, *Rebirth of a Nation: Wales, 1880–1980* (Oxford, 1980) and John Davies, *A History of Wales* (London, 1993).

6   *My Struggle for Life*, p. 59; Paul O'Leary, *Immigration and Integration: The Irish in Wales, 1798–1922* (Cardiff, 2000), pp. 228–31.

7   Raymond Williams, 'The Welsh industrial novel' in his *Problems in Materialism and Culture: Selected Essays* (London, 1980), p. 218. Less charitably, he has been described as 'an obscure pioneer, a precursor of those more gifted writers from the valleys of south Wales who began to emerge at

the time of his death', in Meic Stephens (ed.), *The Oxford Companion to the Literature of Wales* (Oxford, 1987), p. 332.

8   Peter Keating, *The Haunted Study: a Social History of the English Novel, 1875–1914* (London, 1989), p. 313; Kemp, Mitchell and Trotter (eds), *The Oxford Companion to Edwardian Fiction*, p. 368.

9   'Recent novels', *The Times*, 11 Jan. 1911.

10   For example, 'Yanto, the waster', *Everybody's Magazine* (July 1904), 'Shinkin, the strong man', *Everybody's Magazine* (Oct. 1904), 'Tally, the coward,' *Everybody's Magazine* (Nov. 1904), 'William, the inventor', *Pearson's Magazine* (July 1905).

11   'Introduction' to Jean Radford (ed.), *The Progress of Romance: The Politics of Popular Fiction* (London, 1986), pp. 9–12.

12   *My Struggle for Life*, p. 167.

13   Stephen Knight, *A Hundred Years of Fiction: Writing Wales in English* (Cardiff, 2004), p. 29.

14   Dai Smith, 'Tonypandy 1910: definitions of community', *Past and Present*, no. 87 (1980), pp. 158–84.

15   Joseph Keating, 'Genius of Welsh collier,' *Western Mail*, 28 Apr. 1911. I am indebted to Neil Evans for this reference.

16   Keating, *Maurice*, p. 17.

17   'Genius of Welsh collier', *Western Mail*, 28 Apr. 1911.

18   See 'Marriage problem novels' in Kemp, Mitchell and Trotter (eds), *The Oxford Companion to Edwardian Fiction*, pp. 266–7.

19   'The test fails', *T. P.'s Weekly*, 17 Jan. 1913. On Braby, see Kemp, Mitchell and Trotter (eds), *The Oxford Companion to Edwardian Fiction*, pp. 41–2.

20   'The test fails', *T. P.'s Weekly*, 24 Jan. 1913.

21   Ibid. The judgement of Herbert Jenkins.

22   On this point, compare Ruth Sherry, 'The Irish working class in fiction' in Jeremy Hawthorn (ed.), *The British Working-Class Novel of the Twentieth Century* (London, 1982), p. 120.

23   'The test fails', *T. P.'s Weekly*, 17 Jan. 1913. The judgement of Edward Garnett.

24   *Aberdare Leader*, 7 Aug. 1909.

25   *The Times*, 19, 22 Dec. 1906, 11 Jan. 1907.

26   *My Struggle for Life*, p. 155.

27   Copy in National Library of Wales, inscription dated 18 June 1916.

28   See O'Leary, *Immigration and Integration: The Irish in Wales*, pp. 281–96.

29   'Well-known novelist: burial of Councillor Joseph Keating', *Aberdare Leader*, 14 July 1934. The obituary notice in *The Times*, 9 July 1934, claimed that he spoke Welsh. This would appear to be borne out by a close reading of *Adventures in the Dark* (1906).

MY STRUGGLE FOR LIFE

BY

JOSEPH KEATING

LONDON : SIMPKIN, MARSHALL
HAMILTON, KENT & CO. LTD.
1916

SIMPKIN, MARSHALL, HAMILTON,
KENT & CO. LTD.

PREFACE

STORIES of beginnings have always interested me.
Mystery and romance are rooted in them. Whether
a man be a statesman, financier, burglar, poet, or
road-sweeper, his starting-point is so full of mystery
that I love to hear how he became what he is ; and
for me, the most fascinating book ever written,
apart altogether from its divine inspiration, is
Genesis.

If I may be allowed to say, in great reverence, that
the sacred is for ever setting the highest example
to the profane, it will explain one of the main
reasons why I here propose to tell the story of myself.
Two other important reasons have influenced me.
Friends assure me that narratives of actual, personal
experiences and struggles are welcome even in these
tragic days of war ; and there is the chance that my
story, besides throwing a little light on some interesting but hidden parts of our social existence, may be
of use to young men who see the golden flower of
their ambition on the mountain-top, but can find
no way up to it.

The slope of any career is usually very steep.
Some men are lucky enough to be half-way up the
hill before they are born, and are pushed up the
remaining half. Other men start their climbing

lower down. Few commence at the bottom. I
began a quarter of a mile below the bottom.

My adventures as a boy in the coal mines had their
advantages. They introduced me to life in reality
and gave me the privilege of shaking hands with
death every day. Fortunately—(I give my own point
of view entirely)—I am still alive. My head is not
smashed by falling roof-stones ; my back is not
broken by the flight of a cage down a shaft when the
winding rope snaps ; my legs and arms are not torn
from their sockets by tram wheels or machinery ; my
body is not shattered into fragments by an explosion.

Some of the boys and youths who were my colleagues did not escape as I did. Their lost limbs,
twisted spines, gashed faces, or simple, white tombstones on the hillside, are their testimony to our
young days of danger. The marks of peril which
I bear upon my forehead are small. Death was
always polite enough to me to give me fair warning
to get out of his way. But for all his good manners,
I did not like his company.

Yet when I tried to free myself from the pit, and
seek some more acceptable way of earning my bread,
I found myself struggling with difficulties.

I was either too young or too old. I would have
gone navvying, or even scavenging ; but was told
that I was not strong enough for the first, and not
skilled enough for the second. My lack of training
for anything except underground work put me in
the ranks of the hopelessly unskilled on the surface.
Odd jobs I picked up ; but they all came to an
untimely and unwelcome end.

No abiding work of any sort could I find. I was like a willing horse that had fallen down on a slippery road and, having no one to help it to stand upright again, was left sprawling and breaking its knees in the effort to rise. It appeared to be more difficult for a poor miner to get into the sun than for a rich man to enter Heaven. My fate seemed bent on driving me back to the pit.

I was quite determined not to be driven back.

A pitched battle arose between my fate and my inclination. I was young enough to dare destiny, and my coat was off for the tussle. I was willing to starve, but I was not willing to go back to the mine. I had said I had left the pit for ever, and meant it.

Possibly, when fate fails to command, it becomes anxious to obey. Anyhow, at this point a totally unexpected influence joined forces with me, and the fight appeared to be going in my favour. My brother Matthew (who is now Member of Parliament for South Kilkenny) put into my head a way of escape. His plan was that I should become a modern pedlar, and go round the mountains and valleys offering trinkets and domestic utensils for sale.

To this plan there were, in my view, nine hundred and ninety-nine thousand, nine hundred and ninety-nine objections. I loathed the idea of trying to sell anything. I cannot explain this violent hatred of mine towards a harmless and most necessary calling.

There was one thing good in the suggestion. It

offered me a faint chance of betterment ; whereas the pit was, to me, a place of no hope.

How I lived for the next two years is a story to revive the belief in miracles. My greatest agony was that of being compelled to leave home. That almost made me cry.

But I must confess that a youth from nineteen to twenty-one can find happy spots even on the mountain-sides of misery. In the midst of all my wretchedness I was learning to play the fiddle, and was so enthusiastic as to be able to forget my troubles in the joy of the noise I scraped out.

At home, book studies of a methodless kind— shorthand, among other things—had interested me. Now a notion of using the shorthand came into my mind. Time for speed-practice was gained by cutting off the head of morning and lengthening the tail of night. Like poor Macbeth, I "murdered sleep" for my ambition.

After myriads of luckless applications for posts, I found a place on a small weekly paper.

This was my first step forward, after which many of my steps were backwards ; and my zig-zag course from that point was the most painful and, at the same time, most interesting of my experiences.

I began to write novels in the nights, after long days in an office. What set me writing novels no one knows—not even myself ; but whatever it was, it brought me to London, and made me feel the loneliness and the happiness of Grub Street, the coal-mine of literature, where the pen does the slave-

work of the hewer's pick, in underground darkness
that is illumined only by a passing friendly light, or,
perhaps, only by the flame of the writer's own soul
which, like a miner's lamp, encircles him with a
shining ring while he toils. Both grubber and hewer
are slaves of their lamps—though the rays of one
come from inside the man—and both are dogged by
danger ; for slow death by starvation stalks through
Grub Street much the same as sudden death by
violence does through the pit.

My beginning was almost as obscure as that of
the Mother of Eve. Yet at the age of forty-three I
had succeeded in getting a butterfly comedy of mine
produced at a fashionable West-End theatre, with
one, who is said to be perhaps the most beautiful
actress at present on the English stage, in the title
part. And to the first night of my play came an
overwhelmingly distinguished audience of great
authors, great critics, great actors and actresses,
remarkably-gowned women lustrous with jewels, a
medley of social somebodies in pit, stalls and boxes—
the whole brilliant function sprinkled judiciously with
glittering titles. From outer darkness I had leaped
suddenly into the centre of dazzling radiance. With
three dear and delightful friends I sat in the Author's
Box : that little decorated dungeon of torture from
which the creator beholds his creatures being murdered, and wonders if the final curtain will descend
like the knife of the guillotine upon his neck.

I do not like writing about myself. My pen may
appear to contradict this ; but not even the Almighty
can avoid seeming to contradict Himself ; and a man

would have to be superior to his Creator to escape the possibility of being misunderstood. I can only let what I write show whether or not I would willingly reveal, outside the confessional, some of the consequences of original sin.

CONTENTS

CONTENTS

CONTENTS

CHAPTER XXII

CHAPTER XXIII

CHAPTER XXIV

MY STRUGGLE
FOR LIFE

CHAPTER I

My birth : Native place : Our colony of Irish emigrants in
Wales : Dwellers in converted stables : Cellar-houses : My
father's ancient and royal descent : My mother's ambitions :
Remarkable purity of our Irish colony.

I was born on April 16, 1871, in what, at that time,
was a charming, pastoral village, in South Wales,
set in a wooded valley and sheltered by wonderful
mountains which are still my beloved friends whom
I visit on the slightest excuse. I recall mule-teams
picking their way down the beautifully coloured slopes
on a summer evening. The mules carried packs
of provisions, or wood, over the hill-ranges from valley
to valley. Those were primitive and picturesque
days. No coach could travel over the mountains.

The other route for commerce was a canal that
glistened like a silver ribbon fringing the brilliant
robes of the eastern range. A few whitewashed
farms stood out distinctly from the green hillsides,
and droves of cattle plodded up and down the valley
road, the drovers hilariously drunk, and the sheep
or cows occasionally dashing into the kitchen of a
wayside cottage, and creating consternation for the
housewife, and huge entertainment for the children.

By the time I was going to school, railway trains

had begun to run up and down the valley. One went down in the morning and another—perhaps, it was the same one—came up in the evening.

Whenever I saw the train on my road to school, or from a hillside where I was playing, I cheered and waved my cap to it. The rattle of the engine, the white puffs of steam, and the sparks from fire-box or funnel made me enthusiastic. Why the trains were running, or where they went to, puzzled me. I thought they went round the world and back again for no reason, just the same as the birds came to and went from the hillsides every year. If I saw men and women in the coaches I wondered what they were doing there. The trains were full of mystery for me while they were in sight. But as soon as they disappeared between the mountains I forgot all about them, and went on with what I was doing. It took a long time to induce us to travel in this new fashion. We used to forget about the trains when we were going on a journey. We climbed over the mountains and paused on the summits to look down at the steam engine and coaches as mere curiosities. One man I knew would tramp countless miles because, he said, he would not trust himself in a railway train.

No one, it seems, was ever able to translate the name of our Welsh village, Mountain Ash, into the native language. The English name gives a hint of poetic loveliness ; and in my novel " Maurice," I tried to reproduce the old and charming Mountain Ash. Since I was a happy boy there, collieries, and railway tracks hidden under long strings of loaded coal-wagons have given the landscape a new and strange meaning.

On the magnificent slopes are all the wonders of brilliant sunshine and gorgeously coloured foliage. Under the same beautiful slopes human beings are toiling in darkness which might, at any moment, become the blinding light of death by explosion. In the home of my childhood sparkling romance touches the most terrible reality.

The first distinct impression I have of being alive comes from a black, winter evening when my mother was carrying me in her arms, together with a heavy bag of dough which she had kneaded and was taking to the bakehouse to be turned into five or six big loaves for her large family. We were crossing a colliery-yard from one side of the valley to the other, over two railways, a river and a network of shunting tracks, with the glare of pit-lights, blacksmiths' fires, the shrieking of steam-engine whistles, and the clatter of colliery machinery all round us. My mother was a finely shaped, strong, handsome Irish woman, as proud as ten queens and as capable as two prime ministers. Her capacity for managing her household kingdom on small means was a revelation in political economy, brightened by ironic humour. She would tell her seven children later in life, recalling her early difficulties :

" 'Tisn't reared up ye were, but dragged up."

She came from Youghal. Her great ambition was to own the house she lived in ; and how she succeeded was a miracle. She became the owner of a house, but died—God rest her soul !—before she could go to live in it. She had very bright brown eyes, a pale, noble face, and a habit, when she was pensively knitting, of winking her left eye, which she did not intend doing, though it sometimes made my father extremely jealous of her. Everyone who knew her spoke of her as a beautiful woman.

She was one of the grandest mothers the world has ever seen ; and now she is dead, I, like countless other foolish sons, am tortured by remorse, wondering why I should ever have found fault with her or caused her sorrow, when I know that she gave her life for her children. And me she favoured, in her later days, more than all the others, because I showed some glimmering of appreciation by visiting her at far-apart holiday times.

We lived with a little colony of Irish emigrants, a small pool formed by a trickle from the flood of emigration which had been rushing out of Ireland to every corner of the world since the famine in the middle of last century. Ironworks and mines in Wales could provide work and bread. The Irish landed at various parts of the Welsh coast ; and husbands, wives and children tramped away from the ship, until the men found work. Wherever they could earn bread they settled down.

The first comers secured places near the coast. Later groups had to march farther inland amidst the valleys.

They became labourers, navvies, miners, and puddlers. They worked in the dust and darkness of " rubbish-stalls " underground, and in the scorching blaze of steel-furnaces above. They swung pick, shovel, bar and hammer, and handled drills, blasting and hewing tunnels and cuttings through mountains

and valleys. Destiny drove them from their beloved
Irish homes and farms to build railways, sink pits,
and carry the hod up to the tops of boiler-stacks that
seemed to be taller than the hills of this country of
the stranger. The exiles landed with the power to
labour as the sum total of their wealth ; and as they
owned nothing but their poverty and their strength,
they took the poorest dwelling-places as shelter for
themselves and their families.

This was a calamitous thing for a man like my
father, who traced his descent from Heber the
Handsome, son of Milesius, King of Spain. I am not
sure, though my father could easily explain, whether
Milesius conquered the Firbolgs or the Tuatha de
Danann, and became, in consequence, King of all
Ireland. My father was born in Cahirciveen, Co.
Kerry. By that time a British Government had
usurped the sovereignty of Ireland, and my father's
family being dispossessed of their ancient kingdom
were without any revenue. He migrated to Wales
when he was about eighteen, with a Munster brogue
so thick that it could have been cut with a knife. Like
other emigrants, he possessed only the strength of his
body and hands, whereby he might gain the means
of living. Not only does my father trace his descent
from kings, but from men of learning. He is quite
sure that the Rev. Geoffrey Keating, the renowned
Irish historian, is one of his distinguished ancestors.
It is impossible to dispute my father's claim to descent
from kings and scholars because there are no records
for or against it.

Our name, Keating, is Norman. The Irish way

of pronouncing it is Kaet'n. Its correct Celtic spelling is Ceitinn. The Celtic form comes from the fact that the first Normans who went to Ireland became more Irish than the Irish themselves, and intermarried with the ancient Irish families. This is the only thing that lends any colour to my father's regal origin. The rest is purely a matter of imagination.

One important distinction I willingly grant my father : There was never a man in the whole world who could dance Irish jigs and reels with his fascinating gracefulness.

In his youth he had very black, wavy, shining hair, large blue eyes, a good-humoured smile, and, as now, a courtly, fine manner which made his personality exceedingly attractive. He was short, sturdy and lively, and known as " Kaet'n, the Lady-killer." He must have had something undeniably dashing about him to have made a handsome girl like my mother fall in love with him. In his tramps among the Welsh hills he met her at Mountain Ash. He settled down there ; and one fine morning they walked down the valley road, eight miles under sunlight, between mountain ranges, to Treforest Catholic Church, got married, and walked home again the same evening. He was thirty and she sixteen.

I do not know the house I was born in. I think it was somewhere in a place called Nixon's Row. That was not its administrative name. I believe it had a charming Welsh name. But people with imagination like to be intimate with their surroundings ; and Nixon's Row was christened by its tenants after the name of the man who built it, as they named a child after its father. I remember vaguely that we must have removed to another house. I become quite sure of our address when we lived on the Cardiff Road in a row of high, square houses, called The Barracks, a term which accurately described their appearance. Once a year the block was whitewashed. Then it looked like the gaunt ghost of a giant towering formidably over the small, drab houses opposite.

Inside and outside we had space. Huge mountains rose in front of us, and it was only necessary to cross a canal and evade the gamekeeper—an added attraction for boys—in order to have the entire broad woods and slopes for bird-nesting, nutting, poaching, or the fun of Bedlam.

At our back was a railway ; beyond that, the fields of Cwmcynon Farm and the river Cynon—at that time a clear amber stream—for bathing ; and beyond that again still more mountains, which, however, were not considered as desirable as the ones on our side of the valley.

Our house had three storeys, with the top floor entirely unoccupied. Up there we held boxing-matches—boxing was a most admired accomplishment in our quarter—Christy minstrel entertainments, and dramatic performances. A portable theatre, Ebley's, Johnny Noakes', or Norton's, the price of admission to which was threepence, nearly always encamped at Mountain Ash. I was a grave student of the drama, and my brothers, Matt and Maurice, were enthusiasts who could not only appreciate but imitate ; and all our favourite dramas

" Dred the Avenger ; or Alone in the Dismal Swamp,"
"Ingomar, the Terror of the Wilderness," "Maria
Martin ; or the Murder in the Red Barn," "The
Dumb Man of Manchester," "The Maid of Cefn
Ydfa," and countless others were reproduced in our
" top loft." My mother insisted as a great joke
against me that the first words I ever spoke were
uttered when I stabbed our front door with a bread-
knife, and said in a hoarse voice :

" Die, villain, die ! "

I was always hoarse as a child—from so much
crying. I am told I was the most miserable child
ever born. I refused to have anything to do with my
mother after she weaned me, I was so much offended,
and would only allow my sister Molly—Heaven pity
her !—to nurse me.

Three steps led up to our door, with a low
wall at each side to protect us from falling into
the open areas below. The earth had been ex-
cavated to allow light to reach the windows of
houses underneath ours. The street door led into
our big kitchen, which was floored with stone flags.
My sisters washed these flags and freshly sprinkled
them with sand of a lovely red-gold tint every
Saturday. The kitchen was our morning, dining,
and drawing rooms. At the inner end, to the left,
was a pantry spacious enough for a town house.
Around the pantry walls were clean white wooden
shelves, and at the back a wide, flat stone, its surface
very rough. The big " pantry-stone " had been
hewn from the hillside quarry and fitted in its place
without further preparation. A large pantry was

necessary for the never-satisfied appetites of four boys and three girls. The shelves were kept as well-stocked as possible. My mother's pride was a full pantry. She bought her potatoes in sacks, her salt in huge bars like the beams of a ship, her butter in mountains, and her bread in continents. Ever since then, I have pitied people who are compelled to buy half-pounds of butter, quarter-pounds of tea, pinches of salt and contemptible carbuncles called cottage-loaves.

We went to Mass every Sunday morning in the "long room" of a public house called the Scroby Arms. Drink and the devil had possession of the room until midnight, and the Holy Ghost descended upon it in the peace of the Sabbath morning. The long room was at the back of the inn, with a platform at the far end, holding the altar and a piano. Songs and hornpipes had been sung and danced there a few hours previously. Flowers of great beauty decorated the altar, and a tiny red lamp burned before it. When we entered the room we blessed ourselves with the holy water which was placed in a tin can near the door, and genuflected profoundly to the altar and piano. Sunlight poured in from a side window. A few coarse benches, without backs, made seats for the first arrivals. Men and women, boys and girls, crowded in until the interior became warm and suffocating. While waiting for Mass to begin we took out our rosaries and prayed for souls in purgatory.

From a door behind the people the priest appeared, robed in richly coloured vestments, and came slowly forward with great dignity, preceded by one small

altar-boy in black and white. All the stifling congregation went silently upon its knees, as the priest
passed up to the altar. The murmur of musical
Latin words rolled through the silence. The wonderful ceremony of the Mass began ; and, instan-
taneously, the drink-stained long room became, as if
by a miracle, a cathedral of hushed reverence and
worship, from which the sacred had utterly banished
the profane.

Later, the Catholics were able to secure the Workman's Hall on Sundays. Acrobatic and conjuring
tricks were performed in the hall during the week.
A travelling theatrical company might have been
playing there the previous Saturday night, and on
the stage the sacred altar was erected and the holy
sacrifice of the Mass celebrated amidst exit and
entrance wings, and scenery representing a castle
dungeon or a forest glade.

Other houses were opposite us, and farther down
on our side of the valley road. Some were normal
dwellings ; others were situated below the level of the
highway, like cellars, but not so sanitary. A few of
these under-houses had been made by converting
stables into human habitations. " Ben, the shop,"
a kindly, good-natured man with a red face and
brown beard, the only tradesman in the locality, had
kept a horse and cart for his business in week-days,
and for the pleasure and grandeur of his family—a
wife and three children—on Sunday afternoons, when
they went for a drive up or down the valley, to our
admiration and envy. But the difficulty of getting
his debts paid, had influenced him to give up the horse

and cart, clean out the stables, and rent them as homes for his customers.

The horse's stall and the cart-shed became two distinct houses, and the large hayloft above became another two ; so that four families were enabled to live comfortably enough in the space which he had given to one horse. The rent of the converted stables was not excessive, and the people who lived in them were of a joyous, sanguine nature.

At right angles were four or six other cellar-like houses beneath the street above. A branch of the Great Western Railway, and its fence of discarded, tall sleepers opposite the under-houses, formed a quadrangle known as Ben's Yard. I saw two of my uncles fighting fiercely in this yard, one wet Saturday afternoon, over some trivial dispute. They were excellent and skilful fighters of great courage, and the admiration of the Yard was saddened only by the thought that it was a pity to see two brothers fighting ; but no one would dare to interfere. I remember that the fight ended by the appearance of my grandmother in tears.

All the cellar-stable tenants of Ben's Yard and under our house were the most interesting characters. They had pronounced individualities, and were remarkable for piety and independence. Murray, the Cog-sawyer, who had served in the Crimean War as a private soldier, was tall, straight, pale-faced, white-haired, and proudly reserved in manner. His aloofness was a mystery, until one morning, instead of going down the pit to saw cogs as usual, he took his poor old wife to church and married her.

The episode caused great scandal. His soldier-life might have made him careless before he settled down in our Irish Colony ; and, possibly, the atmosphere of piety in which he dwelt awakened his conscience at last to the fact that he had been living in sin.

Mary Grady, grey, shapeless, and living Heaven knew how, also resided in a converted stable. She was sometimes depressed, despite her sanguine temperament, thinking of her dead husband and her scattered family. In those unhappy moments she would weep and say :

" Give me the razor till I cut me throat."

Another tenant, a big strong man, died within a week, because he had quarrelled with his wife, and his children would not speak to him.

One gentle-natured young man followed a girl to America and back again. Then she married him. Like most cases where love is entirely on the man's side, the marriage was a tragedy. In this instance the woman went mad.

Fierce love and fiercer hate, fine chivalry and ignoble revenge, refinement and vulgarity, saintliness and devilry were there. In many ways the cellar-stables were an epitome of the world. Their dominant note was buoyancy, good-nature and good-humour. The young men, besides earning their own livings, some-times got drunk on pay-days and fought with one another. That was a form of amusement.

One of the chief errors I have observed in well-intentioned circles is the tendency to regard working people as a class quite distinct in themselves, and to legislate for them as for the prevention of cruelty to animals. I think there is as much good-nature as ignorance in this view. One remedy only is necessary: Permit the workers to receive the means to live as they desire to live. Then it would be seen that they would like to reside in spacious, wholesome houses, with nice gardens, lawns and woodlands all round them, eat good food, and wear fine clothes.

I have found the same measure of distinct individualities, the same ratio of intelligence and morality, the same standard of civic and spiritual development in the palace as in the slum. Just the same and no difference. There are no classes. The only distinction between the human beings of the world is : Which half is so degraded as to eat and dress at the expense of the other half ?

We were all agreed in The Barracks that those who lived on the profits of our residential and economic limitations—the house-owner who took the rent, the landowner who took the ground rent, together with the employer whose meanness compelled his labourers to seek the only shelter which meagre wages could afford—were undesirable people.

We who lived in The Barracks—which was also a generic name for the whole district—were intensely proud of the place. Its people were hard-working, honest and neighbourly. They gave generously to their church ; of course, there was only one church for them—the Catholic Church. They were kind to one another. If illness or poverty happened to be in one house, nearly every other house proffered help. If one man was killed in the pits, his neighbours helped to carry his dead body from the pit to his home

and from there to his last home on the hillside.
Everybody's home was open to everybody else, and
there was great friendship. There was not a thief
in the district. Loafers and swindlers were not able
to live there. Matrimony was regarded as a sacrament, and the colony had no need of divorce courts.

There was no bawdy talk in the young men's
conversation. I used to feel horribly ashamed when
I went amongst better-off youths and heard them
speak insultingly of women. The girls of the colony
were bright-eyed and pure. And I am merely
repeating statistics when I say that the rate of illegitimacy there would work out at, perhaps, two in a
million ; and in those isolated cases, the man was
blamed and not the girl.

CHAPTER II

AT the age of three and a half I was sent to Newtown
Infants' School, about a quarter of a mile away,
probably more with the idea of getting me out of the
house for a few hours each day than for the purposes
of education, as there was a younger child at home,
and my mother, besides having no nursemaid, did
all the domestic work of a large family. From this
aspect, state-endowed schools were a benefit to
mothers.

This school had the drawback of being a Protestant
one, which caused us acute distress. The souls of
the children would be neglected there, and it was
feared they would grow up in the paganism of
Newtown, a place inhabited entirely by rural immi-
grants from Gloucestershire, Somersetshire, Devonshire, and Cornwall. In Newtown's three rambling
streets there were theosophists, Christadelphians,
Christian scientists, spiritualists, shintoists, method-
ists, baptists, ranters, and shakers. All the fantastic
religions of the world seemed to flourish in Newtown.
In The Barracks there was one dominant religion.

But Newtown had a special street known as The Strand. It ran from a canal up the mountain side into the woods. In this particular street lived renowned poachers, who would not hesitate to shoot any gamekeeper who interfered with them. The Strand appealed to our imagination and we admired it.

I used to go to school hand in hand with other little boys and girls. We climbed a hill and crossed the canal by a one-arched bridge called " The Cat Bridge." At the other side a coal level had been driven into the mountain. My uncle Peter, who had a marvellous gift for playing old Irish tunes on the tin whistle and the accordion, worked in the coal level ; and it was a fascinating moment for us when we were lucky enough to see him coming out from beneath the mountain, all black, riding between his horse and a loaded coal tram, with his little, lighted lamp in his cap, and water dripping from every strap and buckle of the harness.

Some afternoons we were late for school through stopping to watch the women of Forest Level baking their bread. The bakehouse was a low, brick lean-to, against the corner of a small row, above an abandoned rubbish tip. A tremendous bonfire of sticks had to be set blazing in the oven to heat it. The fire pleased the children who stood hand in hand like a chain of cherubs in trousers and pinafores.

I recall my teacher, Miss Julia Shipton, as a handsome, dashing girl with ringlets and brilliant eyes. She used to send me with messages to her mother's house and give me a handful of dried currants as a reward.

One afternoon all the scholars were allowed to climb on the desks and look out through the window to see a boy of our school being carried home with his head cut off. He was a notorious " mitcher." That day he had been playing in a canal boat at the bottom of a quarry incline about a mile down the valley. A tram, half-way up the mountain side and loaded with quarry stones, had run wild down the incline, dashed over the bank across the boat in which Alec was playing, caught his neck against the top of the boat side, and severed his head from his body as evenly as a sword could have done it. We were advised not to be " mitchers " like Alec, and then we should not have our heads cut off.

Something happened one winter. The children of The Barracks only knew that they could not get enough bread to eat, and cried at the harshness of their mothers. It was explained to us that " The Strike " would not let us have the bread, but the explanation could not satisfy our hunger.

Lord Aberdare—whose residence up the valley was a mile from ours—had many daughters who were charming and kind. They filled their ball-room with socks, clogs, clothes, and cake, and invited starving and perishing Mountain Ash to come and be fed and clothed. My mother's pride scorned the notion of eating and dressing at other people's expense. She spoke in profound contempt of the whole scheme.

Practical considerations seemed to influence her eventually. She had extraordinary good sense. She went with the crowd.

She had me by the hand and Maurice in her arms.

My other brothers and sisters could look after themselves. We went through a lodge gate, along a red-coloured drive between big trees to the house with flower gardens and green fields all about it. People and piles of things filled the ball-room. I remember sitting on a shining floor to put on a pair of little white socks and clogs with gleaming brass nails around the bottoms, while a group of smiling well-dressed young women clustered round my mother, admired Maurice, and deliberately picked out some of the finest articles as presents for him. He had fine, fair curls, deep-blue eyes, and splendid audacity. The young women took him in their arms. He told them he could sing ; so they made him stand on the polished floor in the tiny clogs they had put on him, and he sang for them " Fair Ella was a Lady " (a Newtown school song) to their intense delight.

For weeks afterwards the clogs gave headaches to my mother, because she could not get used to the clatter which we made.

Maurice, in the summer, was brought home naked in a clothes basket, apparently drowned. He had been playing near the canal and had fallen in. A man, passing by, had leaped in, brought him out, and lost his gold watch in the water, a misfortune which he accepted cheerfully, because he had reached the child just in time to allow him to be restored to life.

In summer time the youths who came home black from the mines washed and bathed in the canal under The Cat Bridge, with the boats passing up and down, each boat drawn by a horse at the end of the tow rope. Climbing upon a passing boat was a pastime which the swimmers enjoyed and the boatmen resented. They threw pieces of coal at their naked passengers.

My brother Matt, who has since become a member of Parliament, was not four feet high, yet had an ambition to bathe with the big boys. He had the courage of his ambitions. Though the water was a foot above his head and he could not swim on the surface, he used to dive from the bank, swim under water like a fish to the other bank, and pull himself up. One evening, when he was not bathing, I saw him crawling along the steep side of a bank looking for duck-eggs. The bush he clung to gave way and he rolled into the water. Our brother Jack, who was with me on the opposite bank, clapped his bowler hat down tightly on his head and, with all his clothes on, immediately dived in to save him. Jack had an immensely chivalrous nature.

There were plenty of shallow parts in the river and canal. During summer holidays I bathed fourteen times a day. There were no difficulties of toilet, as my attire consisted of shirt, trousers, one brace slantwise over my shoulder, with boots and stockings conveniently left at home. Sometimes all the boys and girls took me with them up to the very tops of the mountains picking " wimbreys." I do not know if the word " whinberries " means exactly the same thing. We carried baskets, jam-jars, bottles, and our relatives' pit food-boxes to hold our pickings, and sang in unison :

> *In the jail his body's buried,*
> *Cold and dead lies young Lefroy.*

Lefroy had murdered somebody.

On warm, dark, autumn nights, after a day's work in the mines, the young men and young women of The Barracks danced quadrilles and waltzes on the road outside our house. My Uncle Peter sat upon our wall and played any tunes that were called for, either on his B-flat flute, his tin whistle, or accordion.

One of the young women who lived next door to us fell madly in love with an Irish navvy who had tramped carelessly into The Barracks and lodged near her house. Her parents would not permit her to marry a man, who tramped from place to place like a gipsy; so she agreed to elope with him. Winter had come and a heavy snowfall had covered mountains and valley with pure white. She was very simple but determined. To get away unsuspected she rolled up her belongings into a bundle and dropped it out from the highest window down into the snow at the back. I saw the girl at the window and saw the bundle fall into the snow. Fate intervened somehow. The girl was kept prisoner in the house, and the navvy got tired of waiting in the snow and went on tramp alone. We never saw him again.

About this time I became conscious of the one murder which had happened in Mountain Ash. Bob Coe, a blacksmith's striker, had invited his friend, John Davies, to take a walk with him up the mountain side on a Saturday afternoon when work was over. In the wood Bob hit his friend on the head with a hatchet, took thirty shillings out of John's pocket, and left the body and weapon in the wood. On Monday morning Bob went up again and was surprised to find John still alive.

" What—not dead yet ! " Bob said, and hit him with the hatchet again.

Then he buried the body and went away from Mountain Ash.   A sheep dog smelt out the decaying corpse, and Bob Coe was hanged outside Swansea or Cardiff jail.   I am not sure which jail it was.   At any rate, he was the last man who was hanged outside it.

After passing all the examinations at Newtown up to Standard 1, I was transferred to The Mount School, to which big boys were sent.   Mr. Dowling was headmaster ; and I see clearly to-day the peculiar white, gristly knobs, as big as walnuts, that stood out all round his head.

A definite memory of my first morning there is the return of boys, who seemed as big as giants, from the mine to school.   Some new Act of Parliament had come into force.   The boys had gone to work in the pits, and Parliament had sent them back to school until they should reach the age of thirteen.   Their indignation and humiliation were a terrible sight. They detested the thought of school, and felt horribly insulted at being compelled to take their places amidst us small boys.   They rebelled openly, and old Dowling needed all his courage and good-humour to keep them in hand.   He, as well as the boys, regarded the Act of Parliament as an act of folly.

Who my teacher at The Mount was has faded from my mind ; but I remember his asking me, as a new scholar, particulars of my social status.   He said to me, as I stood behind my desk, considerably perturbed

at finding myself in such a big school, yet feeling an
unaccountable contempt for it, perhaps because I did
not like leaving Newtown :

" What is your father, Keating ? "

" A hobbler, sir."

" What is a hobbler, Keating ? "

" I don't know, sir."

Neither the teacher nor I could translate the term
into anything socially intelligible. All I knew was
that my father was connected with docks and ships
at Cardiff—eighteen miles away from our house.   He
had gone there because he could earn better wages
than at home.

He had the nature of a rover.   He had been twice to
America.   The first time was about five years after
his marriage.   He had sent for my mother who took
her children, Jack and Molly, with her.   Kate was
born in America.   There my father had, as usual,
gained the confidence of his employer and had been
given control of a lot of navvies, who were making
some waterworks in Pennsylvania.   In Fair View my
mother had provided food and shelter for one of the
gangs.   She became homesick and wanted to return
to Mountain Ash.

My father, always willing to please her, said he
would take her home.

The great waterworks contractors were upset at
the idea of his leaving, and offered him not only the
big wooden shanty in which he lived, but the open
acres of land around it, if he would let my mother go
home alone and remain himself.   He had none of the
practical qualities of my mother.   He obeyed his

emotions, gave up his fine prospects, refused the offer of land, and went home with my mother. That area developed into a coalfield, and my father lost a fortune which would have come to him in coal royalties through his ownership of the land.

When he went back the second time his chance had gone. My mother would not go to America again; so once more he returned home.

We saw little of him as children. Whenever he came home he brought a bagful of books on all conceivable subjects, without any regard for their utility. He seemed to have the impression that the mere sight of books would be intellectual development for his boys. He has always lived the life of an idealist, and found happiness in being a spiritual pillar of the Church.

He sent home from Cardiff all the money he could spare; but even then my ambitious mother worked hard to supplement the domestic income. Her knitting and sewing were said to be of a superior kind, and her beautiful work was prized by local tradespeople who found a profitable sale for it. At the same time she had a houseful of us to keep tidy.

We were seven, as Wordsworth's child said; but we were scarcely as gentle as that child.

" My heart is broke with ye ! " my mother often declared in despair.

Occasionally she put pieces of bread that had been left over from previous meals into our broth, and I did not like that at all. I liked nice, fresh crusts in my broth. My mother would have liked to have been able to please me. Her ideas of living were visions of lavish splendour. But that came of her romantic temperament. Unfortunately the reality of her existence compelled her to live in narrowness.

Before the year was out I left The Mount school. By that time Father Hamlin—an energetic French priest who had been given charge of our parish—had built a new church which was to be used in week days as a Catholic school, and all Irish parents at once withdrew their children from the State schools, in order to send them to their own for the future well-being of our souls.

For six years the pence and shillings of the Irish colony had been contributed towards this sacred cause of building a church. There was not one well-to-do Catholic in the place, and the hundreds of pounds which would be required to pay off the debt would all have to be found by working people. They willingly accepted the burden, because moral purity and natural piety were underneath all the squalor and sordidness of their outward lives. One Catholic man, though, declared he would turn Protestant because he did not get the plastering contract of the church.

The French priest had supervised all the building operations ; and, I believe, besides being his own contractor, had been his own architect. He had taken all this burden upon himself through necessity. If he had not been extremely economical there could not have been a Catholic Church at all.

His French ideas made the building graceful and dainty. It was constructed of cheap bricks, but in spite of that it was the one bit of architectural beauty in the place. It had a tower and spire intended to hold a clock of four faces ; but funds for the clock never came ; white boards filled the gaps ; and four blank faces for ever remained staring north, south, east, and west, at the hills in front, the hills behind, and up and down the valley, as if looking to see if the subscriptions were coming to give them life.

Our church was high up on the slope of a hill, yet we had to go down a long flight of steps to reach the door. The rear part was divided off as a stable for the priest's pony, Mignon, and the trap in which he used to drive down from Aberdare every Sunday morning. After Mass, Mignon, a little bay with very wicked eyes and wild blood, always gave an exhibition of rearing and kicking before it would consent to be driven back to Aberdare.

A house was built by the side of the church. Our new governess—an English girl—lived there. Underneath was a small class-room for infants.

The church itself was our school. There were about a hundred boys and girls of the most curious sizes ; some were five feet tall, and others only two and a half. A few were well and completely dressed, the remainder barefoot and sparingly attired in clothes that were well patched. But all were exceedingly happy.

We had Catechism in the morning and afternoon :

" Who made you ?

" God.

" Why did God make you ? "

And we learned why He did it. We had never heard of God in other schools ; or, at least, the lesson had made no impression on us.

Our worldly studies in the new school were reading,

writing, arithmetic, and geography. I remember that Beachy Head was in Sussex. But distinction of any kind was never won by me. The schoolmistress used to give me three halfpence for cleaning the windows.

Once we were offered a photograph of ourselves— the whole schoolful on a small card—as a prize for the best sums. My low marks put me out of consideration. The schoolmistress ordered me sharply to stand outside in the porch. In a few moments she came down to me. We were alone in the dark porch and invisible to the school.

" Joe Keating," she said, in a severe tone, " why didn't you win the prize ? "

" I don't know, mum."

" Well—here," said she bringing her hand and a small framed picture from behind her back, " is another photograph of our school for you. Put it under your jacket and don't let the others see it."

That was my first experience of the lengths to which a woman will go for anyone she favours.

Some of my best boy-friends in the school had resolved to become pirates. We tattooed blue anchors on the fleshy parts of our hands and arms with Indian ink as a beginning. We took the longest way home on Thursday afternoons in order to study the illustrated placard of " The Police News," which was posted up on a board outside Grier's, the only stationer's shop in the town. Every crime and catastrophe of the week, murder, robbery, explosion or railway collision, was shown in powerful pictures on the poster.

For literature we had the periodicals " The Boys of England," " The Young Men of Great Britain,"

" The Boys of London and New York," " Jack Hark-
away's Schooldays," and " Young Folks." A wonderful story entitled " Ralpho, the young Swordsman of
Warsaw" in " Young Folks " utterly fascinated me.
When that finished, " The Young Men of Great
Britain," had a story called " A Boy from the
Country, or alone in London," which interested me to
such an extent that I used to stand for hours outside
Grier's with my penny, waiting for the train to bring
up the parcel of papers on Thursday evenings. I
could not always get a penny, and when deprived of
a weekly instalment of my story I felt the craving of
an opium eater for his drug.

CHAPTER III

ONCE I had sixpence in silver.

How it came to be mine is forgotten ; but whether
it was a gift of affection or a reward for obliging
somebody, the amount was so large that it seemed
impossible for me to spend it, or, in fact, use it in
any way at all. I had my hand on it in my trouser-
pocket, and felt the silver burning my fingers as I
walked up the street.

Near the Taff Station I saw Jack Lahy, a distant
cousin of ours. He was also called Jack the Swaddy.
He had been a soldier in India, and was such an
interesting personality, gifted with broad humour
and strong, dramatic power, that when, in after
years, I read " Soldiers Three," I felt sure that
Kipling had been studying Jack Lahy. He was tall
and had a broad, fair face and a flattened nose. He
was leaning back against the wall with a discon-
solate expression, and I accurately divined that he
was sober after a spree. He was feeling the terrible
misery of being dry in such cases and having no
money to get a single pint of beer. The sixpence

28

was useless to me and burning my hand ; and I knew what an actual godsend it would be to him. It would pay for two pints. I said :

" Hello, Jack ! " I was seven and he thirty-seven.

" Well, Joe, me boy," he replied dolefully, his wretchedness not in the least relieved by my amiable familiarity.

" Here," said I.

I can never forget Lahy's expression of amazement when my burning sixpence was put into his hand.

" May the Lord spare ye the health, Joe, boy ! " he shouted. The miracle he had been praying for had happened ; and he ran across the road into a tavern nicknamed " The Brickhouse."

Lahy carried the hod and mixed mortar. He was a magnificent workman ; and though he changed his employer frequently, because staying in one place for any length of time bored him, any builders for whom he had once worked always welcomed him back, and allowed him to do just as he liked if he would only remain with them.

At this period, an invasion of navvies overwhelmed Mountain Ash. They were cutting, digging, and shovelling all through the valley. They had horses, wagons, and windlasses. Deep, narrow gullies made in the fields by hundreds of navvies, and the sight of the fresh clay they threw up on each side, captivated me.

A few of my elder intimates had succeeded in getting appointments as " nippers." They received six or seven shillings a week.

I absolutely yearned to become a " nipper " and

to be a real navvy.   There was brilliant romance in
tramping from place to place with the admired gang.

To ganger after ganger I applied for an appointment.   My age was against me, owing to the Act
of Parliament.   I was eight ; and the gangers told me
confidentially that it would mean jail for them if
they gave a job to any " nipper " under twelve or
thirteen unless he had passed the fifth standard.

My love for the toiling rovers—they were fine, tall
men, clean-looking, in moleskin trousers and pilot
jackets, and swung their great, anchor-like picks and
shovels with an easy rhythm—was so strong that
while school holidays were on I rose at half-past five,
just as the navvies did, tied some food up in a red
handkerchief, as they did, and went out to the cutting
in fields or hillside at six o'clock, as they did.   From
six to half-past eight I took an active part in the work,
like an unsalaried Parliamentary secretary, hitching a
horse to wagons which the navvies filled with clay.
At half-past eight the ganger sang out " Ye-ho, boys,"
and we " knocked off," sat on the grass, untied our red
handkerchiefs and ate our " tommy " in the morning
sunshine with mountains in front and behind us.

The navvies were always in good-humour and full
of laughable stories.   Their intelligence was astonishing.   They never lacked a subject.   They were
artists in human conversation and geniality.   They
accepted my companionship as that of an equal.
Entire independence seemed to be the natural thing
for them to feel.   If the ganger unfortunately displeased one, the reply of the navvy was to climb out
of the trench and call out :

" Who wants to buy a shovel ? "

Somebody invariably offered a shilling for the shovel if it were in good condition. He took the shilling, drew what money might be coming to him from the " timey," spent it all the same day in beer, and went on tramp penniless, knowing well that somewhere or other he would come across a navvy colony where he could get a night's " doss." If he had only just joined the gang, and happened to dislike the company, the wet condition of the cutting, or the colour of the clay, when the ganger sang " Ye-ho ! " the navvy came up to the surface and asked :

" Who wants to buy a shovel ? "

What I looked like just at this age did not trouble me. When about eight I had scarlet fever, which nearly finished me. My head had to be shaved. My mother cried a great deal ; and one day from the bed where I lay in delirium, and, strange to say, conscious of my delirium, I heard my younger brother Maurice in the kitchen say :

" If Joe dies, I'll have all his marbles."

My reputation as a marble-player was astounding. The other boys would only risk playing with me at odds. In a single season I had won three hundred and twenty marbles, including glass-alleys and alabaster taws and " bompers." Twenty were in my trouser-pockets when I fell ill ; but the other three hundred were hidden in a tin which Maurice had not been able to find. I did not die, and Maurice was deprived of his chosen inheritance.

The hair on my shaved head began to sprout in short, stiff bristles which had an unwholesome

fascination for my sister Kate who was tall, thin,
and very nervous. She would make me bend my
head towards her. Then she would rub her fore-
finger on the sharp bristles and scream with terror.

In a remarkably short time my hair grew in fair,
shining curls. The contrast was violent. I had
never before had curls. I began to take an interest
in my looks. I had lively, blue eyes, and I wore a
bright blue, silk neckerchief. My mother had given
me the silk neckerchief as a reward for not dying.
I went back to school, and the girls who sat in the
desk behind me used to pull my curls.

About this time I fell in love. She was in my
class. She also had fair curls and blue eyes. Her
name was Ellen Sullivan. She was eight and I was
nine. After school-hours I had to bribe Maurice with
marbles to induce him to go home through The Yard,
so that I should be free to go home round The Mount
which was the route Ellen took homewards. Maurice
would insist on coming with me.

Ellen had no father or mother. She went with
relatives to America that summer, and I have never
seen her since. She was very shy and tearful when
she said good-bye to me. The day the train took her
away I had to adapt "The Anchor's Weighed" to
my grief, and I sang secretly to myself :

> *A tear fell gently from my eye*
> *When last we parted on the shore.*

A great feud arose between my mother and me.
I suddenly felt disinclined to go to school. During
school-time I was up in the mountains. I had often

sat on our doorstep looking up at the hills. A farmer or shepherd riding along the high summit seemed as small as a bird. When rain or snow was falling, any moving thing, a horse, cow, sheep, or man on the mountain-top became mysteriously interesting. (A criminal of some sort once took refuge in our hills, and, for many days afterwards, policemen on horseback could be seen passing slowly against the skyline.) Up there I was out of the reach of punishment or restraint.

Instead of attending school, I roved the mountains in rain and sunshine with farmers, shepherds, gamekeepers, and poachers. I cannot account for this terrible revolt. I became a " mitcher," notwithstanding that Alec Taylor had had his head cut off through " mitching."

In the mornings I slipped out of the house before my mother was up ; that is, up for the second time. She rose between five and six to get breakfast for my father—he had returned from Cardiff to live at home—and for my two elder brothers, Matt and Jack, who had begun to work in the mines. At half-past six or so, my mother usually went back to bed for an hour's rest before beginning the long day's troubles ; and I took advantage of this lull to creep quietly downstairs unseen and unheard, believing that at the first chance she would carry out her promise to thrash me. I admired her for not capturing me while I was asleep. Her sense of fair play apparently would not allow her to take that step.

Sometimes I stayed in the hills till darkness came.

Every night I waited till my mother was either out or had retired to rest, before I ventured into the house. One or other of my brothers or sisters always gave me a hint on the point.

For six entire weeks I lived the life of a hillside brigand whom the authorities were chasing. Food I got in plenty from my mountain friends. Eventually Parliament threatened my mother with a summons for my non-attendance at school. Then, one dark morning—winter was coming on—when Maurice and I were playing cards on the hearthstone by the light of our big fire, my mother made an unexpected entry into the kitchen. She stood over me like a stupendous and terrible goddess. I was leaning on a trembling hand, looking up at her. She had captured me by fair means, and my punishment was serious. I would not take any breakfast, or promise to go to school that day. Yet I went to school. There I had twenty-four " canes," twelve on each hand. I refused dinner in our house.

Outside, only one mother showed any sympathy for me, and she was one of the few in The Barracks who had no respect for laws. Her husband worked in the coal-pits. Her daughters collected sandstones, heated them in their kitchen grate, then pounded them with lumps of iron into the sand which we bought for sprinkling our floors on Saturday afternoons. This woman came from Somersetshire. She had a son who went to school with us, though he was neither Irish nor Catholic. She knew I had had no dinner, so she gave me a huge slice of her bread. The bread was as white as snow ; but I could not

eat it, because I disapproved of the untidy state of
her household. I was fastidious. I made her son
eat the bread on our way to school, though I was
famishing.

Many boys and girls came over the mountains
from Merthyr, begging. Merthyr, to us, seemed to
be a beggars' garden. They sang songs in our street
and " down Newtown."

My two little sisters came picking up my bones ;
And carried them and buried them beneath the marble
    stones.

One street-singer, who came from no one knew
where, was a tall, red-faced man, the skin of his
cheeks broken by impurities of blood. He settled
down in one of the under-houses where, on Sundays,
owing to the Parliament Act which closed the inns,
a cask of beer was on draught sale. This house was
known as a *Cwrw Bach*. When he and his friends
had no more money to pay for the beer on a Sunday
evening, he crossed over to the Miskin, sang hymns
in the street, came back with all the coppers that
had been given to him by pious people, and resumed
the carousal. The woman who kept the *Cwrw Bach*,
whenever she heard the obnoxious word, b——, had
a peculiar habit of challenging the user on its meaning.

A youth, who had come begging from Merthyr, also
settled down in an under-house and worked in the
pits. He had a strange personal magnetism which
attracted me. I would go to the public-house with
him. Many of the young men knew me and, according to a generous custom, filled " tots " (small

glasses) of beer out of their pots to give me a drink.
I remember quite well a craving for these offers, and
bitter disappointment if I happened to be overlooked.
I do not know exactly how an end came to this.   I
think it finished with the departure of my Merthyr
companion.   I remember walking over the mountain
with him one summer day, to a place in Merthyr
named Quarry Row.   We were met, near the rubbish
tips there, by a tiny, sad-faced, little girl who was
his sister.   One of the first items of news she gave
him was :

"—— have gone as a bad girl."

The young woman she referred to was unknown
to me.   What was said was beyond my understanding,
nor did it occur to me to ask the meaning.   I returned
home alone across the mountain that night, and never
saw the youth again.

Father Wilberforce, who afterwards became well-
known in the world, held a mission in our church in
the winter.   He came in sandals, shaven crown, and
the strange dress of his Order.   He taught us the
mission hymn :

> *The snow lay on the ground,*
> *The stars shone bright,*
> *When Christ our Lord was born*
> *On Christmas night.*

His preaching crowded our church.   A large cross,
bearing a life-size image of Christ crucified, had been
specially erected on the altar steps.   I went with
other boys and I fell fast asleep during the sermon.
I woke up at a loud sound, and was struck with terror

at seeing the missioner's eyes. The cross—the largest I had ever seen—was in his hands. He had taken it from its socket and was showing the trembling congregation the bloody wounds our sins had inflicted on our Saviour, and his eyes were shining with tears. We all hated our sins that night.

My interest in school lessons went altogether as soon as I reached the sixth standard. I had worked diligently to reach this height, because failure at the last examination meant that Parliament would force me to remain at school another year—that is, till my age was thirteen. I was nearly twelve. By passing the fifth standard I was independent of Parliament, free to leave school and go into the mines as soon as I was actually twelve.

Two of my brothers were in the pits already. All the boys in school looked forward with longing to the day when they would be allowed to begin work. Release from the boredom of school might have influenced them ; but my happiness was not so much in leaving school as in the idea of actually going to work underground. We saw the pit boys coming home in their black clothes, with black hands and faces, carrying their food-boxes, drinking-tins, and gauze-lamps. They adopted an air of superiority to mere schoolboys. We humbly bowed to this. They had experienced danger amidst thundering falls of roof, and had had mysterious adventures, in deeps, levels and headings, with blue balloons of gas threatening to explode around their lamps. They associated with big men and wonderful horses. They earned six shillings and ninepence every week. Never would

one of them dream of giving up the pits. Life began
to be worth living when once they had gone down.

My mother's feelings on the point of seeing her
sons go into the mine were a mixture of pain and
resignation. She would neither assist nor restrain
us. It was useless for her to deny to herself that
what we might earn would all be needed at home, yet
she would not take a step towards getting permission
from colliery authorities for us to become pit-boys.

For me the prospect of going to work in the mine
contained more glittering romance than if its black
mouth were the entrance to Ali Baba's cave of gold.
The day before I was twelve I had to walk to Aberdare, four miles away, to get my baptismal and school
certificates from Father O'Reilly, our parish priest, a
saint and a gentleman, who, later, rose to be Vicar
General of the Diocese. I walked back, also because
my mother, consistently with her policy, would not
pay my train fare for the purpose I had in view. I
fell in with a travelling circus and menagerie of
elephants, lions and tigers, on my tramp up the valley,
which, years after, made a chapter for my novel,
" Maurice."

My eagerness to go down the pit was so great that
as soon as I came home, I interviewed Dai Morgan
the overman of Navigation Colliery, on my own
initiative, and showed him my qualifications : I
should be twelve years of age on the following day
and had entirely satisfied Parliament that my
education was complete. He said :

" Right you arr, Kaet'n."

Next morning, I was up at half-past five. It was a

grey, sunless morning, but I was thrilling with happiness, and I could scarcely sit peacefully at the table to take my breakfast of bread and butter and tea without milk.

My mother put my food in a small tin box and filled a tin " jack " with cold tea, and said " May the Lord bring you safe home ! " as I left the house.

I went to the pit-head in an ecstasy—the colliery was just behind our house—with a thousand men and boys, amidst iron trams, iron tracks, grease and machinery. I was given a long, gauze-lamp, called a " sprag," entered the pit-cage and, crushed in between about a dozen boys and men, was lowered into the darkness. The swift descent took my breath away and I gasped with fright and clung to my friends' dusty clothes.

CHAPTER IV

THAT first descent into Navigation coal pit, at half-past six o'clock, on the morning of my twelfth birth-day, April 16, 1883, interested me wonderfully. As we dropped below the brink of the shaft, the pale daylight seemed to spring upwards and vanish like a flying ghost. For a moment after that I could see nothing at all. Then faint yellow rays appeared from our lamps, and I could see as well as feel the forms of men and boys with me.

They had ranged themselves in two lines against the iron sides of the " carriage," as they called it. Each man and boy had his hand raised, clinging to a bar. One of the men lifted my hand to a bar, and said good-humouredly :

" Ketch by here, wassy ; or you'll tumble out, p'raps."

They could see me clearly, though I could not see more than their outlines.

My mother had asked one of our friends, who lived near us and was a haulier in the pit, to take care of me that morning. I am sorry I cannot recall his name.

He was with me in the carriage ; but, in any case, the others would have seen to my safety. All were kind to a beginner. They could tell by my schoolboy clothes that this was my first day in the mine.

I soon began to distinguish details. The lamplight illumined only two rows of legs and feet ; but owing to the violent shaking of the carriage, a lamp sometimes swung out, and then its rays flashed on my companions' faces. Some of the men were so tall that they were bent almost double under the iron roof. They were dressed chiefly in trousers of duck or moleskin, which once had been white but was now black, and all sorts of jackets and waistcoats and caps, and carried, like myself, a drinking tin and a box filled with bread and cheese. Some who were particular about their food brought buttered bread and cheese, or even ham sandwiches, and had milk in their tea. Sugar was avoided because the pit was warm, and a sweet drink increased thirst rather than quenched it.

We were going down so rapidly—the pit was a quarter of a mile deep—that our lamplight seemed to me to be always running up. Where the rays touched the shaft walls I saw steam pipes, signalling wires, guide-beams, and iron girders. All the time a terrific wind kept shrieking and blowing bits of coal into our faces. The tiny, flying things struck my forehead and cheeks sharply and painfully. I felt as if I were falling through the earth.

There came a sudden jerk which nearly upset me. Then the movement made me think we were going slowly up again, until a new blaze of light flashed from beneath us, and the carriage came to rest almost as softly as if it were a black cat that had leaped down a coal cellar. I did not know that we had reached the pit bottom.

My companions pushed me out. I slipped awkwardly. The floor about the shaft was covered with large iron plates which were smooth and slippery. My friend most kindly helped me. Lights from somewhere made the plates glitter. I was too confused to have any definite sensation. But I was glad to be there. The quarter of a minute, which was all the time taken for the quarter of a mile drop, had been a magical period in which I had passed from happiness to terror, and back again from terror to happiness. I was delighted to be in the pit.

Crowds of men, boys, and horses were hurrying by. Human beings and animals appeared to be moving phantoms. My eyes could not make anything seem real. The light was, in reality, quite good; but here I could see nothing clearly. My long lamp was still alight; but in this endless darkness my little flame inside the gauze was like a bit of white chalk in a black bottle.

I made out a huge, vaulted roof, formed by a mason's arch, with bright spots high up in the centre and at the sides. The bright spots were wide, flaming gas jets. I could see them; but the spaces between the lights seemed to be blocks of darkness. All the time there was a rattling sound behind me, as the carriages flew up and down the shaft bringing more and more men and boys, who walked past me laughing, chattering, or shouting to others far away in the unseen.

I followed my friend with difficulty. I began to distinguish wires above me and iron tramlines underfoot. I stumbled.

"Don't tumble over the rollers, Joey boy," my friend said genially.

On the ground between the rails were shining iron rollers on which steel-wire hauling ropes were lying; and we passed what were, apparently, two endless rows of coal trams, one row empty and the other loaded.

We stopped when we came to a group of lads. They were laughing and playing noisily under a gaslight, like boys larking around a street lamp.

"Look after Joe Kaet'n," my friend shouted to one of them. "You're all right now," he added to me. And he vanished through an opening in the archway side.

From that same opening came a line of horses—more horses than I had ever seen in any circus. They were black, brown, white, and red. The gaslight shone upon their flanks as they trooped slowly by. Then I knew that I was at the opening to the stable road. The horses were starting out for the day's work, and this was one of the splendid sights I had long wished to see. Behind each animal was its haulier. Every horse carried a nose-bag, and the man had a lighted lamp in his hand. The boys, one by one, joined a horse and man and went off with them.

The lad who had been told to look after me took me with him behind a haulier and horse; and we went in along a tunnel which seemed to have no end. Dust

from so many tramping feet blurred the string of
lights. The air became warm. I was coughing and
perspiring yet entirely charmed with everything,
even with the dangerous-looking roof, upon which
my boy friend flashed his light for my benefit at
special parts, where gloomy caverns with jagged sides
could be seen, and huge stones seemed to be on
the point of dropping as we passed under. He
showed me these murderous things with great pride,
as if they were part of the glory of being in the pit.

"Look at the ragged top," he said. "You won't
find a worse road than the Face Side Level."

I shared the pride he felt, and was honoured at
being in the Face Side Level. There were hundreds
of other roads in the pit; but I was glad I had not
been sent to any but this one. I cannot explain why
I should have found such satisfaction in being connected with places of danger. There seemed to be
a kind of distinction about it which made me
think I was doing something that was very fine. I
was especially proud of being with men and horses.
The good-humoured voices of men and boys, as they
tramped slowly inwards, their laughter, snatches of
song, and lively chatter, the neighing of animals,
jingle of harness, and thud of hoofs in the dust, gave
me a feeling of real happiness.

The exact kind of work I should do in the pit had
been arranged. I think this was done by my brother
John. He was in charge of a hauling engine—an
exalted post—back at the shaft-bottom. He had
been in the mine five or six years, and had begun work
on the Face Side Level, "dooring." Our brother

Matt had also begun as a door-boy in the same district, two years before me. He had since been lucky enough to get a better-paid job, "oiling"; that is, he oiled the iron rollers over which I had stumbled on the way in. Matt's present work would lead to an engine-driver's post, such as John's. It had been settled that I should begin in the same way as they did. I was to be a door-boy on the Face Side. There was a tradition in this similar to the hopeful notion in a prime minister's family, where each young brother starts as a mere Member of Parliament with the intention of gradually rising to the position of political chief engineer.

About a mile from the shaft we halted. The hauliers lowered their horses' nosebags. Men and boys sat in the dust in friendly groups. We were at the "locking-place," where every lamp had to be examined by the fireman before we should be allowed to go in to the coal seams. A defective lamp might set the gas alight and cause an explosion which would kill us all.

The locking-place was a fairy spot to me, with all the lamps, horses, colliers, hauliers, and door-boys. The men around me were smoking.

I knew enough about the mechanism of my lamp to take it to pieces. I had learnt all about its top-gauze, bottom-gauze, and pot, through cleaning my brother Matt's lamp at home. I was told to go to the fireman, a big-faced man with a grey beard, who sat in a hole in the side-wall, with a naked light upon his knee. He tested my gauzes upon the flame, and afterwards locked my lamp.

My boy friend then took me to a man who was smoking. He had an enormous black beard which made his face seem terribly stern. He was examining the horses with his lamp.

" Here's Joe Kaet'n," explained my guide.

" Oh, here you arr," said the man, in a tone so kind and genial that the contrast between his real tenderness and his apparent severity astonished me. He was, in fact, one of the best-natured men I ever knew.

This was the great man—the " gaffer-hauliers," a phrase which was English in Welsh form, and meant " Controller of the Hauliers." It was he who would arrange how and where I should be set to work that first day. This interview was of immense importance to me.

I had heard much of him beforehand. I knew his name, or, at least, his title—Jim Rasswr—a sheer conglomeration of English and Welsh. " Rasswr " meant racer. Jim had been a swift runner, and any distinction was always added to a man's name in our romantic hills, just as in former times characteristic titles were given to Richard Cœur de Lion, and other mediæval heroes.

It was well known to me that Jim Rasswr had won as much as a sovereign a time at racing. I had been an enthusiastic spectator of those running matches. They were held down the valley road in summer time, on Saturday afternoons when work was done. It was difficult to find a flat quarter of a mile along our up and down highway ; but there was a very good part just below Level Rax. Everybody went to see the racing. There was no gate-money taken. We stood in rows on the canal bank, or on the hillside, and looked down at the champions, who were naked except for their spiked little shoes and red, black, or blue loin-drawers. While the race was actually being run, our excitement made the mountains shake in sympathy with us.

"Kaet'n," Jim said, "you shall go with Darling. Take care of yourself, now, mind you. She is nasty sometimes. Tom Pugh!" he shouted, to the darkness beyond. "Joe Kaet'n will door with you."

"Darling" was a little brown mare with one flashing eye and a red hole where the other eye ought to have been. She had run wild once too often in the pit, and had knocked the eye out by colliding with a tram of coal which was in her way. Tom Pugh was her driver, and I was now her door-boy.

As I had often heard the boys speak scornfully of docile pit-horses that would do as they were told and never kick, bite, or run away, I was delighted to hear that I should be "dooring" for a mare that had such a dangerous reputation.

All that day I followed Darling and her vagaries. I rode behind on the coal trams which she pulled. When she stopped at a door I ran ahead, opened it, and stood by it, like my lady's page, while she and her load passed through. Then I closed the door and had another ride behind.

Riding behind the coal trams was in itself a joy and a glory. I had been accustomed to riding behind carts, brewers' drays, and farmers' gambos, with the perpetual expectation of a whip-end reaching me. But here in the pit I could ride behind without fear.

And I must declare that during all the time I was a door-boy I never got tired of that joyous riding.

I was told to close every door carefully before I left it. Some of the doors were made of canvas stretched across a wooden frame. Those were "braddish" (brattice) doors. Others were made of wood only, and were called "plank" doors. I forgot to close one of them, and a few minutes later a collier came running out of his stall, nearly poisoned by gas, almost choking for want of air, his lamp extinguished, and he swearing wildly when he could get breath. By leaving the door open I had cut off the air-current from his road. Gas from the coal had quickly taken the place of air, and the collier had had to smother the flame of his lamp in order to ward off an explosion.

My haulier had lifted his lamp to the man's face and I could see his staring eyes. He was naked to the waist, smudged with coal dust, and wet with perspiration.

As soon as he heard that I was new to the pit, his rage and indignation vanished, and he said good-humouredly :

"Well, we all got to learn, wassy. Give me your lamp and go an' put firre in mine."

When I took his re-lighted lamp back to him, he was kneeling at the coal, hewing it with a big mandrill, and singing quietly. The ground was dark but the layer of stone at the top was as white as bread, and the seam of coal between the two layers glistened pleasantly in our lamplight, like the edge of a blackberry jam sandwich.

We hauled our loaded trams back to a "double-parting." Here our main road resembled an open hand, pointing inwards with fingers stretched apart, each finger a narrow tunnel with a collier "cutting" coal at the extreme end. I learned the names of these tunnels as rapidly as possible, in order to remove the stigma of being a "fresh" door-boy. Dai Vaughan's Deep branched to the left. I worked in The Straight Deep. Timbers held up the roof in parts; but there were spots where the timbers had become cracked and bent under the weight of the hills over us; and in a good many places there were no timbers at all. I could see bare stones above my head.

Soldier's Deep, which we sometimes went into for coal, was the only road that gave me a feeling of fear. I had known long before I entered the pit that there was a ghost in Soldier's Deep—the ghost of the poor old soldier who had made the road, worked in it for years, and had been killed in it by a fall of roof. Soldier's Deep looked isolated and deserted. It ran inwards a long distance, and only one man was working in it. Our voices echoed in a peculiar way through the darkness and silence. Water was always trickling down its timbers which were decayed, twisted, and splintered from top to bottom; and everything within that lonely tunnel looked grey, mouldy, and ghastly under our lamp rays. I shuddered whenever we went into it, and wondered how the man at the inner end of it could go on hewing coal there, so far away from us all.

Dinner-time came, and I sat with the other boys on the ground, in soft, black dust which was very comfortable. Under a timbered roof, we opened our food boxes. My bread and cheese, and the tea from my " jack," had a sweeter taste that day than any food or drink I had ever taken. Rats were running impatiently up and down the dark roadsides anxious to get the crumbs. We could see the rats' eyes sometimes. They were like sparks of fire in the blackness.

We did not recommence work for a quarter of an hour after dinner. We took a " spell." I stretched myself at full length in the dust as the others did, and we talked on some interesting subjects. A rat ran over my face, and the touch of its smooth, cold, little feet on my cheeks made me shiver with fright, and I sat up. The other boys laughed. I soon got used to the rats.

That afternoon, Darling ran away with two trams of coal, down a heading. Her driver was riding on the " iron " between her and the first tram, and I was clinging to the end of the last one. No bit or rein was used for pit-horses except in cases of extreme vicious-ness. Our hauliers established mastery of their animals by voice and will-power. But as there is as much waywardness in a horse as in a human being, even the master's commands were occasionally dis-obeyed. Darling had taken it into her head to ignore the order to stop. She ran through a canvas door, and the loaded trams tore and smashed it.

Then I heard my haulier shout.

" Watch yourself, Joe ! Run back ! "

He had leaped from his seat into the side, where he had to crouch low in order to escape being dragged under the trams, as the road was so narrow. I had run back, and I could see his light coming swiftly towards me.

Then the rumble of the trams stopped suddenly, and the roof came down upon Darling and her load. The trams had been thrown from the rails by her wickedness and had dislodged the roof timber. Countless roaring tons of stone seemed to be falling down. The road was filled with white dust in which the light of our two lamps looked ghostly. The crashing noise from beyond made me imagine that the hills were tumbling down upon us.

My haulier had shown great presence of mind, not only in the way he had saved himself, but also in warning me to retreat. I, not knowing the possibility of danger, should have gone on clinging to the end of the tram, and might have been struck down, smashed, and buried.

When the sound of falling roof ceased, we went forward. We could not see Darling or the trams. I saw only a huge heap of white and broken stones.

" Go and tell Jim Rasswr—quick ! " said my haulier. " Say Darling's buried under a fall."

I felt inclined to cry over Darling. She was really a pretty little mare, in spite of her one eye and her wilfulness.

There seemed to be no way out. My haulier helped me to climb over the " fall."

" Quick, wassy," he urged, when we got over to the other side. " I must go back and mend the door she broke—to keep back the b—— gas ! "

I ran out as fast as I could to the main roadway, and found Jim. I told him what had happened to Darling.

I was much excited. His apparent callousness astonished me as much as his kindness had done in the morning.

" Right you arr, Kaet'n," he said tranquilly. " Go back to Tom Pugh. Say I'm coming."

I was deceived in thinking Jim Rasswr was callous. He arrived at the spot almost as soon as I did, and with him he brought twenty men who carried picks, shovels, hammers, and iron bars. Jim directed the work of removing the stones ; and in what seemed to me only a few minutes' time he had lifted Darling from beneath a mountain. The timbers she had dislodged had fallen in such a way that they had crossed over her as she lay on the ground, and protected her from being crushed.

She was scratched ; and blood trickled here and there through the white coat of dust which completely covered her body. But she merely neighed, when she rose to her feet, shook her head several times, and blew the dust from her nostrils violently. She turned her head back towards us, and, in the lamplight, her one eye gleamed defiantly like that of a wilful child conscious of having done wrong, but in no way sorry for it.

" Damn your eyes, Darling," said Jim Rasswr to her, when he had examined her and found that she was not seriously hurt. " She'll be all right tomorrow," he added to my haulier.

Through all the marvels of that wonderful day my soul was in a state of elation. I felt personally responsible for the working of the entire colliery. Finishing time came as a disappointment.

But there was a consolation : there would be day-light enough left for people to see me going home, black—legitimately black.

That one dominant idea had been at the back of my head from the time we went down the shaft in the morning till we ascended again at half-past five in the evening. My pride in being the associate of men could not be put into words. To be seen returning home at evening time with all the big miners and their boys, stained by dust and toil, was a thing that had, for years, filled my imagination as the most exalted achievement of a life-time. Its heroic side did not concern me. I thought not at all of its being manly, but only of its being mannish. I wanted to be seen going home with the men from the pit, black, vividly black, so black as to be nearly invisible. My desire to be in the mode was much like the enslaving vanity which makes people wish to be in exclusive society.

My wish was granted. I was seen by most of my friends in my black clothes, with my face black, my hands black, and my pit-lamp and " box-and-jack " black, as I came home. My mother smiled at my comical appearance as I went into the house. But there was sigh in her smile.

" God help us ! " she said laughing, as she looked at me. " He's as proud as a dog with two tails."

CHAPTER V

Danger : I hear of Dickens and Byron : Irish politics : Mrs.
Toomey's fireside : I escape death and mutilation : Praying
at my granny's death-bed : The wake : I become a blacksmith :
A collier boy : The pit of darkness : My studies.

BEFORE the year was out I nearly blew up the pit.
I had climbed up into a hole above the roof-timber,
searching for a valuable mineral called mine (crude
iron-stone). We could get two shillings a ton for
this mineral. It took many months to collect a ton ;
but the joy of the chase exceeded the reward. The
skilfully laid roof-timber formed a floor upon which
stones might fall, and not a single one of them could
drop into the roadway beneath. Amongst the loose
stones up in such cavities we often found balls of
mine. But there was no air in those places ; and,
in a coal-pit, where there is no air there is gas.

The gas quite suddenly came down to my lamp,
and changed the gloom into a marvellous blue-green
which made the hole an enchanted cave. Two results
were possible. The gas would either smother me and
my light, or penetrate the gauze, touch the flame, and
explode.

A tremor of the hand that held my lamp would
favour the chance of an explosion. I remember
distinctly that I did not feel in the least afraid. I
had learned the way of the pit. I lowered my lamp

slowly to the timbered floor, and crawled, carrying the blue-green with me, across to the opening through which I had climbed up. There I lowered the lamp still further down, until it reached the air-current, and the danger-colour gradually faded and vanished like an evil spirit up into the darkness of its hole.

During the winter I heard two names mentioned for the first time in our house—also, for the first time in my life : Charles Dickens and Lord Byron.

Our brother John had given up playing ball and other games, and had been passing the time looking at books. He suggested to Matt and me that we ought to get a book called " Barnaby Rudge." I had lost interest in " The Boys of England," and had been reading threepenny book-stories. The title of one was " The Prey of the Tiger ; or The Thugs of India." In this narrative one-half of the characters were silently strangled by the other half, and I liked the book.

The one John wanted to get would cost sixpence. We would do practically anything John suggested ; so Matt and I subscribed three halfpence each, and John provided the other threepence. He wrote the author's name, Charles Dickens, and title of the story, on a torn bit of paper, and sent me to Grier, the stationer, to order the book.

Whether it ever came or not I do not know. At any rate, I did not read the story until many years had passed.

Among John's books at this time was one for which he had given ninepence. Lord Byron's name was on the tan-coloured paper cover. I happened to see a

page headed " The Curse of Minerva." The title was
as attractive as any I had seen, and I read all the lines
under it. The words resembled those spoken by the
actors at Ebley's Theatre (for admission to which we
paid threepence on a Saturday night), and I was
pleased. Nothing else in the book attracted me.

My work in the pit was so interesting that nearly
all leisure time was given to talking about what had
happened during the day ; and, between such discus-
sions and our games of bull-rag, chivvy, cat-and-dog,
and ball-playing, I had not much time to spare for
reading.

Sometimes while playing ball against the pine end
of The Barracks we discussed Irish politics, and
declared our bitter hatred of " coercion." The word
was familiar to me through hearing my father frequently speaking of the government in Ireland, in
terms one might expect from an angel if Satan and
a cabinet of fiends had blasphemously established
themselves in control of Heaven.

Very often on dark, winter evenings I went down
to Mrs. Toomey's. She was a kindly widow with two
sons who had grown to young manhood. They lived
in one of the under-houses. She was very thin, and
had a sweet, singing voice. There was always a group
of youths and boys sitting round Mrs. Toomey's fire,
chatting, telling stories, dancing, or singing " Come
all ye's "—a phrase which good-humouredly described
old Irish street ballads of love, death, and patriotism.
Here, again, we condemned British government in
Ireland and looked with eyes of hope to the Fenian
movement which would free the Irish from political

slavery. Jack McElligott, who lived two doors away, was known to be a Fenian ; and I heard he had learned to drill and shoot for the purpose of destroying Dublin Castle some day or other. I admired him greatly.

On Saturday afternoons in Mrs. Toomey's, I had to read out love stories from some weekly papers for two of the young men who had had no schooling at all, but had gone into the mines when they were seven or eight years old. I could read with ease any book or paper, though I did not know the meaning of half the words.

One evening I imitated a circus tight-rope performer, by walking along the spiked tops of a high railway fence. I heard some one shouting :

" The boy is killed ! "

I had fallen on the railway side, which was covered with furnace clinkers, and men were running to pick me up. I was not dead ; but my head and all the bones in my body were aching. I dared not tell my mother ; and I went to work next day and every other day, as usual, to keep up appearances, though for weeks I could not play any game.

The strange disinclination to let my mother know of any personal mishap was something I cannot explain. One day in the pit I was stretched out on my stomach, riding on top of a tram that was loaded with long timbers. I ought not to have been there, but felt sure that I knew how to take care of myself.

Over-confidence had its penalty. I forgot about a low part of the roof, which caught my back. The obstruction should have stopped the tram. But

Darling pulled harder than ever. When the tram passed under the low part I rolled off with my spine nearly broken.

Tom Pugh lifted me, put me in the side, and made me lie comfortably in the dust for the rest of the day.

Next morning he swore at me for being in the pit when I ought to have stayed in bed. I had gone to work because I did not wish my mother to know that I had been hurt. She always dreaded the thought of an accident happening to us ; but although we had five uncles who were miners, as well as my brothers, not one of our family, with the exception of my grandfather, was killed in the pits.

Some boys and I happened to be in the midst of a wild game of chivvy on a sunny evening, when my mother, her face very white, called me in to recite the Litany of the Blessed Virgin at the bedside of my grandmother who was dying at that moment.

Three or four women and men neighbours were in our house. We all knelt round the little, low bed. My mother put the open Prayer Book in my hand, and I read out aloud, while the others responded " Pray for us," to every line of the invocation. My grandmother had already received the last Sacrament. I could scarcely keep my eyes from the poor old woman's pale and withered face. The last breath left her before we rose from our knees.

She had been called " The Colleen Ruadh " (the red-haired girl) when she was a young woman in Ireland. Before she had been long in The Barracks, her husband was killed at his work. The pit cage had dropped upon his back, and had broken it. He was a big, fine man.

My grandmother had been left with six small children to rear, with no one at all to help her. She had been very handsome ; and, altogether, her story was a sad one. Her favourite son, Peter, who played the flute so well, had died in America from the effects of a blow in a prize-fight. My grandmother had gone to America with him ; but she would not stay there after Peter died.

At her wake we played games and told tales of enchantments. When an Irish Catholic died in The Barracks—either a natural death at home or a violent death in the mines—all who could attended the wake. Our kitchen was crowded with men and women, young and old, till three o'clock in the morning. Two lighted candles were at my grandmother's head and another at her feet. On a table near her were saucers of red snuff and tobacco, and a dozen long and short clay pipes. We played Cock-in-the-Corner, Hunt the Button, and told or listened to tales of leprechauns, giants, and old hags—wonderful stories that had never been written or printed. The characters in them often arrived at lonely mountain tops, so bleak and far from anywhere else that, in those places, the cock never crew, the wind never blew, and the " divil " never stopped to put on his morning gown.

The tales enthralled me.

A few of the old people on coming in would kneel beside the corpse. As soon as their prayers were finished they joined heartily in the games. We talked of everything except the dead. Good-humour, humanity, and religion were mixed together, and the wakes brought relief and consolation to sorrow.

Towards Christmas Day I went round the houses with other boys, and stood outside the doors singing or playing my piccolo—at least, the piccolo was as much mine as my brothers'. Anything in our house was held to be joint property. I had learned music somehow. We never got much money for our performances. Often we considered ourselves lucky if we did not get chased away from a door.

On the following St. Stephen's Day, I rose at six, put on my working clothes, made tea for myself, took my breakfast all alone, filled my box with Christmas cake, and went out to the pit. No one else in the house would think of getting up till noon, after our lively Christmas night.

Few miners were expected to be at work that day. But I had such a liking for the pit that I did not wish to miss a " turn." There was the added attraction of having my box full of my mother's Christmas cake.

No one, in my view, could make Christmas cake to equal my mother's. She baked six or seven loaves of it, a long time before the great Day came ; and would not allow us to touch a crumb of it till Christmas Eve. Then we were all given a free hand, and the big loaves of cake vanished.

She laughed heartily at me when I came home, and said she had been looking for me everywhere, not dreaming that I had gone to work.

When I had been in the pit just twelve months, one of our lads told me an attractive story about a place to be got as " Oliver boy " in the colliery yard. He explained that an Oliver was a big hammer in a blacksmith's shop, and was worked up and down by a treadle. He had been asked to find a boy, and he advised me to take the job. I have not the slightest idea why I suddenly desired to work the treadle of an Oliver. I interviewed Enoch, the man who wanted a boy ; and he agreed to take me, and pay me ten shillings a week. My mother, following her usual policy, raised no objection to my doing as I liked in such matters.

I joined Enoch, and learned to make nuts and bolts at the smith forge, and particularly " dogs " (spikes for fastening tram rails to their sleepers). I was delighted with the new work, the smith's fire, the hammers, tongs, and the Oliver which Enoch and I sent up and down together by putting our joint weight on the treadle.

He was an old and white-haired volunteer, and a splendid rifleman, with hundreds of prizes for marksmanship. Every Monday my duty was simply that of carrying " jacks " of beer to him ; and the next day he would stretch out his right arm to show me how steady his wrist was.

When he was absent, I worked alone at my fine fire, and the fitters and riveters of the yard regarded me with interest, because I was always singing while I hammered and shaped nuts, rivets, dogs, and bolts. I worked from six in the morning till six in the evening ; and one night, when we had orders to make several thousand dogs, and Enoch was still on holiday —though the week was half gone—I went to him at

the public-house to ask permission to work all night
to finish the order. He was so astounded that, after
giving consent, he came out of the public-house and
staggered home. I worked all that night and the
following day.

The heat of the next summer made me decide to
give up the Oliver and go back to the mine. When
I told Enoch he was indignant.

" You must give me a month's notice," he said.
" It's the law."

I gave the month's notice.

" I'll give you another shilling a week if you'll stay
with me," he declared.

I could not stay. At the end of the same day, I
explained that I should not come again. Enoch was
more indignant than ever, but he was powerless. He
had not the least notion of enforcing the law. We
parted.

Years afterwards we met at Barry Island. I called
him by name. He did not recognize me until I told
him who I was. He said in amazement :

" What, Joe ! Why, you look like a gentleman."

When I went down the pit again, I cried. I
realized, then, that my intention a year before had
really been to leave pit-work.

At fourteen I was too old to be a door-boy. But
Sammy Hill wanted a " butty " ; so I went with him
as a collier-boy. My wages were to be fourteen
shillings a week. Sammy came from Devonshire,
and he had joined the Salvation Army in Mountain
Ash. He was short and sturdy, and wore a little
grey beard. He always worked with his shirt off.

" Thee watch me, Joey," he said, " and I'll l'arn thee to be the best collier in the pit."

In a very short time he taught me how to work my own side of our stall. I learned the nature of " face-slips," " back-slips," the special uses of top and bottom mandrels, and the nature of " clod." The coal was not a solid mass, but was full of delicate joinings, the finding of which called for wonderful skill, and unless they were followed carefully a miner might work all day and scarcely hew out as much coal as would boil an egg.

Sammy was all mild good-nature, and would never let me strain myself lifting " cross-bar " lumps, or allow me to work too long without a " spell." After six months, he had such confidence in my knowledge of mining that one day he went out to a prayer-meeting, and left me in the stall all alone, with instructions to fill " one dram " (about a ton of coal) and no more. There was enough time for me to fill two trams. I loaded the first and waited for a haulier to bring me a second empty tram. A shaft accident had happened, which delayed the haulier, and I fell asleep near the warm coal, with my lighted lamp beside me.

When I woke my light had gone out. I was in darkness, and not a sound of any horse, tram, man, or boy could be heard. It was impossible for me to know what the hour might be—whether it was night or day ; but the feeling around me was that everybody had gone home. I was at least a mile and a half from the shaft, in a branch road, with countless turnings to be taken in order to reach the main road, and not a ray of light to guide me. I knew quite well that if I took a wrong turning it might lead into some abandoned workings, where I might wander for ever unfound, or till I dropped from hunger and exhaustion.

I groped about me and found my lamp, jacket, waistcoat, food-box, and drinking tin. Then I turned my back to the coal, and faced outwards. There can be no darkness greater than that of a road in a coal-mine. No crack breaks the black wall which comes flat against the eyes.

My guides were two : my foot upon the tram-rail to keep me in the middle of the road, and the air-current in my face. The wind could blow inwards only from the shaft itself. If I could reach the source of the current I should be safe.

I faced the wind and went forward. My foot upon the iron rail made a hissing sound with every step. My mind was easy though I was fully aware of my danger. I stuck to the tram-rail and moved against the wind, up deeps, down headings, along levels, through canvas doors and plank doors, and around turning after turning. The air-current was the only thing to tell me that I was going outwards instead of inwards.

My first feeling proved to be right. Every horse, man, and boy had gone home, and I had been left behind.

How long I took to travel the distance I cannot tell ; but eventually I saw the lights at the shaft-bottom. Few night workers were in the pit, and none had come to our district. The " hitcher " was the only man near the shaft, and he stared at me as if I were a ghost coming out of the darkness. That experience made a chapter for my first novel, " Son of Judith."

A curious mood came upon me at this age of fourteen and a half. I found amusement in studying a Book of Euclid, which either my father or my brother John had brought into our house. Working out the elementary problems interested me more than any story I had ever read. In fact, I had lost all pleasure in stories just at the time. That might have been one of the reasons why I took up Euclid—to pass the time, and nothing else.

My father was always urging his boys to " study "— a word which to him included all the wealth and power on earth.

" Shtoody, me boys," he said, " is th' grahndisht thing in the whole wide wurrld—excipt th' Cath'lic Churrch itsilf."

He never troubled his head about what subjects we should choose. He could read and write English and Irish. More—he talked Irish, sang Irish, danced Irish, and worshipped Irish. Beyond that, his qualifications as an adviser did not go. But he continued buying bags of books and pens and ink for us. Under his prompting, I decided to attend night-school ; but soon found that, for me, the boredom of school was as acute as ever, and my attendances dwindled down to nothing.

John and Matt were dabbling in shorthand. The queer system of writing attracted me also ; and at the same time I took up French grammar, and a really interesting book about old Greek philosophers.

E

One phrase in the Greek philosophy struck me particularly : " Know thyself." I liked the idea of this, but wondered how the advice was to be put into practice.

We had not the faintest notion, any more than my father had, as to what we should do with all this study. Euclid, French, shorthand, or Greek philosophy would be of little use in " cutting " coal, and certainly, no thought of ever doing any other kind of work had entered my mind. We must have inherited the paternal weakness : a blind love of learning.

My interest in anything was always either hot or cold. I began to sit up till three in the morning, reading by the light of our kitchen lamp. At six o'clock I had to get ready for work ; that is actual work, swinging pick and shovel, hewing out tons of coal, lifting great lumps the weight of which left my knees trembling, and my eyes blinded with sweat. Studying I regarded as no work.

My father now began to repent of having urged me to study. He would make me promise to go to bed early. That promise was seldom kept ; so he brought our parish priest to warn me solemnly that sitting up with books till three or four in the morning, when I had to be up again at six, was very wrong. His reverence made me promise that I would not do it except on Saturday nights, because on Sunday mornings I could stay in bed till time for Mass ; and, of course, a promise given to the priest was sincere and binding.

CHAPTER VI

WHEN my age came near sixteen, Sammy Hill's keen
sense of justice would not let him keep me working
for him at fourteen shillings a week.   He could afford
no more, and he advised me to look for a better-paid
place.   I could not find one in the Navigation pit ;
so was out of work for two days—a humiliating thing
in our quarter.   I was too old to be a collier-boy,
and too young to be a collier.

Tommy Coughlan, an intimate friend of ours, who
was a haulier in Penrhiwceiber colliery, which was a
mile away down the valley, very kindly asked for and
obtained a job that might suit me there.   I was to
work with a collier, " double-shift " ; that is, we were
to work in the daytime during one week, and in the
night the following week ; and so on, in alternate
weeks.   I took the job.

Of all the miseries that were ever inflicted on man-
kind, " double-shift " seemed to me to be the most
inhuman.   At the beginning of the night-week it was
impossible to get into the habit of sleeping in the day ;
and at the beginning of the day-week, it was impossible
to get into the habit of sleeping in the night.   By
the time the capacity for sleeping in the day was

developed, the night-week was over ; and then began the new torture of working all day and keeping awake all night.

I worked with a tall, red-headed and red-bearded Somersetshire man who was geniality itself, and he paid me sixteen shillings a week. His admiration for me made me uncomfortable. He would go round to the other colliers in the middle of the night, repeating:

" My butty d'kno' shorthand."

In the pit, towards two o'clock of a morning, nature seemed to die altogether. The coal fell out in crumbs. The earth seemed to stop moving. A foulness was in the air as if it had come to us through graves and decaying bodies ; and the darkness of the long road beyond our lights appeared to be filled with the ghosts of all the men who had been killed in the pit. My hands became so sore at this hour that I shuddered when I touched our iron " curling-box " to fill a tram.

At five o'clock on winter mornings, after a night of pain, we came out to select big timbers and chalk our number upon the sawn ends. When snow covered the timber, this task was horrible.

During that winter, my brother Matt deceived himself into thinking that my voice would do for singing bass, and made me join our Church choir which he was conducting. We were to sing Webb's Mass in G for the first time at High Mass on Christmas morning. No midnight mass on Christmas Eve was possible, because our priest lived at Aberdare, four miles away. I practised my bass part with more enthusiasm than genius. The sonorous Latin of the Credo was music in itself until I began to sing.

Matt had intended giving me a solo. But I surprised him by my astonishing inability to keep in tune ; and he said I had better not take the solo, but merely join in in the chorus parts.

Music, no doubt, disturbed my emotions, and I fell so deeply in love with a pale-faced, dark-haired Irish girl in our choir, that I could not keep my eyes from her when we were all practising together of a Sunday night in the gallery after Benediction. She was a year over my age. What I felt was so visible to all the world that the other girls frequently complimented me on my taste in beauty.

I asked her one Sunday night, when choir-practice was over, if she would be my sweetheart. She said neither yes nor no, but was very kind.

A Sunday night or so later, when a snowstorm came on as we left the church, she took shelter under an umbrella carried by another youth. I saw the two going down the street, their footsteps silent in the snow. A lighted street lamp was at a corner where she would have to turn to reach her house. Usually she went home alone. This night she stood a moment at the corner, with the lamp-rays changing the white snowflakes into golden feathers, as they fell noiselessly upon the umbrella that sheltered her. Then the youth and herself and the umbrella moved slowly towards her home together ; and as they passed out of sight I felt a knife in my heart.

Before I became a chorister, I had always sat or knelt with the congregation during Mass or Benediction. On Christmas morning I witnessed the celebration of Mass from the height of our choir gallery.

Snow covered the mountains. We could see them from the church windows. Green of ivy and holly brightened by clusters of red berries decorated the church. The white mountains outside, the green walls within, the beautiful vestments of the priests, and the solemnity of the service at the altar, gave me a first impression, which I have never forgotten, of the real, wonderful dignity and grandeur of the Mass. Afterwards, the priest praised our singing of Webb's in G, but advised me to abate my voice a little in the forte passages.

Our big kitchen was a good place for dancing, and the young men and women of the choir often came down on a Sunday night after Benediction. If we had no party at our place, we had one at somebody else's house. We danced quadrilles, lancers and cotillions. I played the tunes on our piccolo. The instrument belonged as much to my three brothers as to me. My brother Matt was the best player of us all; but often when neither he nor I wished to be out of the fun, he hummed the music in perfect tune and time for us while he danced in the set.

The collier with whom I had been working decided, in the summer, to go to another pit, several miles away down the valley. This compelled me to look for a new place; and, as I had always felt a bitter dislike of Penrhiwceiber pit from the first hour I went into it, I would not accept any offer to stay there except one —a place as haulier. The wage for hauling was eighteen shillings a week, and the work tolerably easy for anyone who had the necessary skill. Experience and skill were mine, as the authorities admitted; but my age—about seventeen—made them fear that I was not strong enough to be given charge of a big pit-horse that might play all sorts of dangerous tricks with me.

I was still handicapped by being too young for a man's work and too old for a boy's.

Being out of work was so hateful to me that I took whatever job I could get. I became a stoker of two boilers near our house, at fourteen shillings a week. My boilers provided steam for an engine which hauled the coal out of Forest Level.

Merely shovelling coal into a couple of furnaces was a perpetual rest compared with what I had been doing. Skill in keeping steam up to a required pressure was necessary ; but that skill, after all, was only a matter of judging and observing. The work was so easy that I had time to think, and a vague ambition came to me :

" Could I become an engine-driver ? "

The man who controlled the engine had, in a patronizing way, permitted me to watch him at his work ; and his condescension gradually reached a point at which he allowed me to handle the engine, obey the signals from the electric wires, and haul out the coal. I was as much at ease as himself at the task, and I ventured to mention to him my nebulous ambition to become an engine-driver.

He said only :

" Oh, ahy. I s'pose."

But the words expressed immeasurable scorn and contempt at the presumption of his stoker. He ordered me out of his engine-house and told me to stay for ever down in my stokehole.

Stoking failed me shortly after that. A new scheme had been devised for getting Forest Level coal out, and boilers, stoker, and ambition were left on the scrap heap.

Nothing at all could I get but a place as a labourer in Navigation pit.

My working place in the pit was the "rubbish stall"—any abandoned road from which all coal had been taken, and was now being filled up with dust and stones. My tools of trade consisted of a strong shovel for which I paid two shillings. A horse and haulier brought in trams which had been loaded with dust and stones. I unloaded the trams with my shovel. Each tram held a ton—sometimes two tons. Twelve of these loaded trams made up my "whack." Failure to unload my whack involved my discharge. The wage for this was half a crown a day.

A current of air could not always be arranged in a rubbish-stall, owing to the fact that the road was in process of being stopped up by the rubbish I unloaded and flung behind me. Stripped to the waist, in foul and suffocating heat which made me feel I was perspiring blood, and enveloped by dust, so thick that it darkened my light, I shovelled tons of dust and stones each day until my backbone threatened to snap.

It was not work. It was murder.

Five years previously I had begun in that pit as a doorboy. In five years I had reached the hardest and worst paid job in it. In five years I had reached the rubbish-stall.

One of my colleagues felt the agony of "labouring"

in a more acute way than I did. In order to get light for our work, we drove small nails into side-timbers, and hung our lamps on them. My friend, in his outbursts of despair, sometimes pulled out his nail and flung it into the rubbish. Then followed the difficulty of finding the tiny piece of iron again, as it was impossible for him to work without it; and, with a loaded tram waiting to be emptied, he invoked heaven and hell to find his nail or burn the pit and everybody in it.

If by an accident the wheels of a loaded tram happened to slip over the rails, and could not be brought in to us, we helped our haulier to lift the tram to its track.

One labourer was wiser than we. He could not be blamed for not doing his work unless the trams were duly hauled in. When a loaded tram left the rails, and the haulier invited him to assist in restoring it to its proper place, the labourer sat tranquilly at rest on his rubbish heap, and said:

" Bring 'em in, boys, bring 'em in—and I'll unload 'em."

Two of us were " shifting muck " ; that is, we were removing twenty or forty tons of dust and stone from one spot to another. My colleague, with a long gauze-lamp, was on top of the heap, his legs in sight, his head and shoulders up in a hole.

" ' Heaven from all creatures hides the book of fate,' " he said, coming down the heap.

What bitter and maddening thought had come into his mind, I could not know. He had raised his lamp to examine the roof. The light was on his face, and a smile of hopelessness on his lips. He was tall and thin.

" You are quoting Pope," I said, in astonishment.

" Ahy—me and Pope do agree very well," he answered slowly. He took up his shovel, and said no more.

Reading and study in unmethodical abundance had become a habit with me by this time. One book had led to another. I bought cheap, paper-covered, miserably-printed editions of Goldsmith, Fielding, Dickens, Smollett, Pope, and others. Goldsmith I preferred above them all. I read " Vanity Fair " in weekly instalments, in a half-penny paper called "Dicks's English Library"; and the story made me think very highly of Thackeray, until " Clarissa Harlowe " began to appear in the same periodical. Richardson's overpowering phrases captured all my admiration. Thackeray's simplicity appeared to be a crime, a presumption, when printed in a paper side by side with Richardson's grandiloquence. I had no sense of style; or, rather, I must have had an instinctive sense of style, or my imagination could not have been captivated even by a showman. Richardson's big drum gave me literary deafness for some time afterwards.

One of the Government inspectors of mines sometimes passed by when I was labouring in a collier's stall. He was a young man of our town, and knew that I had been learning shorthand. He was studying the same system. A Government inspector was an exalted person ; yet he sought my advice on shorthand

" outlines " for troublesome words, and we worked them out with chalk on my shovel under the light of our lamps, as we sat on the ground, with our backs resting against the seam of coal.

On Saturday afternoons, during that summer, I went with happy groups of young men and women, picnicking in the mountains. Our favourite place was Raven's Crag, where dark rocks and trees and ferns of the loveliest hues, appealed to our notions of romance. One of my picnicking friends, David Edwardes, was a poet who, in our opinion, would become a new Byron. Another had a taste in fancy waistcoats which rivalled the varied and entrancing hues of Raven's Crag.

We, the men of the party, carried hampers up the steep mountains, and the young women made tea for us. They were charming girls, but they had no serious place in my thoughts; for, about this time, I fell in love.

She lived four miles away. I used to walk the four miles to see her on a Sunday evening. Then, together, we walked many miles on the mountains. When she went home, I walked the four miles back again to our house, and reached there about midnight. Only on Sunday nights could she meet me, otherwise, I should have gone to see her every night. The gap of eternity was between Sunday and Sunday for me. She had come with others to assist our choir on some special occasion; and as soon as we spoke to each other we found that our tastes were mutual. She had brown hair which she wore in a long, heavy plait, down

to her waist.   During our mountain rambles, I talked,
or she sang.   In the intervals we kissed each other.
What cause arose to sever us I do not know.   I had no
wish to part from her at the time.   In after years I
knew that she could never forget me.   She died.

" LABOURING " was slowly destroying me. My youthful body had not matured, and the strain began to be unbearable. I was a boy doing, not a man's work, but an elephant's. I resigned my shovel and my position in the rubbish-stall.

I told Dai Morgan, our overman, that I would take a job as a haulier.

" You be too young to be trusted with a big horse, Joe *bach*," he said. *Bach* was a term which could convey every gentle emotion, from mere good friendship to undying love. The overman knew all the boys in the pit, by name and family-tree. Dai was a huge, bull-headed man, vigorous, healthy, and good-natured.

In his strong desire to oblige me, he added :

" You shall go driving by night. There you arr ! "

He was violating all rules to please me, and he turned away to other more pressing business.

" Driving by night," had one advantage and a million disadvantages. I should be paid eighteen shillings a week ; but the best part of a young man's existence, evening-time, when all the fun of life was dancing before him, would be taken from me. Besides, only " rodneys " (lazy fellows ; also, drunkards) chose " driving by night," as the work was so restful. There was no choice for me. I joined the ranks of the rodneys, and became a night haulier.

My age was nearly eighteen ; yet the first night down in the pit, I hid myself under a dark archway, and cried.

The work itself was pleasant, and so easy that I could do it with my eyes shut and my hands tied behind my back. I remember, one night, wondering why a haulier was paid when his horse did all the work. I merely said a word occasionally to my friend, the horse, and the obliging animal pulled or " backed," went round corners, turned right-about-face, and allowed me to ride comfortably behind on the trams which he hauled from place to place at my request. Compared with labouring, this new work was a pleasing entertainment. In real fact, I sometimes hoped the authorities would never discover that the horse could do the work without its driver.

Ease of body, as it happened, had never had the slightest attraction for me. The confidence, and even the admiration, of men with whom I had worked had been given to me for my activity, skill, and powers of endurance. I do not say that I disliked ease. I say it did not in itself satisfy me. Night-work was loathsome to me because it cut me off from life, my friends, my amusements, and everything that made a leisure hour desirable.

My feeling was that I could be content with such nice work, and such good wages—but not with night employment ; and I thought that if only I could become a day-haulier in the pit, I should be happy for the rest of my life. Into my mind one night came a plot by means of which I hoped to instal myself as a day-haulier, in defiance of Dai Morgan ; or, at any rate, until it was too late for him to object on the score of my age.

Many day-hauliers got drunk on pay-Saturdays, tramped three miles on Sundays in order to qualify themselves as *bona fide* travellers, then got drunk again, and were too ill to work on the following Mondays.

On Monday mornings, after my night's duties, I went home, bolted my breakfast while my mother re-filled my food box —(by this time I had given up carrying a drinking tin)—and hurried back to the pit, into the stables, and diligently sought out what horses were without drivers for the day. My offer to fill a vacant place relieved the " gaffer-hauliers " of much trouble, and was gladly welcomed. My experience as a doorboy, and the skill which I had since acquired in driving, enabled me to evade difficulties which called for mere bodily strength ; and I was able to work on equal terms with any haulier in the pit, except those whose masterful personalities could control wild-natured or very wicked horses. My plan made me known to the " gaffer hauliers," singular and plural, as an entirely competent person.

During one prospecting Monday, Shwni Collier (he owned a real name, John Rees or Jones) claimed my aid. In his district I saw a young man, who was short, slim, and refined in manner. He drove " Turk," a " rubbish horse." Shortly afterwards the same young man was an undergraduate at Oxford University.

On those lucky Mondays I did not go into the pit at night, but went on Tuesday mornings with the idea of being at hand in case of any opening. If I were not wanted, I returned home and went to work at night, as usual. One week I was engaged three days in the same district. On the fourth day, Billy Bola our " gaffer-hauliers " was exasperated by a message which had reached him from the missing man ; and Billy said to me :

" He is gone to some other pit. He was a tidy chap, and he had a tidy job, too, mind you."

I said :

" Well, Billy, I want to drive by day."

" Dai Morgan isn't willing, Joe *bach*."

" You leave that to me, Billy," I said. " I'll see him to-night."

" Right you arr. But, 'member you see him, now ! It's no good without he's willing, see. He'll sack us all."

I repeated my promise to see Dai Morgan, and Billy Bola was satisfied.

Billy was very short, stout, and asthmatical. His nickname " Bola " implied roundness. His raucous coughing could be heard echoing through the long roadways of his district. His big, kindly face was always smudged early in the morning, and in our lamplight his round cheeks resembled a full moon when the shadowy continents across it are plainly visible.

I did not see Dai Morgan ; nor had I the slightest

intention of doing anything but keeping as far away from him as possible, well knowing that he would not allow me to " drive by day." Billy inquired next morning if I had seen Dai Morgan.

My reply was :

" That's all right, Billy."

As I had gained favour by my competency, Billy did not question the meaning of my answer.

Within a week, my absence from night-duty led to discovery ; and Billy Bola damned my eyes for getting him into trouble with Dai Morgan.

" He got black looks on me through you, Joe. Go and see him. Say it's not my fault."

I saw Dai Morgan that evening.

" Back by night ! " he said severely.

Next morning I went with Billy as before, and the following day, and all days. My persistence was beyond all understanding, and authority obeyed. My plot had succeeded. My great hopes were realized. I was allowed to continue " driving by day " undisturbed. The wages were one guinea a week, which I handed over to my mother with unqualified satisfaction and pride. We had always given every penny of our wages to her. She gave us pocket money—two shillings, or more if specially needed—and paid for our clothes.

For me, the change from night work to day work was like bringing a dead man out of his grave to new life. I was completely happy.

The maid of one of Lord Aberdare's daughters wanted to sell her violin. The idea of being able to play Irish jigs and reels on the fiddle appealed to me so strongly that I became the purchaser of the instrument, case, bow, and resin complete, for eighteen shillings.

A clever violinist from Aberdare came down to Mountain Ash to give lessons. I was one of his pupils. Often I had to hurry home from the mine, get rid of all my dust, and rush off without food, to be in time for the lesson. My enthusiasm and incompetency when practising at home reached a stage when my brothers threw their boots at me. Sometimes they hid my fiddle under beds or in the coalhouse, and I could not find it for many days at a time. While at work in the pit I practised the " close-shake " on any kind of stick or " sprag," in order to acquire the characteristic fiddle-tone which women describe as being like beautiful, wavy hair. Unintentionally, the fiddle began to introduce me to Mozart, Corelli, Beethoven, Schubert, and the glories of great music.

My chief companions at this time were five young men and my brother Matt. The seven were very lively students of anything and everything within reach, and had, above all, the delightful habit of reading much and talking much about what they read. One subject was barred : an offensive subject. The talk of my friends was pure, romantic, wild and foolish ; but it was always chivalrous and, if its effect could be felt, ennobling. Only the most lofty and extravagant ideals of humanity and intellectuality had interest for us.

The seven met every evening, without any pre-arrangement, as each was free from any promise on the point ; but there seemed to be a secret, hidden

magnet in our midst, drawing us from other amusements to come together.

One Easter Monday we walked to Newbridge Fair,
eight miles away, to buy books at the second-hand
stall which we heard would be at the Fair. With our
books under our arms we walked home again at night.

One of our laws was stupendous. No one was
allowed to talk about himself. This operated dis-
tressfully on one of the seven, young Edwardes, our
budding Byron, when, to his amazement, he earned
a guinea for a sonnet on " The Soul," which a periodical had accepted and paid for. Our law forbade
him to tell us the astounding news. He told his
secret to somebody, with instructions to reveal it.
Later in life, one of our idealistic seven became so
engrossed in the Public Drainage Act that he was
made Deputy Town Clerk—a development on his
part which disappointed me.

We were brave. We put each other's grammar
right while we talked. If the ungrammatical speaker
defended his phrase, the remaining five friends formed
themselves into a high court, heard both sides fairly, and
gave judgment on the spot. There was no appeal from
that decision. I learned that " between you and I " was
wrong, and that " between you and me "was right ; that
my spelling of " always " was correct, but that my
spelling of " alright " should be changed to " all right."

As a result of our mental milling, Callip Jinkins,
one of the hauliers with whom I worked, was much
impressed. His loaded tram had slipped " over the
road," and he paused to listen to my view as to the
best way of putting his tram on the rails again,

without going to the trouble of nearly breaking his back, and mine, by lifting one end of a ton of coal six inches high. At the end of my speech, he said :

" Joe, you do talk nice."

My horse was named " Bowler," a red-coated, active, useful animal. I had to keep his nose in a powerful muzzle when he was not feeding, or he would spring at and bite anyone, except me, who came within his reach. His eyes, in wicked moods, glittered like yellow lamps. His tail was a short stump which, through some constitutional defect, was hairless, except for a little ragged bunch at the end, and resembled a dark shaving brush. He used his stump in an extraordinary way in vicious moments to express his disapproval of any order I might have given him. He detested being told to push trams back with his hindquarters. During this operation his teeth gleamed and his eyes flashed, and even I dared not get within reach of his mouth, or he would bite me. He did the hated task well all the same.

My acquaintance with miners in various districts made me regard the Welsh collier as a very high type of citizen, good-humoured, kind, skilful, hard-working, and naturally intellectual and pious ; though one collier, when all his genius failed to overcome a stubborn " slip " of coal, would call out to all who were within hearing to join him. Then he would kneel in our midst, and implore the Blessed Saviour to come down and wreck the pit and bury us.

Under my direction, Bowler hauled trams of coal from the hewers' stalls to a " double-parting." At this point an engine rope, made of steel wire, pulled out a " journey " of twenty loaded trams at a time to the shaft bottom. The hauling rope had to be very strong, as the road went steeply upwards.

We were forbidden to ride outward on the " journeys " of twenty trams, owing to the danger of the rope breaking. I was on the middle part of a " journey," half way up the incline, one night, going home. The rope broke. Training and intuition told me what had happened. Experience told me, also, that I should be killed when the trams ran back down the hill, unless I could manage to dismount in a road so narrow that the dust in the sides was always rolling into the middle of the rail track. I stepped off into the dust and half buried myself in it. The trams scraped my coat. They went back and smashed everything in their way, then piled themselves into a heap and brought the roof down in hundreds of tons. I should have been in the heap if I had remained on the trams.

When I was returning from the pit in the pleasant autumn evenings, a young woman would, at the same time, be coming from an opposite direction ; and we could not, in a sense, help meeting. Both of us were going home : she, after a hard day's teaching at school ; I, after a day in the pit. I was in dusty clothes, my hands and face exceedingly black. She was always spotlessly clean, and her white skin shone in the setting sun. Her hair, loose and long, covered her shoulders and waist, like a wrap of bright gold.

She was seventeen or so. She and I were acquainted ;

and we always stopped when we met, just for a moment or two. Her smile when I raised my ragged cap to her, as we met, was very charming. Beautiful mountain slopes were in front of us, and the pit with black machinery and coal wagons behind us. What our fragmentary conversations were about, it is impossible for me to remember ; but I thought it wonderfully kind of her to stop and speak to me. She was always a little late coming from school. Otherwise we should not have met so regularly.

Quite unexpectedly, I began to dislike pit-work. My duties were easy, and the pay satisfactory. My colleagues, the hauliers, were the best-humoured and best-natured fellows. The colliers were in every way excellent. I was on the happiest terms with those in authority over me. I had once believed that if I could achieve the height of " driving by day " my greatest ambition would have been realized. All along, I had desired nothing more than what was now in my grasp. I had no objection to the pit itself ; yet I began to dislike being in it. That was just when I was half-way between eighteen and nineteen. No explanation could I find for my change of feeling.

During the winter my dislike became actual hate.

Formerly, my days in the mine were short and happy. Now an hour there seemed to be a month. The pit had changed into a dungeon of darkness, and my agony in it was terrible. From the moment of going down in the morning I thought only of the moment for going up.

On days when I was not in the mine, I saw men going about their business, in clean clothes. Previously, I had never taken any notice of such men. Now I saw and envied. I thought that if I could be allowed to earn my living, free from the inconvenience of dust-black clothes I should be content.

My two brothers, John and Matthew had, a few months earlier, found pit-work intolerable, had gone away from home, and were seeking a living under the sun. I missed them more keenly than might be believed. We were very fond of one another. I remember, when our parish priest asked me the cause of my despondent manner at that time, I explained that I wanted to go away to my brothers.

A day came in the winter, when the sudden resolve was fixed in my mind while I worked :

"When summer comes, I'll leave the pit for ever."

What should I do for a living ? How could I earn bread ? That was a problem difficult to solve. I knew no trade, craft, or calling except pit-work ; and unless I earned my own living I must starve. If I could not keep myself, no one else could keep me.

"I'll give up the pit, when summer comes," was all my answer to this self-questioning.

I could not wait for the summer. That same winter, within a week of making up my mind, I left the pit.

I had made no preparations for the future. The only prospect before me was one of wretchedness, poverty, and starvation. I risked all that ; and it showed how deep was my feeling. The test of any man's sincerity seems to be in how much he will lose by his action. I was willing to lose everything, in order to escape from the pit which had become my prison.

CHAPTER VIII

My struggle for the sun : My mother joins the fray : I become
a fitter's labourer : I cut my father's hair : Love walks past
my door : My teeth are drawn : A dental miracle.

WHEN Billy Bola told Dai Morgan that I had given
up my "pins," by which was meant that I had given
up horse and pit, Dai swore gigantically, and refused
to believe such an utterly impossible thing.

"He shan't have his money," declared Dai.

His order to the cashiers that the wages due to me
must not be paid, compelled me to seek Dai, on a
misty evening, near the colliery offices. This interview I had wished to avoid. I knew what he would
say, and he said it as soon as he saw me.

"Damn your eyes. Go back to the pit."

The affectionate feeling he had for all the boys who,
like myself, had grown up to be young men under his
eye, made him regard the notion of my leaving as an
unthinkable crime. But he was also deeply concerned
for my welfare, and thought that I was acting merely
on some misguided, youthful impulse.

"I am never going back to the pit again, Dai," I
explained apologetically.

"Don't talk so foolish," he thundered.

One might as well argue with a mountain or an earth-
quake, as with Dai. I said no more, but went home.

My mother's attitude in this crisis was admirable.

She had strictly avoided helping me to get into the pit, and now she would not say a word to induce me to stay there. Her consistency of policy had been unbroken for nearly seven years. Her whole desire was to allow me to please myself in my choice of a career.

She went to Dai Morgan, and made it quite clear to him that she approved of what I had done.

The value of her intervention was : First, the wages due to me—nearly two pounds altogether—would be paid ; second, the colliery management, knowing that my mother sanctioned my wishes, would be willing to listen to any application I might make for a job on the surface. If she had not shown such sympathy with me, the authorities would have withheld my pay and refused to employ me anywhere on their works, because I had left the pit without giving legal notice. My mother was a great diplomat, and she made my offence seem a virtue. This was important. It would be a serious thing for me if my employers sent word to the various colliery yards, as was done in such cases, that I was not a desirable person to engage.

Then began my blind search for the sun. I tried everywhere for work on the surface. There were four collieries within a distance of two miles. Hundreds of men were employed coal-tipping, coal-trimming, coal-weighing, and so on, about the pit-heads. Coal, and only coal, was the industry of Mountain Ash. Yet nowhere amidst the hundreds was there one small vacancy for me, though I applied for all sorts of places, such as greasing railway wagons, driving hauling engines, and tipping rubbish. Surface work was so keenly desired by all sorts that men waited in invisible queues for other men to die; and as soon as any kind of post became vacant, the first man of the line stepped forward to claim the gaffer's promised favour. I, at the far-off end of the long tail, had no chance.

One of the vague notions in my mind as to how I should earn a living in the summer time, was that of carrying the hod. I knew that special training was needed for this, and hoped that, somehow, a means of acquiring the necessary skill would come my way.

A week of idleness and utter wretchedness went by. I hated being out of work.

My mother once more showed her superb diplomacy. Many years before, she had declined to help me into the pit. But she was quite willing to do all she could to help me out of it. She came home one night and said to me:

"Joe, I've been talking to Price, the mechanic, about you; and you are to see him at six o'clock to-morrow morning."

Price, the mechanic, had charge of all the machinery of two collieries. He had known me since the days I had worked at the "Oliver," in the Yard. I went out at six next morning, in my working clothes, to be ready for any miracle.

And the miracle happened.

Price sent me up to the Duffryn pit, with George, the bugler, who was a fitter, and had only one thumb, the other having been torn off by a cog-wheel. I was to carry tools and sections of machinery for George, the bugler. I became, there and then, a fitter's labourer.

That was an enormous advancement for me. I was elated. Whether my wages would be seventeen or eighteen shillings a week did not trouble me. I should be working in the light of day.

We repaired winding engines and hauling engines, fly-wheels, cog-wheels, piston-rods, cylinders, and boiler-valves. I carried every necessary item that was portable, to George, the bugler. He, as the fitter, would not dream of carrying anything but his steel rule, which he kept in a little, narrow pocket at the side of his trousers, like a long dagger in a sheath. While he worked we discussed music. He was a clever corner playet in the volunteer band, and, by his genius would, perhaps, have become bandmaster, but for his erratic tendencies.

During the following six weeks, my days were pleasant. Being under the sky, instead of under the mountains, was a joy in itself.

We were kept so busy that we had to work much overtime, which pleased me, because it brought increased pay. But on the night of the Monday before Whitsuntide I was not pleased. That Monday was the day on which Mountain Ash Fair was held. I wanted very much to go to the Fair, and we were told to work all night at repairing some engines. I made a strong appeal to be set free, but was informed that the engines could not wait. It was the first Fair I had ever missed, and I felt sad all night.

In The Barracks we played cards at one or other of the houses, from Saturday afternoon (when all work finished early) till Monday morning (when work began again), with one short break on Sunday morning for going to Mass. Twenty-fives required much finesse, especially with such clever players as Ned Murphy, the cobbler's son, who was a cripple, and had all the cunning and daring which seem to go with physical helplessness.

On other nights I attended an institute, which had recently been opened by the Anglican Church people for their young men. A few Irish Catholics were permitted to join.

The institute contained a library of useful books. I spent all my time in the billiard room. We paid ninepence for a "hundred up." As I always lost, I always had to pay. Before the week was half out I had no money; but the fascination of the billiard table for me was so overwhelming that I frequently pawned my waistcoat for ninepence, in order to get a game. On each pay-day I redeemed the waistcoat, until the time came when it was too old for Jacobs, the pawnbroker, to risk his money on it any more.

One Sunday afternoon my father wanted me to cut his hair for him. He preferred my style of hair-dressing to Mike, the barber's. Three or four times a year my father had his locks trimmed, and I was always his barber. He sat with his back to our front window, with a red handkerchief across his shoulders. His hair had once been shining black curls. It was still long and curly, but quite white. I had my coat off, my sleeves turned up, and, with scissors and comb, was taking the greatest care to give my father the kind of cut that would satisfy the dandy in him.

Half-way through my task I looked out of our window. The afternoon was sunny. My glance out was quite unpremeditated. At that same moment a young woman was walking slowly past our house. I put down the scissors and comb, put on my coat, said :

" Wait a bit, father."

Something suddenly compelled me to go out and follow the young woman down the valley road. She was Lala—(Her name was not Lala)—the girl with the fair, shining hair, who used to meet me so regularly when I would be on my way home from the pit in my black clothes. Owing to my change of work, I had not seen much of her lately. I believe we had met at one or two dances in the Drill Hall, during the winter, and I had been thinking a great deal about her.

I secretly regretted that she was neither Irish nor Catholic ; but I had a vague hopefulness that I could get over the religious difficulty by making her a Catholic.

The distance between us when I reached the road was not more than thirty yards. She was walking quite slowly, but I was not bold enough to overtake her in view of the houses with their doors open to welcome the sunshine into the kitchens. I walked steadily behind her, and forgot all about having left my father with his hair only half-cut.

At the end of our street, she turned up a hill to the left. I had guessed correctly that she was going to Sunday School. There was an easier way along the canal bank, by which she could have reached her school without passing our door. I did not think of that at the time. I thought only of how pretty she looked in her dress of delicate grey, and the trouble which her extraordinary personal charm had been giving me since last autumn. The feeling had gradually become intolerable. At the same time, her manner towards me had always been graciousness itself.

On the hill we were hidden from the view of our street; and I overtook her just as she was beginning to cross the one-arch bridge over the canal. I could not tell whether or no she knew I was there; but when I called her by name, and she turned her head and saw me, she did not seem to be in the least surprised. She smiled very amiably, and stopped, with one foot on the hill, and the other on the cobbled edge of the curving bridge floor. Beside us was the canal; in front of us were the mountains; and behind us, across the valley, more mountains. Sunlight and wind put shining ripples in her long, loose hair.

"Lala," said I, "will you come out with me?"

She scraped the cobble-stones of the bridge with her toe, looking down at it, and hesitated.

Her hesitation offended me.

"Say yes or no," I said.

My impatience touched her pride.

"No," said she, her lips pursing resentfully.

I turned away and went down the hill.

When I reached our house my father was raging with his hair only half cut. And as it was time for him to go to Benediction, and his duties as custodian of the collection plate made it impossible for him to wait, he went to church as he was.

My brother Matt organized many kinds of entertainments—Christy Minstrel, theatrical, and musical —for our church and charity. He gave me a part as the hero in Lover's " White Horse of the Pepper's," a two-act play. I was admired for my pair of black silk knee-breeches, white shirt, and blue waistband. All my costume was made by my mother. My sister Annie was the heroine, my brother Maurice an important character, and Matt the impresario. Annie was almost a child. She was a child of genius. She sang old Irish songs with a pathos that brought tears at every note. She mimicked every character she met, in a way that made us helpless with laughter. She danced Irish jigs and reels delightfully.

We held a concert in the town hall. I was to play the " Bohemian Girl " overture on my fiddle, with a nervous pianist. He started before I was ready, and no power on earth could stop him. I was not able to put in a single note throughout the whole overture. The audience applauded both of us when he finished.

Toothache had perpetually haunted me like an invisible, torturing demon. A travelling dentist happened to call at our house, and my mother thought it a good chance for me to get rid of my worst troubles.

" This one," said the dentist, holding up a tooth in his forceps, " is fairly good. I will stop it and put it back."

We all looked on in amazement while he repaired

my tooth. When he had stopped it, he put it back into its own socket in my jawbone. It remained there, and was a more companionable tooth than it had ever been before. It did its work, and never bothered me.

CHAPTER IX

GEORGE, the bugler, by some mishap due to his erratic
genius, was removed from the Duffryn, and sent to
work elsewhere. This left me without a fitter to
assist, as no one was put in George's place.

For a time I cleaned engines about the pit-head. I
admired the magnificent sections of the big winding-
engine. The cleaning work, unfortunately, could not
keep me busy all day. I had hours of idleness which
were most painful to me. I dared not risk being
seen reading, sleeping, or even sitting down. I had
to seem to be working. If an official passed through
the engine-house, I unscrewed a harmless nut and
screwed it back again, until the man had gone out of
sight.

In the Ventilator building one afternoon, my
boredom became actual agony. It seemed to me that
nothing could be harder than a job which was too
easy. I tried to think, but no thought would come.
My brain would not work while my hands were idle.
Deadliness was creeping into my life. I felt limp and
spineless, and sat down for a moment on the iron

foundations. Steam from the cylinders made the engine-room warm, and the huge fly-wheel went round with a drowsy hum. I was still trying to think, but fell fast asleep. Price, the mechanic, above all people in the world, the man who had so kindly found the job for me, came into the Ventilator and woke me up.

" Don't do that again, Kaet'n," he said warningly, and passed on.

It was impossible for me to excuse myself on the score that I had fallen asleep because there was not work to keep me awake. The answer would have been that, in such circumstances, my services were unnecessary.

Price was a good-natured man. Instead of punishing me, he sent word to me next day that I was to take charge of a pumping engine at the riverside.

Now I tasted joy. In a little shed with a brown canvas top, down at the water's edge, I oiled my engine, regulated valves and levers, and pumped the river into boilers, to make steam for all the engines of the pit, on the surface and underground.

No one inspected me, and my hut became a study, library, and a university. I brought what books I liked, and I read all day. I learned, in ten minutes, how to control my engine without giving it constant attention ; and my mind was free. I read Thackeray, Swift, Goldsmith, Byron, Shelley, Keats, Sheridan, Fielding, Smollett, and Dickens.

Even when my hours were changed from day to night, I was happy. Night duty had compensations. It was summer-time, and my shed was snug. All through the long night, by the glare of a big oil-torch,

I read poetry, philosophy, and stories. No library was big enough to satisfy my appetite. The sound of running water, the purr of my tiny engine, the darkness and solitude, the red light of my torch, the book in my hand, an occasional touch of the oil-can for the bearers, and a glance or two at valves and levers, were the romance of my riverside nights.

A Sunday night free from duty was arranged for my convenience at irregular intervals. On one of these rare occasions, I met Lala, accidentally, near the railway station. It was late. She had been with her cousin who had gone away by train. I raised my hat, and would have passed on without a word. But Lala walked by my side down the dark road. We were both going the same way home. I was surprised to find Lala remaining so near me and, evidently so contented to be near me, after our quarrel.

I said :

" Lala, why did you say ' no ' that Sunday ? "

" I didn't mean it," she answered. And the star-light seemed to be in her smile as she looked at me. I put my arm round her waist, and kissed her lips ; and we were very happy.

By some freak of my fate, all my good-fortune was taken from me before the summer was half-way through. The coal-seams of the Duffryn pit were declared to be unprofitable. The miners were taken out, the shaft was closed, the boilers that drank my river were shut down, my tiny engine was dismantled, and I was discharged.

Price did his best to make room for me elsewhere ; but, owing to the number of others who had prior claims, he failed. I was out of work, and my hopes were scattered to the four winds.

The dreary work of looking for work had to be faced again. I tramped up and down the valley, willing to take any miserable job on the earth but not under it. Nothing except unchanging refusal rewarded my asking.

In my desperation, I applied for a place as shorthand clerk, at Abercwmboi. My qualifications were scanty. But sheer hopelessness of securing anything else drove me to the attempt. How the advertisement of the vacant post came to my notice it is impossible to say, because newspapers had no meaning at all for me at this period of my life. And as for their advertisements, such a method of seeking or finding was a development of civilization that had not reached me. If anyone in The Barracks wanted anything, he or she went looking for it in person, or told someone else to tell someone else of the want.

This particular advertisement requested applicants to write a letter, stating age, office experience, and the amount of salary expected. I wrote ; but my letter avoided any mention of office experience, as I had had none ; nor did it refer to salary, because I would take whatever I could get.

In a few, simple words, I said that my age was nineteen, and that I would like to get the appointment.

While the letter was being written, the priest called at our house to make the kindliest inquiries, as usual, regarding our temporal welfare. I showed my letter to his reverence. He corrected one or two points for me, said it was a good letter, that I was to give his name as a reference, and wished me luck.

A reply came from Mr. Hann, asking me to call and see him. I walked two miles up the valley road to his colliery offices. He examined me with a stern and patient eye. He was a dark-bearded, pale-faced man. His genius as a mining engineer had made millions of money for his company. He dictated a letter. My father had never tired of reading out to me for practice ; so my speed satisfied Hann. He told me to transcribe the letter, and he sat watching me while I did it.

My shorthand was as easy for me to decipher as ordinary print would have been. But, as I had used the pick oftener than the pen, I could transcribe in longhand only very slowly. My writing had the angularity that is always found where the strength of the hand has been developed for heavy work. Suppleness of wrist is destroyed by manual labour. The words of my letter seemed to have been formed with the iron bar which I had used for levering out tons of coal.

Hann looked a long time at my transcription. He inquired where I had learned shorthand, and where I had been educated.

" Oh, at home," I replied amiably.

He said that as I had had no experience in office work he could not give me the appointment ; but that when I had gained experience he would be very glad to do what he could for me, as he wished to encourage young men to educate themselves as I, evidently, had done.

His talk seemed to me to border upon idiocy. In the first place, how was I to get the experience he mentioned, unless someone had more sense than he, and allowed me to start in an office ? His stupid attempt at patronizing me, when he spoke of " encouraging " young men such as myself, while he was refusing to be of any use at all to me, I regarded as a display of the worst kind of manners. He ought to have held his tongue, instead of claiming a merit which his action belied.

I had too bad an opinion of him to express it ; so I went away in silence.

There was a wagon-shop near our house. I asked Rennish, the gaffer—a thin man, with a red, flowing beard and one eye—for a place as a helper.

" Do you know anything about making wagons ? " he inquired.

" No ; but I could easily learn how to do it," I answered.

My calm reply seemed to exasperate him. In a fury, he gripped me by the arm and rushed me into the wagon-shop.

" Do you see those men working with lathes, saws, rule, and straight-edge ? " he asked, his quivering finger pointing to the busy wagon-makers.

" Yes."

" Do you think you could easily learn their work, you foolish young man ? You have not had any training."

" I didn't ask for a job as wagon-maker," said I, " but as a helper. Look at those chaps carrying planks. Do you think I couldn't carry a piece of a tree from one place to another without any training ? "

" Go away—go away ! " he shouted.

Somehow I found a place as a spare-hand scavenger under the Local Board, cleaning street lamps, digging drains, weeding the surveyor's garden, painting railings, and doing other odd jobs. My wage was a pound a week ; and I feel sure we were paid fortnightly, because, every pay-day, I had to sign a stamped receipt, and the wretched authorities were mean enough to deduct the penny stamp from my wages.

Amongst my duties came the task of painting a huge gasometer. For weeks I was splashed from head to foot with red paint.

One day, when I was on top of the gasometer, and pressure had sent the upper part to a tremendous height, I wanted to throw myself off—a trick of the nerves which has, possibly, in other cases, sent persons over high cliffs into the sea.

Nothing but flinging myself down to be killed would satisfy me.

Yet behind that wish was a clear idea of its absurdity. Between Providence and my sense of humour, I gained strength enough to crawl around the edge, to our ladder. I went down to earth slowly instead of suddenly. When my feet touched the ground I fell in a heap. A story of mine called " The Pinnacle," which made editors in America and England ask me for more of its kind, came out of that terrifying moment.

After I had finished colouring the gasometer, I was

sent out with shovel, brush, and wheel-barrow, sweeping and cleaning the streets. I was glad to have the work to do. When I went home, recently, I found a Welsh poet at the same kind of work there. His poetry had the glory of genius in it.

My sorrow was that, being only a spare hand, my job could not last. The end came within a few weeks. The Local Board gave me and two others notice that our services, though valuable, were no longer necessary to the well-being of the community. And for reasons of public economy we were discharged.

No other employer in the district wanted me, except for underground work. A hundred times I was offered well-paid jobs in the mines. In fact, some of the colliery authorities urged my mother to advise me to go into the pit again ; but she was all in favour of my keeping out of it. I felt the hopelessness of my position. Everything I had tried had failed. I was as unlucky as the man who said that if he put a duck in the water, his duck would drown.

After months of struggling to get free of the mines I was no further away than at the beginning. The shadow of the pit was stretching out its black hand to drag me back to it.

I had said, on giving up the pit, that I had left it for ever. My fate laughed at me. My future would be that of a half-starved rodney, an idler, a brother to the few lazy, drunken, red-faced, pimple-cheeked wastrels who were bywords of scorn and contempt to all my friends. I challenged my fate. I was helpless, but not beaten. Let starvation come, I would not go into the mine again.

CHAPTER X

THOUGHTS of enlisting as a soldier came to me now, when there seemed to be no other way of keeping out of the pit.

" I'd rather wear the red coat than black coat," was my reply to the objections of my friends.

My brother Matt came home one night, when my crisis was near its agonizing climax.

Matt was a surprising youth. He had run away from home, at fourteen years of age, with Gadnor Coyne's theatrical company. Matt had great acting talent. The company was stranded in a fortnight. Matt had found a job for himself in Bridgend, with some navvies who were digging out the foundations of a lunatic asylum there ; but his whereabouts being discovered, my mother sent our brother Jack as an ambassador, and he brought Matt home. Recently, Matt, sick of the mines, had run away from home once more. How he had managed to live no one knew exactly. I think he had been, among other things, a cattle drover, in Cardiff. His adventurous career had made him a collector and salesman for Jones and Jones, a Rhondda Valley firm of general merchants.

He sold pianos, mangles, harmoniums, perambulators, and jewellery, on the hire system, collected the instalments, received a commission on all his work, and his earnings amounted sometimes to three pounds in a week, sometimes twenty pounds, because he had a genius for selling things.

Now, in order to get me out of my difficulty, he wanted to take me over to Jones and Jones, and make a salesman of me.

The notion of my going round the valleys, knocking at miners' doors, trying to sell trinkets, mangles, and musical instruments, made me writhe with pain. I declared it impossible for me to do such work. Matt said I was a fool, and that he would prove it.

The sun was setting over the hills behind our house when we started the discussion. The sun went round the world, under the mountains, and up again over the hills in front of our house before we finished. Matt won. I agreed that I was a fool, and consented to become a pedlar.

He took me away by the first train down the valley, that same morning, to show me how I ought to begin. During the day he gave me some of his own stock of watches and chains, so that I might try my hand. He observed my methods, when I knocked at doors, and the housewives appeared. He told me that my expression of disgust and horror, as I introduced my articles for sale, would ruin the business. I must control my face, he said, and smile, or I should never be a successful salesman. I tried to smile. He watched me, and said that my smile was worse than my look of horror.

All the same he would not despair. I wanted to go home and pitch the whole business out of my sight. He practically kept me handcuffed to him, and led me, like a prisoner, over the mountains, to his firm's premises. His employers were impressed by his recommendation of me. I could not belie his glowing description of my ability. I signed an agreement to become a " salesman on commission."

Strange to say, for the first three months, my new work was quite tolerable. My earnings were from two to four pounds a week (I could never hope to equal Matt's brilliant achievements), and going round the mountains in the sunshine was itself a pleasure. I had something of the simplicity of " The Vicar of Wakefield's " son, Moses, in my commercial outlook. In an Aberdare Coffee Tavern one afternoon—I had turned in out of the rain—the subject of fiddles somehow arose between a pale-faced young man and me. I could have talked all day and all night in my enthusiasm about fiddles ; but my business became mixed up with our conversation, whether through an inquiry from my companion or by my own wish, I cannot remember. He said he was thinking of buying a watch, and would be glad to see my stock.

He liked one, the price of which was four guineas, and would take it, but had no money at all at present to pay the deposit of one pound. Any fiddler was, in my opinion, a person to be trusted entirely. He wrote his address on the hire agreement, and signed it in proper form ; and I was only too pleased to hand him the watch. We arranged that I should call upon him on the following Saturday for the first sovereign ;

and, afterwards, he would pay five shillings a week, until the total amount was cleared off. I called at his address in Abercwmboi on the next Saturday, but he was unknown there. I never saw him or the watch again. I had to pay for the net loss, and my enthusiasm for fiddlers cost me three pounds, five shillings.

Towards winter my distaste for peddling came back so strongly that I hated it. Some days I would force myself to tramp five or six miles to reach a village in the hills, with the intention of exploiting the district conscientiously ; but as soon as I knocked at the first house door, nausea would blind and sicken me, and I would turn away before the door could be opened, and walk back home again.

A trivial quarrel arose between my mother and me, early in March. I left home, and took rooms in the Wood Road, Pontypridd. What caused the quarrel I do not remember at all ; but my agony at leaving home can never be forgotten. It made me ill. Living in the house of a stranger was torture to me. I would have gone back to my mother ; but just at this very time, my employers added to my work certain duties of collecting, which compelled me to remain at Pontypridd whether I would or no.

The people with whom I lived were kindness itself. But it took many months to harden me to the idea of tolerating residence in another person's house. I became resigned but not reconciled ; and not all the years that have passed since then have been able to lessen my dislike of living away from my own home.

My brother Matt lived with me. That fact and the good-nature of the young couple who owned the house helped to make the change bearable.

My mother called to see me one afternoon. Matt was away for the week, travelling. I was alone in our room. There could be no doubt that my mother desired to make up our quarrel. I was just as anxious to do likewise, but felt greatly embarrassed, and my manner had an aloofness which offended her pride so much that when I asked her if she would have tea with me she declined, and went away at once.

My fiddle introduced me to new friends. I played for the great Caradog, when he organized oratorio performances. Frank Southwood and I played duets all night, up at his house on the hill, to the annoyance of his mother and sister who could not get any sleep. Frank and I blamed each other for not playing in correct time, and we kept the table between us to prevent ourselves from fighting.

He arranged concerts, and I helped him to collect fiddlers enough to form bands. Chapels and churches of every denomination sought us out, and we were always fiddling somewhere or other up and down the valleys. Matt had given twenty pounds for a flute. I performed solos on it at concerts. Once I played The Cuckoo solo on my fiddle at a chapel. Once, also, at a Cymanfa, some puritan extremists denounced our fiddles as " instruments of the devil," and the whole orchestra was bundled out of the chapel.

At this period I became acquainted with some of the glories of chamber music. We were never short of a 'cello, viola, double-bass, or clarionet ; and at

Frank's house, every Sunday, from three in the afternoon till three in the morning, we had quartets, trios, quintets, sextets, and octets. Russian, Italian, French and German music were all in our repertoire. Girls not out of their teens sat at the piano, and read the difficult scores with ease.

My clothes had become a matter of importance to me. I was careful about the cut of my coat, the hang of my trousers, the shape of my bowler hat, and the smartness of my collar.

My dandyism reached a point where it offended people who had no understanding. Matt and I were out for a Sunday afternoon stroll on Pontypridd common. My clothes and walking stick brought jeers from some hilarious young men. I had no desire to be a laughing-stock, and suggested to Matt that we might as well return. The scoffing youths dogged us and collected a crowd. They followed us up the Berw road. They began to mob us. And as there were nearly a hundred of them, I thought it unwise to go too far up the valley, and Matt agreed with me.

Our difficulty now was, how were we to get back through the crowd which quite filled up the space between river and hillside ?

I faced the jeerers, lifted my stick and said :

" Open out a passage for us, or I'll break your heads."

" Will you put your stick down and fight me ? " said one from the front rank.

" Certainly."

I gave my stick and coat to Matt. The other fellow had taken off his coat. We closed. I believed that if I fell, the senseless tempers of the youthful mob would break loose altogether, and I might be kicked on the ground. I took care not to fall. Boxing had been one of our home-studies. In three seconds, my man was down, with his nose and mouth much damaged.

A second challenger took his place immediately. I knocked him down as soon as he had finished speaking, and he was in no hurry to get up.

A third stepped forward.

" You won't knock me down ! " he said, springing at me.

My fist hit him so directly on the jaw that he dropped and crumpled up on the ground like an empty sack.

It is impossible to explain where my precision and strength came from. Matt was staring at me in amazement. So were the others. I was just as much surprised as anybody else.

An extraordinary silence followed. The crowd allowed me to put on my coat. I went towards them. They opened out automatically for me, and did not move as Matt and I passed through the gap. Nor did they utter a sound while we were within hearing.

Reading of all sorts—philosophy, history, politics, poetry, and novels—was mixed up with my music and other amusements. I was tremendously alive at this period. Everything interested me. Every hour, every minute was crammed with my activities in one direction or another. New, mysterious emotions and passions seemed to be breaking out like little flames from all parts of my body. As soon as the morning sunlight touched my bedroom window, I woke. I did not rise. I leaped up. I flung the bedclothes away from me. They seemed to be burning my flesh. A glorious feeling within me, as I got out of bed, made me sing. My singing was never in tune, but my impulse of joy had to express itself.

The authors whom I read were nearly all a century old. Some were older. Volumes by living writers were too high-priced for me, though that obstacle would not have prevented me from getting a book if I had had any idea that it might be interesting. Our school-books had never mentioned living writers ; and the impression in my mind was that an author, to be a living author, must be dead ; and that his work was all the better if he had died of neglect and starvation.

Matt brought home two volumes. They gave me the first hint that authors might be good writers even if they were alive. He had picked up a paper-covered book of stories, " Soldiers Three," by a writer with a name which I regarded as being barbarous. The central character was my cousin, Jack Lahy the Swaddy. In the book he was called " Mulvaney ; " and I was astonished at the fascinating way " Mulvaney " told his stories. Reading them was nearly as good as listening to Lahy himself, when he would be sitting on a low, long stool, which he had nicknamed " Longbody," talking of his " sojering " in India, down in my granny's kitchen of a winter's night, with no light but the red glow of the fire on our faces.

The second volume Matt bought was " Three Men in a Boat." The book made me laugh. I had thought that only Smollett and Dickens could make a reader laugh ; and I was surprised to find that a man who was actually living could write in such a genuinely humorous way.

Only two other modern books had I read : Edna Lyall's " Donovan," which made me cry ; and " The Mystery of a Hansom Cab."

Father Smith, our parish priest, and his curate, Father Stansilaus, often called to see my brother and me, and we felt greatly honoured by this friendship. Father Smith was a big, soldierly, Irish priest. He had been a chaplain in the Indian Army.

Father Stansilaus was very stout and round. I was particularly fond of the big priest, who was simple and gentle. At the same time, I liked and admired the little priest. He was well-read, knew the world, and told interesting stories about famous bishops and cardinals. He enjoyed talking to Matt and me, because there was no one else in the parish who took such a keen interest, as we did, in intellectual things that did not concern either spiritual or temporal welfare. He was transferred to another parish.

Father Smith, shortly afterwards, went away also. I was the only one at the railway station to see the big priest off. He was almost in tears.

New influences had caused me to be negligent in my religious duties, until a mission was held at Treforest Catholic Church. The missioner was a young Welsh priest, with the Cymric music, emotion, and poetic imagery in his voice and phrases. I had never missed Mass, but a Catholic must do more than regularly attend Mass, if he wishes to remain within the fold. The austerity of Catholicism gives the conscience no rest until the soul is purged of sin. The missioner's eloquence startled me into examining my conscience. It had become blacker in the few months since I had left home than it had ever been in all the nineteen years before that.

Long afterwards, I learned that the priest whose piety and fervour had made me fear for my soul's safety, had defied God, broken his priestly vows, and married a Welsh widow.

Fiddle playing brought me into favour with the local post office. A badly-paid place there was vacant, and I, being still disgusted with peddling, asked my friends to give me the appointment. They consented at once. I was to assist with the distribution of the mail at four o'clock in the morning, and learn to be a telegraph clerk.

Here I saw the spark of ambition fly up before my eyes. I desired to be first in anything I undertook. I wanted to be the pinnacle—the head. I would become Postmaster-General. I did not know that it would be necessary for me to become a Member of Parliament. In any case, that would not have bothered me.

My feeling was the true, wonderful, inspired ambition that desires a thing, and is not hampered by any thought of obstacles. The Postmaster-Generalship idea was merely a symbol. Anything that was at the top would have done just as well for my satisfaction. The reality was my ambition.

Up to this period I had merely thought of getting a living. Now, living, as living, became of no account at all. I forgot it. I thought only of the glory of achievement. The glow within me came from a flame that blazed without any need of oil or wick or substance of any worldly kind.   It was the pure fire. Let dark misfortunes and disappointments be piled upon it, and it would go on burning.   Let black despair weigh down on it like a stifling damper, and the fire would still live.   Nothing had lit it, and nothing could put it out.

CHAPTER XI

GETTING up at four in the morning to go on duty at
the post office was not much trouble to me.   But to
keep out of official reports for mistakes about mail-
baskets was beyond my power.

One morning, in the grey and misty dawn, a
subordinate struck our superior in the face.

Tempers were short at such an early hour.   Mail-
bags and baskets were in everybody's way.   The
slightest misguided word made my colleagues irritable,
and they quarrelled, while hands, arms, and mouths
were full of letters, parcels, and registered packets.

" I'll report you for that," said our superior, wiping
the blood from his lips.

Hot words were exchanged and it seemed as if blow
would be followed by blow, for the continuous strain
keeps one's nerves at tension point.

But the quarrel between the two was somehow patched up satisfactorily and the blow struck
that morning was never mentioned in the official
reports.

The Gloucester Mail very soon entangled me.   A
dark morning came when I could not find the bill of

contents which should have been in the parcel-basket
from Gloucester. It was my duty to send the thing
on to a sub-office. The sub-office reported me to
St. Martin's-le-Grand. St. Martin's-le-Grand reported
Gloucester. Gloucester reported half a dozen inter-
mediate offices, and the half-dozen reported me once
more. The inquiry went all round the United
Kingdom, until I found the bill on a shelf in our office.
Our chief clerk privately advised me to burn the
document.

The final report fixed upon me as the real culprit.
I was instructed to forward answers to an endless
series of questions regarding age, health, intelligence,
length of service, and the number of times I had
already been reported. The chief clerk's advice to
me was : Admit nothing, and deny everything. I
looked at the long, blue sheet steadily for five minutes.
Then I tore it up. The questions were, to my mind,
impudent and offensive ; and I decided to have no
more to do with a General Post Office that could be
so rude to me.

The immediate problem of how I should live did
not trouble me. The future was my present. Vanity
without experience made that future shine so daz-
zlingly that I could not see the shadows around me.
I thought I was walking forward, with the light on
my face, and did not know that I was standing still,
and in darkness.

In order to get food, I took a place as the one and
only violinist in a music-hall orchestra. The other
instruments were a piano and double-bass. Our hall
was at the back of a public-house, called The Bunch

of Grapes. There I earned fifteen shillings a week. On that amount and my hopes I was perfectly happy. I laughed so much at the comedians on the stage in front of me that I often failed to pick up my cues. The performers forgave my errors, because they had never before seen a member of a theatre-orchestra laugh at anything, and they confessed to me that I was paying their genius a very high compliment. Our pianist—who was the musical conductor—never laughed ; and he resented my merriment so bitterly that, as soon as another fiddler applied to him for a job, I was discharged.

Following this disaster, Matt and I had a grave talk—another all-night debate—at our rooms, on the subject of our future. My brother had always wished to be an actor. I had not the smallest doubt that his career on the stage would rival that of Garrick. Matt suggested that both of us should become actors. I did not feel in any way Matt's equal, as far as acting was concerned, but had no objection to making the attempt, providing we should always be together. He said that there might be some difficulty in that respect ; and he put his own inclinations aside, in order to find out what was to become of me.

We tried to dig out a solid foundation for my future. Matt quite agreed with me that I would eventually be a great man. At what ? That was the thing we had to settle. I was undecided whether I wished to be a great fiddler or a great journalist. Probably the example of Dickens put journalism into my head.

Matt pointed out that it would be difficult for me to live on nothing while I was preparing myself to be a great fiddler ; whereas, I could earn bread and cheese, as a reporter, while studying to be a great journalist.

I decided to become a great journalist.

My studies began at sunrise that same morning, with Justin McCarthy's " History of Our Own Times." At mid-day I walked up the valley to the offices of the general merchants, for whom I had previously been a salesman, and asked to be allowed to work for them once more. I still loathed trying to sell goods, but was willing to do anything to earn my living while studying. The firm was kind enough to re-engage me.

Shorthand, French, Grammar, English and French literature of all kinds, and the leading articles in newspapers, were my subjects. At six in the morning I was up reading and writing. Afternoons were devoted to earning enough to pay for my food and lodging. At evening time I returned home and studied till midnight and, sometimes, beyond it. My days and nights were happy.

Speed-practice for shorthand had to be gained. An offer of threepence as wages, for an hour's reading aloud to me each day, tempted a boy to undertake this task. He began with enthusiasm. But it soon became evident that an hour was much longer than he had imagined. Reading out bored him horribly. Yet he was a loyal lad and stuck to his engagement. He came day after day. The work was agony to him. He wriggled in his chair, the book dropped from his hands, he yawned and looked out of the window at other boys who were playing in the street, and sometimes he fell fast asleep while I was trying to find a suitable outline for a strange word.

Within three months, I was replying to advertisements of vacant junior reporterships. The hundreds of letters sent by me brought back only one response : a request for proof of my experience as a reporter. I had had no experience, and could not send what was wanted. I offered my services to the local journals in order to get experience.

One editor passed my window at eleven o'clock each morning. He was a short, thin, grey-bearded dandy, his back as straight as a wall. A black satchel, which he always carried in his right hand, gave him an important air. He engaged me to report sermons at half a crown a column. For six weeks he printed my reports, but I could not get a single half-crown out of him. I did reporting for the other newspapers. Not one of the offices ever paid me. Experience and the friendship of various reporters rewarded me.

Evans, a reporter on the staff of a well-known local weekly paper, published at Cadoxton, recommended me to his editor, who I was told, had just left Oxford University, where he had gained distinction. I visited the offices, and saw the editor. He was sitting at his table, writing, in purple ink, on loose, square sheets. His pen formed the most beautiful letters I had ever seen. He was a fair, youngish man, thick-set, with a scowling expression like that of a flat-faced bull.

He engaged me as a junior reporter, at fifteen shillings a week.

This was entirely satisfactory to me. It seemed to be a real step forward. Now I should gain the right experience. The salary would pay for enough food to keep me alive, and that was all I wanted.

Cadoxton was a forlorn town of empty houses and closed shops. Barry Dock, a mile nearer to the Bristol Channel, had attracted all the trade, and Cadoxton streets echoed desolation.

In our ramshackle office in a decayed street—I forget its name—I helped to read proofs. Outside, I reported mothers' meetings, tea meetings, temperance meetings, concerts, and entertainments. Everything that was dull and tiresome interested our readers. The work bored and stupefied me. It was a relief for me to go home to my lodgings, and study till four o'clock in the morning. My landlady and another woman gossiped in the kitchen late at night, while I read in the next room, with cups, plates, and dishes piled around my books and paraffin lamp on the table. Only a closed door separated the women from me, and their whispering voices sent out a persistent " chew chew " to accompany my studies.

My diet was largely bread, butter, tea, potatoes, boiled bacon, and cabbage. I was not particular about what food I ate, so long as it kept off hunger. Still, the limitations of my table reminded me of the genial satire with which my cousin, Jack Lahy, had often described the scanty and monotonous menu of our poor Irish people, at home, in The Barracks.

" Man ! " he would exlaim, " write home and say
we have fine living in Wales——

> *Bread, butther an' tay,*
> *Three times a day*
> *An' very often, a bloather av a Sunday.*

Many families of newly arrived Irish emigrants in
The Barracks—" Shawn K'nops," we called them—
were quite satisfied with a sack of potatoes and a
bar of salt as their food.   White bread was a luxury
in itself for them.   A very hard-working Shawn
K'nop was asked by his landlady should she order a
pound of butter for him.

" Butther, m'am ? " he inquired,   in   surprise.
" What 'ud I want butther for, wid fine, fwhite
bread ? "

The " bloather " satirized by Jack Lahy was a
staple dish in poor times.   A good-humoured Irish
lodger amongst our people asked his landlady to read
out his bill to him, when he was paying her for his
week's board.   She put on her spectacles, held up the
bit of paper, and began :

> " Moonday marrnin', brikfist, wan bloather.
> Moonday, dinner, two bloathers.
> Moonday, supper, wan bloather.
> T'choosday marrnin', brikfist, wan bloather.
> T'choosday, dinner, two bloathers.
> T'choosday, supper, wan bloather.
> Widinsday marrnin', brikfist, wan bloather.
> Widinsday, dinner, two bloathers.
> Widinsday, supper, wan ——"

" M'am ! " he interrupted. " Yerrah, blot out the bloathers, an' put down a whale."

Bloaters I never liked ; but thought my boiled bacon and cabbage the most delicious dish anyone could desire. As for my wardrobe on fifteen shillings a week, I left clothes altogether out of my list of necessities.

CHAPTER XII

Reporting : An immoral case : A murder : I am in danger of
being drowned : A street fight : My great hopes : Publishing
day : My mistake : My editor's revenge : My tragic destiny.

ONCE, the editor instructed me to report police court
proceedings at Penarth—a seaport town that produced
strange sins.

That day, a case of immorality was tried. The
revelations were not only horrifying, but damaging
to the reputation of a small, pretty woman. When I
saw her in the prisoner's dock I felt sorry for her, and
for her husband ; and I decided that it would be
painful for them to have any mention of their shame
made public. Beyond that, I believed that the story
was too improper for any paper to print. I sent in no
" copy " to my editor concerning this case.

Our next issue came out blamelessly. But another
paper—our greatest rival—made a special feature of
the case, with large headlines, beginning : " Domestic
Infelicity at Penarth." Details were faithfully given,
and the report created an unusual demand for the
paper.

My editor wanted to know why I had not " written
up " the disgusting thing. I explained that it appeared to be wise to suppress it for humanitarian and
moral reasons.

The success achieved by our rival that week was a

black mark against me. Never again was I sent to report police court proceedings.

A procession of some society was to be followed by a dinner at a public-house behind Cadoxton Hill. I was instructed to get the news and the names. A tall man in his shirt-sleeves was leaning against the public-house door when I arrived there.

" What is the name of the landlord ? " I asked.

" Me."

" Oh," said I, with the friendliest smile. " Are you the boss of the shanty ? "

My amiability had serious results. The word, " shanty," offended the landlord. He refused to permit me to cross the threshold. Not an item of the news would he allow me to gather. I returned with an empty notebook. My editor laughed when I explained the reason of my failure. But, all the same, it was a second black mark against me.

That night a crowd near a public-house in Barry Dock attracted my attention. Any sort of paragraph was welcome, and I sought information. A reporter from the other local paper was talking to three policemen. The officers marched off as I came up. I asked my colleague what had happened.

" Nothing—only a drunken row."

Both his editor and mine were correspondents for daily journals, and we reporters acted as jackals, tracking down prey for our lions, and receiving a bone of praise as our share of the feast.

The next issue of the paper for which our rival editor was correspondent contained a sensational column, describing a murder which had been committed inside the public-house. I had seen only the crowd outside.

Not a word of this murder appeared in the daily for which my editor was representative, because I had taken the other reporter's word that nothing worthy of notice had happened. It had not occurred to me that he had wished to prevent me from making any further inquiries, so that he could keep the news to himself. He had shown particular skill in doing this. He had chatted with me for a little while, and walked me slowly away from the public-house, and his friendliness had made me forget all about the crowd.

For failing to report this crime, my editor was censured by the daily paper which he represented. Had I not been deceived by the other reporter, I should have gained favour. My error made our editor morose. His sullen nature never allowed him to be furious. He and his local rival were always eager to get news and be first with it. My editor always walked heavily, with his head bent, frowning, as if he had lost his soul and was looking for it in the gutter. The other editor trotted about the streets with his head up, and a look of surprise on his face, as if asking Heaven why there was nothing new on the earth.

Yellow fever had been brought into Barry Dock. All ships arriving in the harbour were put into quarantine—a regulation dating from 1448 when Venice was the sea-mart of Eastern trade, and ships carried various diseases as an ordinary part of their cargoes. The Barry Docks custom-house officers and I were out every night, in a rowing boat, visiting the vessels. Nothing pleased me better than rowing round the harbour of Barry Island at three o'clock in the morning with moonlight on the water. We clambered up the sides of enormous ships, and searched every nook and corner of them for Yellow Fever. The chance of finding the disease and keeping it, did not mar my happiness. The captains feasted us. When a ship was permitted to go into dock, I stood on the bows. Owing to the down-channel sweep of the current, no one could ever know whether the vessel would smash its nose against the outer walls, or not ; and I had all the thrill of waves and danger, as our big ship rose and plunged through the narrow opening to the dock gates.

A terrific storm had lashed sea and shore for a week. On Saturday the rain ceased, and I went down to Barry Island for a swim. Not a sail or a human being was within sight, owing to the gale, which made waves that seemed to be as big as the island. I loved swimming, and the storm had kept me out of the water for six days. I stripped on the sands, and dived in.

The fine waves lifted me to the sky. Never had a bathe seemed so pleasant.

When I had had enough I turned to swim to the shore ; but found that, in my joy of the big waves, I had allowed myself to be carried out to a point where the current swept down channel, past the island. I put all my strength into the attempt to swim through the sweeping line which was cutting me off from the shore. I swung arms and legs till no feeling was left in them, and I was exhausted. I lay like a helpless bit of wreckage on the surface. I accepted the evident truth that I should be carried out to the middle of the Bristol Channel, and drowned that afternoon.

A wave would lift me up so high that I could see all the island ; but no man, woman, or child was there. Then the wave would fall, and I seemed to be taken down to the bottom of the Channel, where I could see nothing at all but grey water.

My thought was :

"My card is in my waistcoat pocket on the sands. They will know who was drowned."

Then came a more bitter thought :

"After all my struggle to get a start reporting, I am to lose it so soon."

Floating on the waves rested me. Strength came back. I had always felt that a man was never beaten till he gave up fighting.

Now I made another attempt to get through the current, which was like an elastic line against my chest. The line would bend but not break. I was in no way panic-stricken. If drowning was to be my end, I had no objection to it, but, at the same time, would do what was possible to avoid it.

Suddenly I noticed that some progress had been made and that I was in a part of the current which slanted towards the shore. I at once gave up trying to break through the line, and swam downwards, on the Channel side of it.

Three quarters of a mile south of the island I found myself nearer land, in easier water, through which I swam until my knees and toes scratched themselves on hidden rocks. I waded out, a mile or so from where I had gone in, my legs trembling so badly that I could not walk or stand.

A week or so later, my editor sent me for a photo-block of some unfortunate person who had either been stabbed or poisoned. On my way back to the office, a dock accident (which would be good " copy " for our paper) kept me two hours getting details.

Outside the docks, I stopped to watch two of my countrymen fighting. They were Irish sailors, one red-headed, the other as dark-skinned as a Spaniard. They had just been paid off from their ship, after a long voyage, and had been carousing together. Now, their coats were off, and they were hitting each other fine, ringing blows, yet with the most extreme courtesy, taking no advantage of any slip or awkward moment, but standing fairly up in an excellent combat, passing lively comments on their own fight, praising, in a delicious brogue, any particularly well-placed hit by one or the other.

The one who was effectively struck shouted his admiration for the skill with which the blow had been delivered.

" Goold rings on ye ! "

And, at the same, he drove his fist into his opponent's face.

" Aha, me bucco ! Ye got me that time," commented the staggering victim.

Their reckless courage and good-humour made me laugh. But I stepped between them, separated them, and inquired of the red-head why they were fighting.

" He don't come from my county," he protested, pointing indignantly at the other who had, apparently, claimed to have been born on some part of Irish earth which was sacred ground in his friend's estimation. I fully appreciated the subtle and serious difficulty; and suggested that the argument could easily be settled if they did not take any further notice of it. They accepted my view, shook hands fervently, put on their coats, and went off arm in arm, singing. And I wrote an interesting paragraph, with the absurd episode as my subject.

Twenty years of such varied experience, I thought, would complete me. Twenty years were set as the exact period for my training. After that, I would be editor of the *Times* or the *Daily News*. Those two were the most important journals. I had not decided which of the two I should edit and control, as the greatest journalist of my day.

At the moment, I had not been quite three months at newspaper work; but my plans for a brilliant journalistic future were entirely ready. Three months were only a minute in my time-table of experience. I would continue studying, now that luck had given me a chance, learn all that I could, and, by hard work, achieve a splendid reputation. I would remain on my present paper for some years; so that when the time came for me to make a change, I should be able to go away with glowing testimonials that would make editors feverishly eager for me to join their staffs.

That day was Thursday, our weekly publishing day. Our paper was ready to go to press, but for one item: the photo-block of the stabbed or poisoned person, for which I had been sent. My delay of two hours at such a critical time seemed to be the final proof of my incompetency. My editor's face, when I arrived, was the ugliest I ever saw owned by man.

On the following Saturday when he handed me my fifteen shillings, as he sat at his table with the pay-sheet in front of him, he said :

"We are reducing the staff. The paper cannot afford your salary. You must get another post."

I looked at this scowling, bull-faced man. His statement that my fifteen shillings a week was too heavy for the finances of the paper to bear did not seem to be true. I felt that some other reason had prompted him to get rid of me. Possibly, he had been annoyed by my mistakes. On the other hand, I had worked hard and willingly, and had earned my small salary. He had never found fault with my work, except in one instance where I had wrongly used the apostrophe in a possessive pronoun, and had written " their's " instead of " theirs." Other re-porters were guilty of more and worse errors in grammar. Considering all things, I concluded that he was dismissing me because he did not like me. No doubt he felt justified in ridding himself of any subordinate who displeased him. But the thing was serious for me. I could see no justice or human feeling in conduct which, apparently, was based on so trivial a cause that a lie had to be told in order to hide the mean and brutal truth.

While I looked at him I was saying to him in my mind :

"Oxford gave you distinction ; but you give no distinction to Oxford. With all your education, you cannot understand that I am struggling, night and day, to keep alive and train myself for some sort of desirable work. You do not know what trouble it has cost me to get this start which you are taking from me. You see nothing of all my years of labouring for a living—while reading, writing, and figuring—all my years of tussle to reach, without tutor, guide, or method, a crude and simple stage of training that might have been gained in a few months with the help of friends and their money, such as you had. The same number of years that you spent in school and university, I spent in the mines. I have to do two men's work. I have to earn as well as learn. You do not know the nature of that difficulty. You have not written hundreds of useless letters applying for jobs, to receive only one reply asking for proofs of experience which I could not send, but had hoped to win here. You are driving me away, and I shall not have those 'proofs of experience' to give, when I again write hundreds of futile applications. You do not see that what you are doing is as bad as strangling me, because you are dismissing me before I have had time to earn a satisfactory testimonial which might get me another post. When I was near being drowned the other day, my only regret was the idea of losing this job that had come to me as a miracle. The waves were too merciful to let me become a bit of floating wreckage. You will do what they refused to do. You are less mighty than the sea, but you are more cruel."

I made no appeal to him. He had no sense, and I had no servility.

I said, with an air of indifference, though I felt sick and heart-broken :

" All right—when can I leave ? "

" Oh, you can take a fortnight."

At the end of the fortnight he said :

" You can stay another week."

At the end of the week I was out of work and hope-less. My hopelessness, indeed, was like a stupor blinding me, as I packed up to go away from my lodgings. I had not been able to save any money out of my salary of fifteen shillings ; and, after paying for my last week's food, shelter, and washing-bill, I had eightpence left.

CHAPTER XIII

I seek refuge in Cardiff : An elder brother's view of a younger
brother's ideas : A damper on my fire : I am a shorthand clerk
in a fish shop : The fishmonger's daughter takes away my job :
Rent-collecting : I refuse to be a blackleg : Pawning my
fiddle : I meet an angel in the rain.

My belongings, when all had been packed up, did not
need a carrier's van to take them away. One small
handbag and a fiddle-case were my baggage. My
books, wardrobe (except for the clothes I was wearing),
and all my possessions, were in the handbag and the
fiddle-case. The fiddle went everywhere with me. I
was in no humour to play upon it at present, though I
had a fine opportunity of playing to the dance of
despair in my heart. I carried bag and fiddle, one in
each hand, when I left my lodgings that Saturday
afternoon.

From the door of the house where I had lived, the
Bristol Channel, with big ships at anchor, waiting for
the tide in Barry Roads, was visible. Sunshine played
on the sea, and put more silver on the waves than I had
in my pockets.

With sevenpence out of my eightpence, I took ticket
at the railway station for Cardiff.

Cardiff had great importance in my eyes. Many a
ton of coal I had " cut " in the mines, to be sent there
and taken to foreign parts from its docks. Nearly

all the coal of our valleys was shipped at Cardiff. That accounted for its being the biggest coal-port in the world. At home, we had talked of the town in awe and veneration, just as pilgrims of the two great creeds might talk of Rome or Mecca. Anyone from Mountain Ash who had been to Cardiff was regarded as a traveller, and anything he or she had to say about it was listened to with deep respect.

It was a clean, bright place, quite flat, with wide streets of shops and offices, and tall, dark buildings, some of which were even four stories high. Two daily papers were published there. Not only were there horse-trams for people to ride in from one street to another—so large was the town—but horse-'buses were there as well ; and, besides all this, there was a monument of the Marquis of Bute in the middle of one of the streets. When I came out of the railway station at Cardiff that afternoon, the first thing I looked at was the monument ; and I forgot my troubles while staring up at it, with my bag and fiddle, one in each hand.

Twice previously I had been in Cardiff. The second time, I had deliberately stayed the night at a coffee-tavern there, in order to experience the sensation of waking up in a town. The coffee-tavern bed was damp and clammy, and it was a wonder I ever woke up at all. I did not get rheumatic fever ; nor did I feel any after-effects of any sort. I was about sixteen then, and had gone there by train.

But the first time, I had walked to Cardiff from Mountain Ash—nearly nineteen miles. I was not thirteen years old. Some accident had made the

pits idle one day. My younger brother, Maurice, and
I had gone out nutting on the mountain side, near
The Black Houses. We got tired of our sport when our
shirts were bulging out with the nuts we had picked,
and Maurice suggested the daring idea of walking all
the way down the road to see Cardiff. It was on the
steps of the monument that we sat, utterly worn out,
after a six hours' tramp. I had a penny. We bought
a bun, broke it fairly in half, and ate it while we rested
on the monument steps, and gazed at all the people,
traffic, and other wonders in Cardiff streets. Lamps
were being lighted in streets and shop windows when
we thought of returning home. I was for walking
back. Maurice began to cry.

He said he would see our sister, Molly, who was an
assistant in a draper's shop. We had stood outside
the shop, looking at it, for a long time. We wanted to
see Molly, but we had not gone in because we did not
wish her to see us in our dust and perspiration. Now,
however, the thought of the horrid tramp of over
eighteen miles home was too much for Maurice. He
went into the big shop, while I waited outside. Molly
came to the door with him, blamed me severely for
what we had done, and gave me a two-shilling piece to
buy two half-tickets for the railway journey home.
I was over the age-limit for half-tickets, but did not
look it, and the booking-clerk was not too inquisitive.
The full fare was only one and sevenpence, and
Maurice and I enjoyed ourselves magnificently on the
extra fivepence.

At home, we had often talked of how fine it would be
for us if we could live in Cardiff—how glorious, when

anyone asked us where we were working (always the
first question after " How be ? " in Mountain Ash)
to be able to say :

" Oh, I'm working in Cardiff."

As on my first tramp to this great town—I had now
come to it with a penny. Then, my visit had been a
brilliant adventure. Now, my coming was a black
misery.

Carrying my bag and fiddle, I walked up St. Mary
Street to Cardiff Castle, the grey-vaulted stables
of which I mistook for a romantic banqueting-hall,
through Duke Street and Crockherbtown, to Castle
Road. Trams and 'buses rattled past me, but I could
not think of giving any one of them the only penny I
possessed.

In Castle Road I inquired of some " corner boys "
for Arran Street ; and at the door of No. 4 Arran
Street, I knocked timidly.

A thin, fair woman opened the door.

" Does Mr. John Keating live here ? " I asked.

" Yes."

" Will you tell him, please, that his brother Joe is
here ? "

" He is not in."

" When will he be in ? "

" I don't know.   But you can come in and wait for
him, if you like."

" Thank you."

In the front room I sat a long time, staring out of
the window, waiting for my eldest brother. He had
left home three years previously. After various ups
and downs, in different parts of England, he had,

through his knowledge of machinery, become the South Wales representative of a Manchester Engineering firm, and had made Cardiff his centre.

He came in towards dusk. He was dark and rather good-looking. We had a very high opinion of John.

" Hullo ! " he said, surprised at seeing me.

" I've had the sack," I explained.

" I thought as much."

This reception was not encouraging. His tone implied that he had been wondering how I could ever have expected to keep any job that was worth having.

Still, when he found that I was not only out of work, but had neither money nor lodgings, he said kindly :

" You can stay with me while you are looking for work."

Two nights afterwards, we were sitting together by the fire, which had been lighted because the evening was chilly. We discussed my prospects. I unfolded my intention of trying to become a journalist, despite all difficulties. He asked what chances there were in my favour. I said that during the past three weeks I had written twenty applications for reporting jobs, but had had no reply.

" You can put it out of your head," said he, " that you will ever be a great journalist."

My answer was that with twenty years' experience I could not help being a success.

" Put it out of your head," he repeated. " You just think of earning a living. Don't bother me by talking of anything else."

As, at that moment, I was living on his generosity, and any word of his had the utmost importance for me, what he now said went burning through me, as if a red-hot poker had been thrust into my brain. He did not realize how dangerous a thing it was for an elder brother to speak slightingly of a younger brother's notions. I could scarcely sleep that night, owing to the agony of my thoughts. I made a vow that I would never study again, and that I would think only of living, just as if I were a pig.

Next morning, I went out, and found a job as shorthand clerk in a Hope Street Fish Shop.

The proprietor was a wholesale dealer. He had advertised in the morning paper for a boy " with a knowledge of shorthand." I persuaded him that my services as a correspondence clerk would be valuable to him. He agreed to give me eighteen shillings a week. He had had less schooling than I, and could not write or dictate a sentence with anything like a meaning in it. I gave form to his ideas, and he was more than pleased with me. He respected my power over his words. He could not understand how I was able to make them convey sense.

This attitude of deference on his part gave me a first hint of the enormous advantage which anyone who knew how to use words effectively had over those who lacked that gift. He made me see that the world was controlled not by wisdom, but by words ; and that our rulers were not philosophers but word-jugglers. I saw that the wholesale fishmonger had a million times more genius, sense, and experience, as far as his affairs were concerned, than I had ; yet he regarded me with admiration, merely because I knew how to make his words express his thoughts.

White fish, red fish, pink fish, and blue fish were all around me, as I sat at my desk, with notebook and pencil, at work ; and the various tints seemed to throw off various smells. The pink fish, when alone, had a totally different aroma from that of the green fish. Even in the darkened storeroom at the back of our shop, it was possible to tell, without a light, in which corner the smoked haddock was hanging, and in what other corner dried codfish could be found. All the smells combined had something of an orchestral effect—a harmony of many themes.

A black-haired, dwarf-boy whose eyes squinted and flashed horribly, worked in the storehouse. Our employer trusted him so implicitly that the dwarf seemed to be the fishmonger's soul. He was a violent, vicious boy. He came to my desk and demanded my name. I had not asked him his name. My self-respect prompted me to resent his impudence, and I tried to ignore his existence. He grabbed my notebook with his dirty, fish-scale covered hands, and his cross-eyes moved wildly to and fro in their sockets.

" The boss told me to get your name," he shouted.

" He knows my name," I answered, in a severe tone. I adopted a dignified manner with the intention of quelling him.

" But I don't," he roared. " And the boss told me to get it—and I'm goin' to get it."

" If he wishes me to tell you my name," I said, " that is a different matter. My name is Keating."

" That's your second name. I want your first name."

" My first name with anyone who has manners," I explained, " is 'Mr.' "

" You won't get no ' Mister ' here," he informed me. " Is it Tom, Bill, or Jack ? "

That dwarf-boy did not know the kind of shorthand clerk I was, or he would not have set out to domineer where I was concerned. His vigorous personality chastened my conceit a little, but I resolved to make him mend his manners. I told him very clearly that I allowed none but my intimate friends to address me with familiarity, and that my Christian name would be of no service to him.

He declared he would find it out for himself and use it. He kept his word. By the next morning he had discovered that my name was Joseph, and from the darkness of the storehouse he would yell out :

" Joe, two dozen smoke 'addick, Lizzie Murphy."

Part of my duties was that of booking orders from Irish girls who went round the streets with baskets, selling fish. The dwarf hid himself every time I went looking for him. I could see his flashing eyes behind the stock of dried cod in the dark storeroom, but consideration for my clothes would not allow me to grope through the fish pile to reach him. I retired to my desk. I was patient, but still firmly resolved that I would find some means of putting a stop to his annoying conduct.

A fantastic twist in my vanity revealed itself here. Despite the fact that I had violently broken with ambitions, my old notion of becoming the head of any enterprise in which I was engaged arose instinctively in the fish shop, notwithstanding the obnoxious nature of my surroundings. I saw myself in breeches and leather leggings, shining with fish scales, controlling vast fishing fleets in every sea.

On the following Monday my employer went to Bristol to arrange for supplies ; and, in his absence, his daughter took charge of Hope Street. Our place had scarcely any business to do on Monday. I had some account books to set in order, but the daughter insisted on remaining close beside me all day. Her nearness interfered with my work. In fact, she was in my arms throughout most of the day. She was about my own age, and was rather a pretty girl.

When her father returned in the evening, the account books had not been set in order. He was furious at my idleness, and asked me why I had not carried out his instructions. His daughter had gone back to her own desk. I could not explain why the work had been neglected, and he told me to leave his fish shop for ever.

During the remainder of the week, I called at hundreds of offices in Cardiff and about its docks, seeking a place as shorthand clerk. I could not afford to wait for newspaper advertisements of such a post. I tried, also, to get into the local theatre orchestra as a second fiddle. By the end of the week, two successes came from my energetic seekings.

One place was offered me by a Docks Engineering office at seventeen shillings and sixpence a week ; and the other offer came from an auctioneer's office in Westgate Street, at one pound a week.

Although I felt that by going to the docks I should gain interesting experience of ships and sea, the difference of a half-crown was so important that I accepted the one pound a week post without hesitation.

Besides using my shorthand in the office, I learned to work the typewriter there, and went out collecting rents in the poor districts of Cardiff, on the first two days of each week. Collecting rents from the purses of poor tenants was like collecting drops of blood from their hearts. I found that the people often had to choose between hunger and house-room. If they paid the rent, they were compelled to do without food. If they could not live without food, they were compelled to do without shelter. Our office kept a bailiff who was always busy making families homeless. Fathers, mothers, children, and furniture, were flung into the streets every week.

Our chief corresponding clerk, a fair young man with a massive head and a good baritone voice, frequently invited me to walk with him, when he would be going to meet his sweetheart. Whenever he made an appointment with her, he always put on a tall, silk hat ; but had not the courage to walk through the streets, alone in his tall hat.

He had journalistic ambitions, which made me pity him. He wrote an article describing a marketing street on Saturday night in Cardiff. The article was printed in a local paper. He did not receive any payment, but the reward of seeing in print what he had written was enough. He was overjoyed at his success, and bought many copies of the paper to show to his friends. This amateur joy, too, I pitied.

For my own part I was mostly alone. When I left the office of an evening, and walked over the river bridge to my lodgings in Tudor Road, my thoughts were chiefly of suicide.

I had good food, decent clothes, and comfortable lodgings ; but I had given up studying, thrown aside all my fine intentions, and was thinking only of getting a living. I found that merely living had no attraction for me. Something besides life was necessary to make it worth living. I never kept a diary ; but I remember writing in some book at this time : " How long—how long—how long ? "

The instinct of patriotism in our family had made myself and my brothers members of The United Irish League at home, and we joined the local branches of the league wherever we went.

One of our colleagues was a handsome dandy. We often bantered him over his irreproachable dress and appearance and asserted that a beautiful girl, who was said to have been fond of him, was only attracted by such a " Beau Brummell." But the poor girl went into a decline and her sudden death was great grief to many of us.

At Christmas time I went home ; and, after the holidays, returned to my lodgings in Cardiff, with one of my mother's largest Christmas cakes in my portmanteau. I disliked carrying any kind of bag or parcel, as a rule ; but would carry anything if it contained a loaf of Christmas cake made by mother. To my taste, nothing in the world could ever match her cake. This one she had specially given me for myself alone, and the thought of eating it slowly, day by day, brought me ecstatic joy. While the cake lasted my life would be happy. The loaf was beautifully browned outside.   The inside was loaded with raisins, currants, lemon-peel, and spices.   Her secret was somewhere in the delicious spices.   Munching her cake was like reading a poem by Keats.

That same evening I cut the loaf for my tea.   I was sparing, because I wanted the treasure to last as long as possible.   I gave a piece to my landlady's daughter when she cleared my table and took the loaf out to the pantry.

Next day I went to the office.   At six o'clock we finished work.   Thoughts of the cake made me hurry to my lodgings.   My landlady's daughter brought in my tea, but there was no sign of the cake on the table ; so I said :

" I'll have some of that cake for tea."

" What cake ? " she asked, with an air of surprise that mystified me.   She was a dark-haired, red-cheeked, pleasant young woman of nineteeen.

" The cake I brought from my home last night," I explained very distinctly.

" Oh, there's none left," she replied, still with an air and tone of amazement.

" None left," I repeated, almost trembling with dread.   " How do you mean—none left ? "

" You ate it all for your tea last night," she answered.

In my horror I tried to show by quoting the immense size of the loaf and the measurements of the pieces I had actually cut from it, how impossible it was for me to have eaten it all.   Reason and argument, however, failed to shake her.   I never saw another crumb of the big cake.

Kelly, a dark-featured clerk in our office, resigned, and his work was added on to mine. His wages had been thirty shillings a week. When pay-day came, I was expecting to receive the increased salary, but was paid only my usual one pound. I would not do work for which thirty shillings a week had been paid, unless I received that amount. My point of view was that I should be doing a mean thing in taking a job at less wages than the other man had earned. I applied to our manager for the increase of ten shillings. He referred me to our employer, who, in turn, referred me back to the manager. I could get nothing but evasions. This annoyed me so much that, one day, when the head of my department criticised my work I told him to go to the devil.

He complained to our manager who, instead of giving me an increased salary, wrote me out a week's notice to leave the office.

For four weeks I was out of work. No application of mine for employment met with success anywhere. This was a curious thing, as I had had nine months' office experience. My late manager had refused to give me a testimonial. He had said he would answer direct any inquiries as to my capacity. I referred several prospective employers to him. None of them engaged me. I was bound to think that the manager's replies to inquiries about me were bad.

A pound or thirty shillings was all I had saved. That money was spent in the first two weeks.

To buy food in the third week, I had to pawn everything I possessed, except my fiddle and the suit of clothes upon me. The fiddle I kept because it might secure an engagement for me, if no clerkship could be found.

But, in the fourth week, the fiddle itself went into a Bridge Street pawnshop for fifteen shillings.

As the pawnbroker would not advance a shilling on the fiddle-case, I brought that away with me ; and a heavy shower coming on, I took shelter under the Theatre Royal portico, with the fiddle-case in my hand. I was quite aware that I looked forlorn and dejected. The overcoat upon me was ragged and shapeless.   I stared at the rain and my thoughts were melancholy. The fifteen shillings would keep me in food and lodgings for one more week.   After that—what would happen if no employment came my way ?   I saw myself passing from one shaky job to another, with hunger always haunting me, as if I were an unfortunate monkey leaping from tree to tree in the jungle, with the jaws of a tiger always open below him, waiting for him to drop in and be swallowed up.

A man in a brown bowler hat was hurrying down the street, his head bent against the rain.   He caught sight of me, under the portico, and turned in beside me.

Once, only, had we met before.   I had been taken to his house by my friend, the clerk who wore a top-hat when going to meet his sweetheart.   My fiddle had gone with me and we had had a pleasant evening of singing and dancing.

The man in the brown bowler remembered me, shook hands, and asked me why I was not at my office.   His manner was exceedingly friendly and good-natured.

" Oh, I have left that office," said I, casually, as if it did not matter.

" What office are you in now ? "

" No office at all."

" How's that ? "

" Can't get a job."

" Funny."

" Yes."

" Would you care to apply to the *Western Mail* ? "

" I'd apply anywhere."

" Well, try the *Mail*."

There was a peculiar confidence in his tone, as he made the suggestion. All I knew about him was his name, Watkins Thomas, and that during my visit to his house he had struck me as being one of the best-humoured and best-natured of hosts.

" All right," I agreed, " if you think there's a chance. Do you know anyone at the *Mail*."

" Yes. I work there."

" To whom shall I apply ? "

" Oh, to me."

Who or what was responsible for this extraordinary meeting ? My friend, the clerk in the top-hat, my fiddle, the pawnbroker, or the rain ?

When misfortune was reaching its worst point with me, I met a man whose good-nature and utterly disinterested friendship put an end to my difficulties at once. So fine were his qualities, so well-bred was he, that I had not had the faintest notion I was talking to one in authority.

It is a mere fact of my life that I have met men of the noblest natures, and experience has forced upon me the conviction that good men are in a large majority in the world. Bitterness or misfortune may make people declare that they have no illusions about human nature, by which is usually meant that viciousness and selfishness are the ruling tendencies. That view is based on a narrow experience. Angelic natures are always revealing themselves unexpectedly in our midst ; and I should be inclined to say that the man who has " no illusions " about his fellow creatures has the greatest illusion of all.

CHAPTER XIV

Good-fortune comes my way : I am described as being "just an ordinary clerk" : Gambling my week's wages : Fatal scholarships : A Channel trip : A soldier's misfortune : A cynic : A gentleman : A dozen young women are under my control : I break my oath : The woman in the street.

My application to the *Western Mail* offices for employment was elaborate. All my talents were clearly catalogued.

A formal postcard came in reply, requesting me to call at nine o'clock on the following Monday morning. I obeyed. That was in the middle of 1893. I was astounded to find that my friend was the business-head of the immense establishment. He handed me over to one of his hundreds of subordinates, and set me to work there and then, at a better salary than any other office had paid me.

If I had been one of the inspired Psalmists of Holy Scripture, I might have been able to express my joy and gratitude to this Heaven-sent friend at that moment. He had lifted me out of despair, and given me work when everybody else had refused me.

As it was, I merely followed his subordinate's instructions, wrote figures on account sheets, and filed correspondence.

In a pile of letters which I had to index for future reference, I found one from my late manager.

" DEAR SIR,—In reply to your enquiry respecting Joseph Keating, he was in our employment nine months. He is just an ordinary clerk.

" Yours," etc.

Such a grudging, miserable testimonial explained why all my attempts to find work had failed. Every would-be employer had read between the lines that I was undesirable. The letter did not say so. But because it said nothing good of me it implied everything that was bad.

The damaging consequences that might have come to me from such a letter—it might have ruined me—made me feel that men in responsible positions should be extremely careful in dealing with a subordinate's welfare. No personal animosity ought to be allowed to influence a recommendation. Whatever merits an employee possesses should be fully stated. Their absence makes the testimonial a death-warrant.

In my case, fortunately, the mean letter served only to show the ill-nature of my late manager and the superb good-nature of my friend, who refused to be influenced by a questionable credential, though he did not know that I should discover his kindly feeling for me. I could never forget that beautiful revelation of human goodness.

A magnificent fire had burned down the old offices of the *Mail* ; and, for the time being, we were housed in a rambling, decrepit building, divided off into innumerable rooms, all the floors of which were lop-sided and rickety. The temporary printing works and editorial offices were about a quarter of a mile away. My duties were entirely in the business department. In my room, a dozen clerks were figuring around me all day, in huge ledgers, on shaky desks, under a white-washed ceiling from which fragments of plaster were always dropping.

We worked late at nights at the end of June to " balance the books." There were millions of accounts in the big ledgers. Within two months, we struck a " trial balance." 3d. was missing out of about £200,000. We perspired in the stifling heat of autumn nights, for three weeks, looking for the 3d. When we found it, we all adjourned to the nearest public-house to toast the discovery.

On Friday nights, after drawing our pay, we played cards on the creaking desks, till Saturday morning. I had much skill but little judgment, and frequently lost all my week's pay at penny Nap, and had to live on credit until the following Friday. There was scarcely a trick of the game that I did not know, yet I always lost. I never blamed my luck, but I believed that my luck ought to have been better.

At the time, I was lodging in Keppock Street, with Frank Nicholas, who had won a Welsh University scholarship and was studying Sciences at Cardiff. He had worked about the mines at Mountain Ash. Another friend of ours, Tom Phillips, who had worked with me in the mines at home, lived with us. He, also, had won a scholarship. Most of the scholarship money went in fees and text books, and left the students with nothing to eat worth mentioning. In hot summer evenings, they would be lying stretched out upon the floor, on their hungry stomachs, with text books under their noses, studying hard. I would not study. I was still keeping to my bitter oath on that point.

Tom Phillips was short and bulky. Frank was tall and lean, with glossy black hair and bright black eyes. The scholarship killed poor Tom. He fell ill, and died suddenly. Frank won honours, left his college, and starved for another twelve months, looking for a place where he could use what he had learned. He had no one to help him, and the university authorities had no system or method for guiding scholarship students into positions where their education could get them a living. In some cases the university ruined students for ever, owing to defects in the system when applied to the needs of a scholarship winner who happened to be the son of poor working people. Frank disappeared. Years later, I heard he had been killed in a South African gold mine.

Through our advertisement department, the privilege of a free trip on the Bristol Channel came my way. I chose a Saturday afternoon, when the boat went to Ilfracombe. The week had been stormy and the channel was greatly disturbed. It was my first " sea-trip." I became ill almost as soon as we left Cardiff pier. The boat took over three hours to go down to Ilfracombe. I was ill all the time. We disembarked and remained on shore for half an hour. I was ill during all that half-hour. The return voyage took up another three hours. Night came and the moon rose. Most of the passengers were admiring the beauty of the Channel in the moonlight. I was so ill that I wished the boat would sink. I was leaning over the bulwarks, gazing at the waves, wondering why the ship would not go down and put an end to my agony.

Seven hours of sickness and pain I endured ; from the time we set out to the moment we returned I was ill. After that I was laid up for a week.

Ever since, even when I am on shore, the mere sight of a swell on the sea will bring back memories of that horrible free trip to Ilfracombe, and I have to turn my back on the waves, in order to overcome my feeling of nausea.

The great Irish rebel, O'Donovan Rossa, called at our office to see me. The heads of the United Irish League (I had become Secretary of the local branch) brought him to the room where I, with a dozen other clerks, was writing and figuring, and introduced him to me with as much ceremony and deference as if I were an important personage. The visit had the air of a meeting between two celebrated characters. I was twenty-three, with smooth, fair cheeks, and untroubled blue eyes. O'Donovan Rossa's eyes were blue, but they were faded, watery and restless with the memory of many sorrows. His small body was shrivelled, his hair white, his pale cheeks withered and heavily lined, and every dark hollow hid a darker pain. His small hand was trembling pitifully as I held it in mine. He had just come out of Portland prison, where he had served a sentence of fourteen or fifteen years in horrible torture. He was a simple, good man, who had willingly risked life and liberty for his ideal of smashing the shackles that had made Ireland a slave to British misgovernment. He had been arrested for plotting to blow up the House of Commons with dynamite. I admired him, and deplored the misgovernment that made men so desperate.

The office boy came to me, just before finishing time, one Wednesday evening.

" Mr. Keating, a man downstairs wants to see you."

" Who is he ? "

" A man. I can't pronounce his name. He wouldn't come in. He's outside the door, on the pavement."

Downstairs and out I went. The evening was warm, and the setting sun threw a beautiful red glow over the street, trams, horses, and hurrying people. All the world looked happy and comfortable.

On the pavement, outside our office door, stood a man with the most miserable and wretched expression imaginable. He was my cousin, Jack Lahy. I guessed that he had in all likelihood visited Cardiff on the previous Saturday, his pay-day, had spent his last penny in a carousing outburst, and was stranded.

" Hullo, Jack."

He shook hands with me in silence. He wore grey corduroy trousers, a battered, black bowler hat, and a tattered coat which was buttoned up to his chin to hide, as I knew, the absence of waistcoat and shirt. All that was pawnable he had put away. His coat was too small. Clearly he had pledged his own, and borrowed this.

" I ought to burr'ned," was the first thing he said. " Joe, could ye give me me train fare—to take me back to Th' Marrdy."

He gave no further explanation. I offered him more than his train fare, but he would only take two shillings.

" No," said he, " I want to get out av this blasted town. The Lorrd f'rgive me ! I kem down last Sathurday, an' not a mouthful av annything but beer have I tasted. I'm ashamed av me life. An' luk at me leg ! "

He had broken his right leg since I had last seen him. He had a tall, soldierly figure ; and this calamity of a bent and deformed limb had hurt his pride more than anything else could. There were tears in his eyes, as he drew my attention to it. I should not have allowed my gaze to turn to it if he had not invited me to do so. The accident had happened to him up at The Mardy—a mining village, far up among the hills at the top of the Rhondda Fach. Some scaffolding had given way whilst he was carrying a hod of mortar up a ladder on a new building, and he had been flung to the ground.

" I've travelled the wurrld sojerin'," he said bitterly. " An' tuh think I shud go to a God-f'rsaken place like Th' Marrdy, to get me leg broke ! "

Poor Jack Lahy ! Never again did I see him. He went back to The Mardy, and died there. God rest his soul !

Near our offices, to the west, was a small, common-looking public house. Outside it, during a luncheon hour, I met Dinny Riordan. Dinny had studied much. He was a cynic. He had known me when I was a boy at Mountain Ash.

" And what are you doing in Cardiff, Joe ? "

" I'm a clerk in an office."

" I'm a pitman's labourer in Maesteg," he said, sneering at himself. He swayed a little. He was not sober, but he was not drunk. He was tall, well-built, and good-looking. I had admired him at home for his extraordinary talents. He danced hornpipes as brilliantly as he debated on intellectual subjects. He detested manual labour, and had tried in all sorts of ways to shake himself free of the mines.

He looked down at me, his eyes half-closed, a contemptuous smile twisting his lips, in the true manner of a man addressing an inferior :

" Joe," said he, " I've tried many trades. I've been a weigher, packman, policeman, and Heaven knows what. And now I'm a pitman's labourer. You think you are getting on, I suppose."

" Oh, I don't know, Dinny. I've got a good job, and I'm doing the best I can with it."

He paused, swayed, and nodded pityingly at me.

" Believe me, Joe," he said. " In ten years time, you'll be worse off than ever you were."

His prophecy struck me as being of an undesirable kind, considering all the bother I had had to get a tolerable job. We shook hands. I wished him the best of luck. His parting admonition was :

" Mark my words. Joe. You'll come to no good."

A serious family matter took me home. My mother had decided to send our youngest brother, Maurice, to America. Maurice had grown into a handsome young man, with shining, fair hair, finely shaped features, a remarkably good taste in clothes,

a fascinating manner that made him a favourite
wherever he went, and an aristocratic dislike of doing
any sort of work for a living.

His inclination to be a gentleman was inherited.
All his brothers had it. But, for our part, we bowed
to the inevitable and earned our bread. Maurice
declined to soil his hands in such a demeaning way.
He had given up every job that had been found for
him.

My mother could not afford to keep him, and the
problem of what was to be done with him had been
long argued. We had suggested to our mother that
she should refuse to shelter him. We could not
understand why she did not send him away. It did
not occur to us that of her seven children only two,
Maurice and Annie, lived at home. We could not
realize how it pained her to see her sons and daughters
forsaking home, one by one, and the house becoming
more and more lonely for her. One of the cruellest
things my mother had to bear was the thought of
her children scattered about the world, leaving her
to dwell in silence and loneliness. Her pride and her
love were equally wounded. We did not know what
heart-breaking pangs had been endured when she,
at last, agreed to send Maurice away.

Our sister, Kate, had married and gone to America.
Her husband was a farmer in Iowa. Maurice was to
work on the farm, and the experience would make a
man of him. He had held out against the idea for
some time ; but the finer instincts of his character
overcame all his jaunty notions and he eventually
consented. We had no doubt that he would reveal

the manliest qualities when necessity compelled him, whether he would or no, to earn his living.

Matt and I, between us, made up his passage-money. As the train went out of Mountain Ash, Maurice cried. My mother wept hopelessly. Her last and youngest boy was going away from her. Now, only one child, out of her seven, remained at home.

Matt, who, at this time, had no thought of politics or Parliament, stayed with me at my lodgings one night, and told me that he was starting out as an actor in a touring company. Their play was "The Grip of Iron." He was engaged as a gendarme, as a baggage man, and as a piccolo player. Every night he would perform in those three distinguished capacities. I was entirely pleased, and said it was time that one, at least, of the Keatings set out to make the fame which was due to our exalted lineage.

My own personal ambitions were dead ; but my family pride, like Pooh-bah's, was enormous ; and I was so simple, thank God, as to believe that my brother's genius for acting would lift our name to its proper pinnacle.

Matt and Lyn Harding went off together next morning. Lyn Harding's home was only a few miles away, and he worked at Cardiff. He and Matt had become friends, and had decided to begin their stage careers at the same time. Matt was destined for a different sphere. Lyn made his name famous throughout England and America.

Near the fish shop in Hope Street, where I had abandoned hope, was a dark and dusty public meeting place called The Colonial Hall. On an idle afternoon, in the summer of 1894, I went there to hear what Welsh Nationalists had to say about their ideals. A small, young-looking man was on the platform, addressing a scanty, scattered, and apathetic audience. In appearance the speaker was insignificant. His black, morning coat was badly cut, his trousers bagged at the knees, his long black hair was disordered, and dust and perspiration had soiled his white collar and hollow cheeks.

Yet this untidy young man interested me. In spite of the depressing conditions, his phrasing had the glow under it which turns ordinary words into eloquence. His voice was musical, and his ideas poetic. His clenched hand, when he waved it in a gesture, seemed to draw a line of flame through the air. I looked at a bill to find out his name, and read that a Mr. D. Lloyd George would address the meeting. I had never heard of him, and had not come to listen to him that afternoon. But the impression he gave me was that he had the genius of a great orator. Later, I saw him many times at our offices, though our journal was utterly opposed to his politics. He and Willie Davies, our editor-in-chief, were close personal friends. They would have a long chat together, and the next morning our paper would come out with a couple of columns of the most violent abuse of D. Lloyd George, his policy, ideals, intentions, and all his fondest hopes.

In our new offices—fine buildings, with shining, white walls—I was set in authority. About a dozen young women, whose ages varied from eighteen to twenty-two were under my control. Some of the girls were good-looking. I was twenty-four. The ribald clerks used to call the department my harem.

My assistants did all the correspondence and copying work for our offices. Typewriters were clicking around me all day. I had become quite used to typewriting. I took down correspondence from dictation, on the machine, so rapidly that the letters were ready for signing as soon as the one dictating them had finished speaking.

My girls, in details of personal appearance, were all neat, clean, and correct. In their work, the majority were slipshod, untidy and unreliable. A misplaced curl in their hair, a wrong kind of brooch or trinket in their decorations, or an ink smudge on their faces, was a serious thing ; but a misplaced word or figure, or a smudge on their copied pages, was nothing. They were a great trouble to me, until I found that mistakes in office work did not strike the feminine mind as being of any importance. After that discovery, careful supervision enabled me to keep the department running smoothly and pleasantly.

Patience, in small things, I never had. Yet in some ways I was patient. I never hinted at dismissal to any one of the young women, no matter what errors she made. I had had too much of " getting the sack " myself to think of being harsh in that way towards unintentional offenders. My notion of discipline was not the cruel bludgeon of dismissal. My tone and face became very stern and terrible over mistakes, and some of the girls cried.

Once, I remained stern for three days towards one

of the young women. She had been wilfully careless. On the third day, she rose from her typewriter desk, came to mine, and said she could not bear it any longer. There were tears in her eyes. She promised that she would never be careless again. She kept her promise —till she forgot it.

Altogether, more than a hundred young women, possibly, two hundred, passed through my department. They only left when better-paid posts had been found for them, either by our office or by themselves ; and not one went away in any doubt about receiving a full and fair testimonial, with all her merits put at their highest value, and none of her faults mentioned at all ; so that she might get another post if she disliked the one to which she was then going. Supposing she had some fault which would cause inconvenience to an employer ? That did not matter to me. To my mind, the well-being of an employee was more important than the convenience, profit, or loss, of an employer.

My vow that I would not study was broken. I had kept away from text books for nearly three years, and had defied every impulse to learn anything, except new ways of amusing myself. I had countless friends, musicians, singers, actors, journalists, politicians, business people, and liars, rogues, and rodneys of all sorts. A million experiences, some of which must never be recorded, had made me a student in spite of myself. I talked copiously, and expressed curious views with such learned self-confidence that a woman friend once asked me :

" What subject are you studying ? "

" The world," I answered, laughing.

In one of the streets through which I had to pass in order to reach our office, very lamentable phases of life existed. Every morning I saw a certain girl kneeling on the pavement, with bucket, brush, and soap, washing and scrubbing the steps of a house. It was common knowledge in the district that within the house dwelt a young woman who lived in the worst manner possible. It struck me as being curious to see this poor scrubber soiling her hands, doing rough and unpleasant work for a livelihood, while the mistress who employed her gained a livelihood by soiling everything that God had given her but her hands. The servant was bound to know what all knew about her mistress. I believed that, one day, the evil influences around the girl on the doorstep would blind and stain her soul, and the thought would come to her that she need not continue doing this unpleasant work when, by imitating her mistress, she could live in luxury, and keep a servant herself.

My analysis of the motives at work in that girl's heart, as she scrubbed and washed the steps, was based on what I had observed in Cardiff streets. My deductions were crude, and, perhaps, cruel.

But I thought of her home, her childhood, her up-bringing, her lack of education, and the deadening effect of squalid surroundings upon her mind ; and I believed that unless she had the support of a spiritual and moral training, familiarity with vice would be certain to make her ignore its real sinfulness, and desire its apparent advantages.

Without knowing it, I was thinking a novel, with

herself as the heroine ; and I was trying to find a way by which she could be saved, in my story, from the inevitable and terrible degradation that awaited her in life.   In my thoughts, I found a way of escape for her ; but in her own destiny there was no escape. I was horrified to see the poor scrubbing girl, within three months, decked out in flaunting finery, foolishly painted cheeks, and cheap jewellery, plying the bad trade of the woman in the street.

CHAPTER XV

A SECRET upheaval had begun to distress me. A confusing storm of thoughts was lashing me towards the strange idea of writing novels. This disturbance arose from nothing at all.

None of my acquaintances in Cardiff had any kind of literary tastes. I knew no one at all there who had ever written anything but news paragraphs. Never in all my journalistic efforts had I intended trying to write any story, or novel, or anything in the nature of literature. Not even in my boyhood had such a dream been mine.

No notion of achieving fame or riches was in my mind. My wish to write had no worldly ambitions in it or cravings for monetary reward. I had no hopes of gaining anything but a living by whatever work I attempted to do. With all my vanity, I was modest in the presence of literature. Nothing else in the world (except religion) could make me feel humble in any way. I had no respect for wealth, kings, dukes, lords, statesmen, social distinctions, success, power, or authority of any sort. But I never could avoid feeling shy and hesitant when face to face with the impulse to write a phrase which might be worth reading for its own sake. A man is always shy when he is about to kiss the woman he really loves. I had evidently found my true love.

My desire was to construct huge pictures of life, with real details of what I had seen, felt, and thought, all moulded into wonderful harmonies of story, truth and characterization. I saw each of my books as if it were a human heart telling its story.

My ignorance of the names of colours, trees, flowers, pieces of furniture, and the various parts of architecture was a joke to my friends. I was not much interested in these external objects. I saw only the things that were invisible. My vision tried to go through the body to the hidden heart. I wished to understand why a man and woman sinned and repented. What were their motives ? What were the mysteries of their passions, their love and hate, their selfishness and their generosity. What they felt and thought was more to me than what they did. The outside world I scarcely noticed. The inner beauty held my eyes. I was like a lover who could not see the pretty dress worn by his sweetheart, because he saw only the grace and charm of the girl herself.

Men and women of my acquaintance, when out for a country walk, would step aside to avoid treading upon a snail which, with its house on its back, happened to be crossing the road. But those men and women raised their eyes to the sky, as if asking Heaven to mark their tenderness of heart. The snail had not attempted to bite their feet, or molest them in any way; and I wondered why people could seek credit for not doing such a wilful injury as that of destroying the life and home of a poor crawler.

One woman regularly gave her used-up tea-leaves to starving families, and informed us every day:

" Oh, I am good to the poor ! "

Names of other friends of mine often appeared in printed lists of charitable subscriptions. The fact that they allowed the world to be told of their generosity did not take away in the least from their good intentions.

The curious, subtle mixture of charity and vanity in the hearts of my friends interested me. Big and small motives appeared to be hidden under every human action. If a jealous woman spoiled the life of a man she loved, or a trusted man ruined a family whose money was in his care, such tragedies were usually due to the best intentions.

The motive under the action was what I sought. But I felt that I knew less about the truth of life than anyone else in the world. Who was I, to think of revealing the unknown ? My education was a subject for laughter. I believed that everybody knew more about everything than I did. And as for attempting to put my ignorance into books, could any idea be more daring ? Yet something was urging me to do it.

Knowing how hopelessly undeveloped was my mind, how untrained I was in art of any kind, how greatly I lacked the clearness of thought that comes from certainty of knowledge, the grace of phrase, refinement, taste, and breadth of imagination that make literature, I had to face the question : Was the gift in me ?—was I a diamond in a dust-heap, and I had only to cut my own way up through the obscuring rubbish, under which accident had buried me, to shine brilliantly on the top ? That was a terrible question to answer.

The impulse to write made me rather afraid of myself. All other desires that had come to me, I had welcomed boldly and confidently, without diffidence or timidity. Such things as being a great journalist, or the head of the Government or of any big enterprise, had seemed to be easily within reach if I cared to stretch out my hand to grasp them. But in presence of the idea of writing my wonderful novels I bowed modestly and very humbly, scarcely able to look at the brilliant radiance I felt around me.

For a long time the temptation pursued me, and I dared not turn to look at it. It followed me to the office, as Mary's lamb followed her to school, and home again. It went out with me to my amusements. In music-halls, theatres, concert-rooms, at card-parties, political meetings, at Mass, and when I was talking to my friends in street or field, it was always hovering about my head, trying to whisper in my ear ; and while I was resisting, I was yielding.

I said :

" Very well, young Keating. This is 1895. You shall write for five years. If you do not get a novel published before the end of the century, you are not a novelist, and you shall write no more."

My shortcomings were clear to me. They were so numerous that if I began to learn the alphabet, as a first step towards writing literature, I should not be going too far back. I decided to learn grammar, and study psychology.

To master English grammar was not my hope at all. I did not believe that anyone could master it, since I had noted errors in the best writers as well as in the worst. But I wanted to get a working knowledge of how words should be arranged so as to form an intelligent sentence. After that I would trust to Providence. As for psychology, I had observed the confusing and mystifying conduct of men and women, and I wished to see the scaffolding and ladders by which their thoughts built up an action. Psychology I regarded as the grammar of motives.

The intended base of my studies was, therefore: To learn how thoughts made actions, and how words made sentences to express those actions.

I had never been familiar with money; but at this time, a sovereign could be spared for amusements each week out of my excellent pay at the office. My spare money should go towards lessons in grammar.

Only the best instruction would satisfy me. I applied to the Professor of English Literature at the University College, asking him if he would teach me to write grammatically. He advised me to take lessons from Mr. Dore, a friend of his, who knew all that could be known about the structure of the English language. Mr. Dore asked me to write a few pages on any subject I cared to choose. I wrote some character-sketches and short stories. When he had read them he said he would be my tutor, would take no fee of any sort, but would do the work for the pleasure of helping me to express my ideas accurately. This was an astonishing compliment. Altogether, the exalted mind and fine friendship of Mr. Dore was an inspiration to me.

Psychology entangled me in a terrible fashion. From Cardiff Public Library I borrowed the two volumes of Herbert Spencer's "Principles of Psychology." The books were magnificently bound in brown leather. Their print was bold and distinct. But before I read half of the first page, I met words that were utter strangers to me. My cheap dictionaries were quite useless. I bought a huge dictionary. It cost me thirty-five shillings. Twelve months study in spare time of the two volumes gave me a picture of the mind as a thought-machine, bearing a strong resemblance to a telegraph office into which impulses came like people handing in telegram forms, and the messages were sent at once to the eye, leg, hand, finger, or any part of the body to which they were addressed.

Psychology was not the only thing in my mind. About this time I fell in love. Often while my fingers were turning over the leaves of my big dictionary, seeking out the meaning of some monstrous word, I forgot the subject I was studying. And when I had found the word, I could not see it or its meaning. The page would be filled with the face of a very beautiful girl. She had recently come into my department at the office. Never had I seen such sweetness as was in her smile. She had large blue eyes, pale and slightly hollow cheeks, and scarlet lips. She was nineteen, and her form was exceedingly graceful. But her charm was her look, her smile, and her manner. I saw her every day, but had no intention of telling her that she was interrupting my studies, or that I was thinking more of her than of Spencer's psychology.

A piano and mandoline also interfered with my studies. I lived with my married sister, Molly, in a little street near Roath Park. Next door to us dwelt a young man and wife, who were childless. They appeared to have learned "Marche aux Flambeaux," which they played together on the piano and mandoline. A back room had been given to me as a quiet place for my work at home. By ill-luck the next-door couple had chosen a back room for their performances. As sure as I sat down to read and write the piano and mandoline began to jangle. Only a jerry-built wall of lath and plaster separated the two houses. The noise, which seemed to be in my room, put me into a state of the most horrible irritation. They knew only this one tune, and they played it so often that the paper broke loose from the wall, and the plaster cracked and fell upon my books.

The first hint that anyone else in Cardiff was writing came to me in a curious way. Our editor sent down to my department an enormous pile of manuscript, with a request that I would let the owner know how much it would cost to get it type-written. I looked through the pages in order to estimate the cost of copying the work, and found

that it was a poetic tragedy. There was so much
of it that the price of one typewritten copy would
be five pounds. An ordinary business letter was
sent to the owner stating this fact.

While one of my assistants was writing the letter,
I was reading the manuscript, because it was such
fine poetry. The author's name on the title-page,
J. E. Patterson, was quite unknown to me. But
Keats, Shelley, and Shakespeare were in some of his
big lines.

A day or so went by, and a youngish man attired
in a big, black mackintosh—the day was wet—
came into the office and, after first explaining
that his name was J. E. Patterson, asked for the
tragedy.

It was handed towards him, and from the abrupt
manner in which he took it, I judged that our high
estimate of five pounds for copying it had offended
him. But I told him of my admiration for his
poetry, and our interview ended in an invitation
from him to call and see him at his rooms on the
following Saturday afternoon. I called.

He was writing. His attitude and appearance
reminded me of Victor Hugo, only that Hugo, I
believe, always stood when at work. Patterson sat.
Manuscripts of novels and poems were heaped around
his desk, as if they were the delicacies of a fruit-
stall. He interested me greatly. He told me he
had been a sailor, I told him I had been a miner,
and we spent a very pleasant evening, talking about
ourselves.

Another poet, my friend, the new Byron of boyhood

days at Mountain Ash, visited me. I introduced him to Patterson ; and, in the cool of evenings, we three roamed fields and woods, and talked mightily. What walks ! What talks ! A sigh and a smile to their memory !

Seven chapters of my novel were written—by which I mean that the actual writing of the seven chapters had been done seven times over, at least. In between, I had written short stories, character-sketches, and articles for the purpose of making the point of my pen flexible. I also read every kind of book or essay I could borrow from the public library, dealing with dramatic construction. I tried to analyse De Maupassant, Tolstoy, Thomas Hardy, Stevenson, Flaubert, and Meredith, so as to find out what principle guided them in shaping their stories. I discovered that more delicacy was required to keep the balance of art than the balance of justice.

In form of phrase, I looked for the right word to express what I meant. I did not look for style. To me, style was like long hair on a man. I felt that any man who wore long hair was either humbugging the world, or humbugging himself.

My writing and reading could only be done at home in the evenings, or on Sundays. I plodded every week-day at my office work, which sometimes kept me busy till ten o'clock in the night.

How my seven chapters managed to become written is now beyond my understanding. I remember only that the eighth could not be started at all, though my heroine, " Merva Brully," had great attractions for me, because she was the girl whom I had seen scrubbing the bad woman's doorstep, and I had found in the story a way of saving the poor girl from the evil which, in actual life, had overtaken her. In fact, on my way home, late from the office, thinking of the happy future I was making for her, I would see her under the electric lamps in the streets doing her best to ruin herself, body and soul.

But I, also, was nearly ruining myself in body and brain, by doing too much work. When I went to bed, my heart seemed to be trying to beat a hole through my ribs. The throbbing in my head made sounds come from my pillow like the full-speed puffing of a locomotive. About two o'clock, one Sunday morning, I could not even remain lying down in bed. I went out, and lay down in the fields near our house.

The morning moon was warm. The dew on the grass and the fresh air soothed me. I saw a group of phantoms carrying what seemed to be a beer-barrel, on their shoulders, across the field. The shadows were not silent. They swore terribly and laughed noisily, and the hill beyond sent back the echoes of their oaths and laughter. I could distinguish the moving figures from the dark and motionless trees, though their footsteps made no sound on the wet grass. Before they were quite out of sight they stopped and began to sing. I rose and went slowly up to them.

They were a drunken gang. They had brought out a cask of beer to finish a Saturday-night carousal. The cask was on the grass, and they were drinking from the tap, one by one, and dancing around.

The hideous scene interested me, but my presence was not welcomed.

" You clear off, mister, or you'll get shot," shouted one.

Having no desire to be maltreated, I retired. I heard no shot, but something stung me in the side, and a bullet fell near my feet. They had fired at me with a catapult. The pain in my side was acute, and remained so for many weeks afterwards.

A policeman in uniform and a tall detective in plain clothes stopped me at the edge of the field, on my way home. They were evidently searching for the gang, and arrested me as a member of it. I had only an old suit on, and a loose muffler round my neck. Lack of sleep made me look as if I were half-drunk.

At first, they laughed at my explanations, and were going to handcuff me. But some element in my tone and manner induced them to give me the benefit of the doubt. They told me I ought to be ashamed of myself, and went swiftly across the field. I turned to see what would happen. The two officers with truncheons and handcuffs rushed into the midst of the dancing shadows. Then came yells and cries, and much livelier dancing, to the tune of the truncheons, which reminded me of the line in Longfellow's " Psalm of Day " :

And the night shall be filled with music.

Owing to pressure at our office in the previous year, I had had no holiday. Now, with his usual kindness, my chief allowed me to take a month's holiday. I went to Carmarthen town, the home of a close friend of mine—the auctioneer's clerk with the tall silk hat—and took rooms in a market-gardener's house, near the river. In my bag were the seven chapters of " Merva Brully," and in my head were the remaining twenty chapters, which had been most elaborately planned out. All that had to be done was merely the writing of them.

Between the piano, mandoline, and " Marche aux Flambeaux," at home, and the heavy work at our office, I had no hope of being able to complete the book unless I did it during this holiday. It was with this in mind that I had asked for a whole month.

One day only was my actual holiday. Every morning, at nine o'clock, I began writing. Outside was sunshine, mountains, river, fields, and gardens. I remained inside, usually, till darkness came.

My good-natured hostess was astounded at my strange holiday-making. One morning she brought in for my breakfast a delicious-looking sewin (the Welsh name for a kind of salmon-trout ; though it is said, also, to be distinct from the salmon species).

Like every good Catholic, I hated fish. I would not touch the sewin.

She pressed it upon me in a sad manner.

" It is very good for the brain," said she, glancing mournfully at the pile of loose sheets which were on my table waiting to be filled with words.

One night when I was returning to my Carmarthen lodgings, a most musical voice said :

" Good night, Mr. Keating."

Janet was standing in the dark doorway of a small house. I had passed it without noticing her. We had been introduced to each other a few days before. She was such a nice girl, slender rather, with clear, grey eyes, that I had imagined her owning too many sweethearts to be able to spare a thought for me. I saw her home that night. After that, she made all my evenings happy. Like most Welsh girls she had a very affectionate nature. Some afternoons I gave up work, and she and I went away into the mountains till nightfall. She spoke in Welsh to the farmers' wives who made tea for us amidst the hills, and her clear, lovely voice revealed to me the music of her native language.

By writing sixty thousand words that month I finished my first novel, " Merva Brully."

If what I had done was valueless, if I had made the mistake of a lifetime, the glow in my heart as I looked at my completed story was worth all the toil. No pain of disappointment which might be in store for me could equal the pleasure I felt that night. Whether I had been wrong or not in giving my holiday to this task, or foolish in attempting to write, in such a short time, this terrific number of words to express my ideas, even should those ideas prove to be less extraordinary than the pains they had cost me, I felt that my achievement was glorious.

When I put " The End " under the last line on the last page of the last chapter of my book, it seemed to me that I had done the impossible. I had written a novel out of nothing but an impulse. I had made a picture of a vision. I, who should have been content to think only of coal-mines and rubbish tips, had been imagining wondrous things of life, earth, and heaven. I had forgotten my natal environment, yet was thinking and feeling as I did amidst the mountains and mines of my boyhood. I had seen the old pastoral life of our village being buried slowly under a mantle of black dust, like the burying of good by evil; and though I had written about an altogether different world, the beauty and ugliness, the romance and realism of my home were in my book, because the heights of the mountains and the depths of the mine were in myself.

Was I great or small in my novel ? I cannot say. A great man is greater than his environment, whether it be the courts of kings or the courts of beggars, of ancient spacious homes or modern suffocating slums. The test of his greatness is the power to see beyond his social horizon. If he is ordinary he will be the slave of circumstance. If he has genius, he will be the master of circumstance. Because genius is the seed of an extraordinary flower that requires no care or guidance; no prepared earth, favourable conditions, special climate or hot-house substitute; it is its own gardener, and will grow to its full glory and beauty in rich or mean soil, and, like the soul of an angel, find nourishment even in stones. For any man's intellectual development, the world itself is a university.

To return to the office with one's face so sunburnt that the skin peeled off was our idea of a triumphant holiday. When I came back, my chief gazed at me in great disappointment.

" Keating," said he ; " you don't look a bit brown."

My face was reflected in the mirror which hung upon the wall of his room ; and for the first time I noticed that I looked pale and jaded.

CHAPTER XVI

My novel seeks without finding : An afternoon in London :
Sausages and mashed potatoes : The Baron : The poet : A
prize story : Every man should have a valet : A novel of mine
published : I go to hell : A trick of the nerves : I go to Paris :
My short stories accepted : I go to London.

My novel went looking for a publisher in London. My
agent was the General Post Office. The typewritten
copy went away by post and came back by post, over
and over again. I introduced " Merva Brully " to
every publisher whose address was printed in the
London Directory. The result reminded me of the
countless hundreds of useless letters I had once written
applying for work. I had never found a job through
all my letters ; and, now, " Merva " could not find
acceptance.

Still, it must be recorded that one publisher wrote
me to say that he had been utterly fascinated by my
novel, that it was, undoubtedly, a fine piece of literature. He would be altogether charmed to publish
it, he said, if I gave him seventy-five pounds.

Fortunately, I did not own this amount. By some
means I had learned that the only people who paid
for publication were writers whose work was either
too good, or too bad, for ordinary readers. I thought
that my book was too good. And if the required
sum had been mine, it might have put me amongst

the biggest fools on earth—that is to say, I might have given money to a publisher.

It is useless for me to try to say what agony I felt when, month after month, the postman, knowing nothing of the situation, calmly and methodically handed me my brown-paper parcel of rejected literature.

But, as surely as it came back to me, it went away again. I had started, and would go on submitting the manuscript for publication until the Post Office itself rejected it, refused to sell me stamps for it, and put an armed guard on the door to keep me and my novel out.

A colleague asked me to go with him to London. I went there for an afternoon, and did not care much for the place, though I had heard a great deal about it.

The only thing I remember of the visit is that some London friend of my friend met us at Paddington, and took us to a shop where mashed potatoes and sausages were stewing inside the window, upon trays overflowing with bubbling, frothy, brown gravy. Three lots of sausages, mashed potatoes and gravy were piled into plates, and put before us. My companions seemed to regard the dish as a luxury. They ate heartily, with joy in their eyes. I had become rather fastidious about my food. The appearance of my sausage made me ill. I tasted it, and had to go out quickly. I waited outside, some distance from the shop window, till the other two joined me.

The last Baron of Loughmore called upon me, at our office in Cardiff, on a wet, winter evening, just at finishing time. All the electric lamps shone brilliantly.

One of our messenger boys brought the Baron down to my department, at the lower end of the huge office, where I, unusually busy, was surrounded by young women and typewriting machines.

My visitor was the first really picturesque person I had ever seen. He was tall. He wore a big, dark, wide-brimmed hat, and a black cape which the rain had wetted so completely that the electric lights shone glitteringly upon its surface, as if it were a lake reflecting stars. His brown-skinned face, bristling, black moustache, his tall, proudly straight figure, combined with his broad sombrero and cape, made me think that he was a Spanish hidalgo of many quarterings.

"Mr. Keating," said he, with a slight, pleasing stammer in his speech, "Ted Burr-dett is a frind av mine, and—and, I undherstand that y'r a gr'ate frind av—av his. And—and he to'ld me that I was to call at th' Westherr'n Male and—and make mesilf known to ye. Me—me name is Purr-cil."

His soft-toned, refined brogue, of course, put his nationality beyond doubt. Though he looked like a Spaniard, he was, in fact, an educated Irishman.

We shook hands and leaned against a high desk to discuss the subject of his visit. He had travelled in South America, had been editor of a Spanish newspaper there, had acted as "advance agent," in various parts of the world, for a famous quack doctor, and had returned to England as poor as he had gone away from it. He told me he came of a distinguished Irish family that numbered kings, princes, and lesser nobility amongst its members; and that, although his ordinary name was Purcell, he was, in reality, the last Baron of Loughmore, an estate somewhere in Ireland. I introduced him to our chief editor, who engaged him to write stories for the " Evening Express " (our evening paper) at so much a column.

The Baron could produce more fiction than any half-dozen men I ever met. He wrote a two-column story every day. He assured me, and I believed him, that he could write a million words a year. Often, when he had arranged to spend an evening with me, I found him, at seven o'clock, in bed. He would rise ; and, on the point of going out with me, he would remember that he had not written the story due to appear next day.

" What, in th' name av th' Lorrd, will I write about ?   Give me a title ! "

A title would be given.

" Wait awhile, now, till I write the story."

When he had finished we went out for the evening. He had the most courteous manners, and all his talk was about cardinals, statesmen, and journalists. His companionship was delightful.

" Keating, me bhoy," he said one day, " y're doin' too much worrk, and y're not looking well. Y' ought to get married, and thin y'd have no responsibilities."

In his friendship for me, he wanted to teach me Spanish. I had no time to learn it. I played old Irish tunes for him on my fiddle and he declared I was a magnificent fiddler. He read my novel and told me that I was a genius, but that my story developed wrongly, and that he was trying to find out where it failed. Before he succeeded in doing this he went to Ireland, and wrote telling me that I was to go there at once, as he had arranged for me to edit the local newspaper, represent the county in Parliament, and marry the daughter of the widow who owned the newspaper.

A poet came to sell typewriters. He was sent to us by a London typewriter company for whom our office acted as a local agency, and he was instructed to make my department his headquarters. His name was Jack. He came from Scotland. He was very young and stout, with a fair, moon face, and light, scanty hair. Every day, he drank beer—quantity irregular—and saved a definite sum of money each week. I did not drink; yet I could not save any money at all. He assured me that he only drank for the good of his health.

He arrived at our office late in the evening. He told me his name, and his mission. The next thing he did was read me his poetry. He carried his verses—which were written in a sprawling hand on loose sheets—in an inside pocket. In manner and appearance he was an ordinary man. In his verses he was altogether extraordinary. He described himself:

> *I am the first of ages,*
> *The cry of primal years !*

He went home for a holiday to Scotland, and as soon as he crossed the border he

> *Slammed the door on England.*

He reached some lochs amidst mountains at twilight and said :

> *Wait !   See yon steely glitter ?*
> *'Tis Day's ghost upon the water.*

The poet, the Baron, and I had lively evenings together. Jack—that is, the poet—for all his boldness in metre was timid in himself. He and the Baron were together in a public-house, in Tudor Road, one night. The landlord, a huge, bulky, proud-necked man, insulted the Baron by refusing to sell him any more beer. The Baron, furious at the unwarranted affront—his natural exuberance and good-humour had been mistaken for alcoholic excitation—struck the offender in the face. Great personal courage was shown in doing this. One blow from the big landlord could have broken the Baron's match-stick body. The poet's moral support was necessary in such an unequal quarrel but he ran away.

It was inevitable that I should bring two such immortals as Jack and Patterson together.

Jack's immense stoutness, his big, fair face, round and smooth, and his hair light and thin, like a ragged, straw thatch, marked him off dramatically from Patterson who was short, slim and wiry, with a tremendous mass of raven hair shining like a black aureole behind his small and delicately shaped features. Jack, beside him, suggested a mountain with a blackbird singing half-way up the slope. Patterson's poetry was of a musical and precious genius. It differed entirely from Jack's robust lines. The clash of schools brought a clash of tempers, and the meeting of the two poets was a jangle of pre-dilections, a tune on a big drum and triangle. Once only, I believe, did they foregather.

Dai Edwardes, my Welsh friend, the poet from Mountain Ash, who had written two or three promising books, got on well with Jack. When business became too greatly a bore they spent afternoons discussing poetry.

Whether Jack sold typewriters or not did not really concern me. He was not under my control; but, as I was head of the department, he regarded me, in a way, as being in authority over him; and some afternoons he would come in merely to let me see that he was actually attending to his duties. My desk was near the door. He had to pass me, in order to reach his own desk. I would look up casually at him. If I saw his fair face slightly flushed, I said nothing.

Whenever I was silent he tossed his papers savagely about his table, went out rapidly and indignantly, and told Edwardes, who, at such times, would be waiting patiently for him outside our office:

"There's Keating in there—cocking his damned eye at me—measuring how many glasses I've had! I don't like it, Edwardes!"

Then Edwardes would be invited down to Jack's rooms in De Spencer Gardens, where the chief orna-ment was a small, plaster bust of Robert Burns, on the mantel-piece. Jack worshipped Burns. In tears he would take up the sacred bust, speak to it, and place it in the hands of Edwardes, who held it reveren-tially, while Jack, still weeping, went down on his knees, and kissed it.

The office girl, whose beauty, smile, and charm had disturbed my studies, soon began to trouble Jack's poetry.   He fell deeply under her spell, but she did not respond ; and he wrote :

> *Care put a furrow on my brow*
> *In writing out this line :*
> *I would not now be thus alone,*
> *If she were pal o' mine.*

The acuteness of his suffering at the thought of her was shown one night. I was working late at the office, alone. He came in. The electric lights shone on his large, smooth face.

He commenced to bewail his lonely fate and pour out his sorrows in true poetical fashion, but finally broke out into a fury of passion and said :

" Joe, you're a pig—a pig! I love her—and she loves you ! "

His fantastic behaviour made me decide to have him taken home at once, in order to save him from being seen by my chief, who was also working late in his own room at the top end of our floor.

By skilful management I was able to get him into a cab. I paid the driver, instructed him to take my friend to his rooms, and went back to my work. The poet was driven home ; but, for some wild reason, he returned, hatless, to the office, that same night (I was told) after I had gone.

Our leader-writer, an excellent Welsh scholar, who kept hard at work all the week until Saturday mornings when, as there were no articles to be written that night, he would invariably seek for relaxation in the corner public house in the company of many old friends—urged me strongly to enter the 1898 National Eisteddfod competition, where a prize of fifty pounds was offered for an English novel of Welsh life. The Baron had told our editor that I had written a novel, the editor had asked his leader-writer to read it, and the leader-writer had reported that my book had power in it. From that moment, our editor had been most encouraging in his attitude towards me, and showed his kindly feeling in a thousand ways. He joined with his leader-writer in advising me to try for the Eisteddfod prize.

In secret, my pride was utterly against the idea of entering into competition with anybody on earth. I made plausible excuses, such as want of time, pressure of business at the office, and so on. My friend, the leader-writer, persisted, and, in the end, I wrote a novel of the mines called " Gwen Lloyd " and sent it in. Ernest Rhys (afterwards editor of *Everyman's Library*) and William Edwards Tirebuck, the novelist, were the judges.

My novel did not get the prize ; but Tirebuck privately wrote a long and kind letter to the author of " Gwen Lloyd " (he did not know my name) saying how great was his admiration of my pictures of mining life.

The winning book appeared weekly in a local journal the proprietor of which had paid the prize-money ; and I saw that those who had drawn up the competition rules specifying " a novel " had been ignorant people. What had been really required was not a novel but a newspaper serial, a special form of story.

My novel would have been of no use at all for news-paper purposes.

Now I had two volumes troubling the post. In addition I wrote short stories and articles and sent them to editors in London. A cheque for three guineas came to me for one story. That was all the payment I received for three years' work.

Still, my mind was quite made up. I would earn my living as a novelist. My notions of an income were not extravagant. To our editor, one night, after he had spoken enthusiastically about some story I had written, I said :

"If I could make a pound a week at writing I'd be happy."

His face expressed deep doubt as to the likelihood of my earning that sum.

The figure in money was not the measure of my other hopes. I believed that the novels which were in me and not yet written would be great, immortal books, that I would be regarded as a master, and my name spoken throughout the world. I saw myself famous for all eternity. Yet, not once did I see myself rich. I did not think of making a fortune. I thought about making literature. The idea of money only came into my mind with the question of how I was to live in this world while I was writing my masterpieces. Money as money, I never bothered about. If my landlady and tailor were not always placing their bills before me, I should not have known the meaning of money.

With my career clearly fixed, I was happy in the present, and immortal in the future. Outwardly I was just an ordinary young man who went to an office every day, reading his morning paper on the top of a penny omnibus, paid grave attention to the choice of his ties, socks, and hats, saw that the crease of his trousers was perfectly straight with the centre of his shoe, spent occasional week-ends in adjacent country villages, played billiards badly, and took a fortnight's holiday in the summer at some seaside place. Inwardly I lived, moved, and worked in a halo of enthusiasm and glory.

An urgent letter from my mother took me home. An accident had happened to my father. He had had a narrow escape from being killed by machinery in the colliery yard. When I arrived at our house in Mountain Ash, he was lying upon a bed, downstairs, in the front room. He was pale and weak. The doctor had ordered him brandy. My father refused to touch alcohol of any kind. When a young man he had taken "the pledge" for life. He would not break the pledge. Our parish priest, Father O'Reilly, had visited him, and had urged him to obey the doctor.

"Con," said Father O'Reilly, "there is no sin in taking brandy when the doctor advises it."

"No, father. I wouldn't tashte a drap av it. I wuddn't brake me plidge."

"If you don't take it, Con, you might die."

"That's God's will, father. Glory be to His holy name!"

My father disobeyed the doctor, and lived.

My mother explained to me that she thought he would be compelled to give up work, and in that case my brothers and I would have to send her enough money to keep the home going. Maurice was in America, and nothing had been heard of him. Our brother John had not had much luck in London, and very little money could be expected from him. Matt's good-fortune had deserted him for the time being. I was the only one of the four of us doing well. I said :

"Very well, mother. I am not earning enough to keep two homes. But I will take a house in Cardiff, and live with you, father, and my sister Annie. I can manage to keep us all, that way."

She agreed, and I returned to Cardiff and found a suitable house.

This plan, I realized quite plainly, meant the destruction of all my brilliant future ; because I should have to think first and last of earning money instead of immortality. Study and novel writing would have to be put aside for many years, my best years—that is, the time of youth, irresponsibility, inspiration, vitality and enthusiasm. Perhaps, when the opportunity to resume my studies came, it would be too late for me to make use of my freedom ; when, though from my hands and feet the shackles might have fallen, they would still, as it were, be on my heart and soul.

But I was a student of other people's tragedies, and I accepted my own.

"The well-being of my mother, my father, and my sister," I decided, "is more important than my immortality."

Whether there was a blessing or not in my good intentions I cannot say. But when I wrote and told my mother that I had taken the house, she replied explaining that neither herself nor my father could face the idea of leaving Mountain Ash, where old associations had endeared the place and the people to them, and that I was to send home what money I could spare, and they would manage as best they could.

In 1899 I began to write "Son of Judith."

The plot of it had occurred to me two years before, while I was taking a holiday at Carmarthen. I had outlined the story to my friend there. He had said:

"What a horrible idea! For God's sake, don't touch it."

During six months of the writing, neuralgia was boring holes in my brain. I was fool enough to let bad teeth remain in my jaws to torture me in bed and out of it.

In my time I have suffered many kinds of pain, physical and spiritual; and I know that pangs of conscience, horrors of muscles twisting themselves into rheumatic knots, despair of failure, or grief for a beloved one's death, can never equal the gnawing, relentless, malignant, night-and-day agony of neuralgia. Hope and the meaning of life are taken away from the victim. A bad tooth in the jaw is a thorn in the soul. A pair of pincers can pluck the evil out, but the sufferer has not even sense enough left to use that simple remedy.

In spite of my idiocy, I finished my novel in the spring of 1900. I had taken rooms in Penarth in order to get quiet and isolation at nights for my task. I sent the manuscript to William Heinemann. He

said that my story " over-stepped nature." I knew
that it did nothing of the kind. Six other publishers
rejected it.

Five years (1895 to 1900) I had set as a period
within which a book written by me must be accepted.
If no publisher took a novel of mine by the following
October, that fact, according to my test, would prove
that I had not the creative gift, and that I must give
up trying to be a novelist, or break my word. Thoughts
of writing twenty novels had come to me, and I was
not sure that I could abandon the notion.

Another serious anxiety troubled me. I had become mightily fastidious about my personal appearance. My suits of clothes, ties, boots and shirts
increased in number and variety. But the bother of
keeping these things in order was unwelcome. I
wished to appear well-dressed, but begrudged the
time necessary to satisfy this wish. There was a
running fight between my vanity and my indolence.
I realized that only a very hard-working, gifted person
had energy and ability enough to be a dandy. I
decided that every man ought to have a valet ; and
I promised myself that that would be the first sinful
luxury I should get, if ever I could afford it.

The eighth publisher to whom I sent " Son of
Judith " wrote me saying that if I would not demand
any sum in advance, and would allow him to sell five
hundred copies free of charge, he would publish my
novel, and pay me a ten per cent. royalty.

The letter was in a girl's hand, and contained a
lot of details ; but I was so overjoyed that I could
read nothing below the words of acceptance. When

I walked down the street to our office that morning in the sunshine, I pitied each man, youth, girl, and woman I saw on my way, because he or she had not had a novel accepted by a publisher.

This offer reached me less than two months before my five years were out. The test was in my favour. I regarded myself as a novelist.

The editor of "The Western Mail" was almost as pleased at my success as I was myself ; and, in his kind way, he told the news to many journalist friends of his in London and the provinces.

When the book came out, the important notices given to it in responsible newspapers surprised the publisher so much that he wrote me saying how gratified he was. According to the reviewers, my story was an Icelandic saga, an Æschylean tragedy, a Zolaesque reality, and a romance by Victor Hugo, all rolled into one, and my delineation of Welsh character more accurate than Shakespeare's ; while " The Times " review declared that the Welsh intonation of English was so faithfully reproduced in the book that it ought to be set to music as an oratorio.

My most distinct memory of this period is that I had four ghastly back teeth levered out of my jaws.

While I was unconscious under gas, with the dentist operating on me, I went down to hell and had a sensible, friendly chat with the devil, who seemed to be a pleasant, amiable fellow. The place where he sat on his throne was dark, but it had an attractive red glow in the background. I came up in time to see a thought in the dentist's brain travelling down through his arm to his hand, from his hand into the bright forceps which was hauling at my tooth. The thought went from the instrument into my tooth, and from there up to my own brain. The thought which I saw was,

" I hope he won't wake up till this tooth is out, because I've broken it."

When consciousness came to me, I asked the dentist if he had thought what I had seen him think, though I did not tell him of what I had seen.

" Yes ! " he answered, in amazement, breathing hard from the tussle. " How did you know ? You were unconscious."

I was ill. A doctor-friend warned me :

" Keating, you are living on your nerves. You've been overworking, and you'll smash up if you're not careful."

This was good advice, but I did not know how to use it.

Christmas time of that year I spent at home in Mountain Ash, as usual. My sister Annie went with Matt and me to Midnight Mass. She was in the choir. I think they sang Haydn's No. 3 that night. In the middle of the " Et Incarnatus " Annie fell to the floor, unconscious. For many years a malignant illness had been haunting her.

We carried her home. She did not regain consciousness throughout our holiday. I went back to Cardiff, and, on New Year morning, a telegram came to me at the office from my mother, telling me that Annie was dead. She had never awakened from that last falling faint.

She was a talented, lovely girl, with wonderful,

dark-brown eyes, and a charming, affectionate manner. She would sing the saddest of old Irish songs, and make us all cry. We knew that she was singing her own sorrows. I had often tried to induce her to choose only cheerful melodies. She would laugh at me, put her arms around my neck, and hold me as closely to her as if her heart were breaking. Her life, ever since the malady had begun to show itself, had been a brooding tragedy. Her death at twenty-four was a greater tragedy. I did not know until then that I was so fond of her. I sat all night in the room where her beautiful body was laid out. I could not believe she was dead. I could not leave the room, for fear that she would be lonely. God rest her poor soul !

Two weeks after we had buried her, I met, in Cardiff, an acquaintance who told me that since I had last seen him he had been out of his mind, through over-study of old Irish texts.

This harmless statement was responsible for the queerest trick that nerves ever played on anybody. My nerves were like fiddle-strings, frayed and strained by too much use, and on the point of breaking. I immediately believed that some horrible calamity was about to destroy me.

It had already been arranged that I should visit home for the week-end. I went home. All Saturday night and all day Sunday, I was trying to hide my terrifying secret from my mother.

At two o'clock on Monday morning, in bed, I felt every inch of my body quivering. A doctor was brought. He held a light close to my eyes, went away, and sent medicine that was of no use at all to me.

For six weeks I was sleepless. During the whole of that period, I heard our kitchen clock strike every hour of day and night. My nerves were so raw that the tinkle of a teaspoon upon a saucer gave me excruciating pain.

What my friend, the doctor, had warned me about, was happening. I had been living on my nerves and the breakdown had come, at last. The enthusiasm of five years had brought its penalty. My book was out, and the frightful reaction from an unnatural strain had set in. The death of my sister had been the final, unbearable shock.

Against everybody's advice, I decided that the only way to cure myself of this dread of noises lay in going into their midst. Back to Cardiff, and to my office work, I went. My chief stared at my ghost of a face, and ordered me home again. I went to my sister Molly's house in Cardiff. She brought Doctor Shepherd to me. He had practised in India, and, probably, my state was nothing new to his experience.

" The first thing I will give you is sleep," he said, genially.

It took him forty-eight hours to put me to sleep. But I shall never forget that he gave me unconsciousness for the first time in six weeks.

My illness lasted over four years altogether. I was not outwardly ill. I went to the office, visited my friends, played the fiddle, and was apparently a normal person. But I dreaded being alone. I walked the streets late at night because I was afraid to go to bed.

I felt that I could never write again, and this painful thought added to my secret misery.

Once, many years before, my friend the auctioneer's clerk who was too timid to walk the street in his top-hat when he visited his sweetheart, unless I accompanied him, had nicknamed me :

" Keating, the Man of Great Laughter."

Now, I had lost my sense of humour, the most terrible calamity that a nervous breakdown could have brought upon me. I could not laugh.

Change of work and place of living, I thought, would help to enable me to laugh. To my chief's indignation I resigned my post. I joined my friend, Frank Southwood, at Swansea, in a business which we believed would be profitable. In two months I was forty pounds in debt. My brother Matt found a job for me with a London firm. I was to sell wall-paper to wholesale dealers. I went to Paris for this firm. Instead of trying to sell anything I took the opportunity of learning to speak French like a Frenchman. This unprofitable effort brought me notice of dismissal. I returned to Cardiff, penniless, and my best of friends at "The Western Mail" was kind enough to re-engage me.

Though I had failed in everything else, my plan of improving my health had been a success. Change of scene, and new experiences, had brought back a little of my strength of mind and sense of humour.

Doctors and friends had made me promise that I would write no more. But I could not keep away from writing. Authorship is not a profession. It is a disease. The temptation of drink or vice is nothing compared with the temptation to write. As soon as energy began to come back, I wrote another novel.

Probably the crisis through which I had passed made this story abortive. At any rate, no publisher would accept it.

Then I wrote many short stories of mining life. Six of these stories were sold at three pounds each. My royalties on " Son of Judith " had amounted to one shilling and five pence, which the publisher had sent to me in stamps.

In the autumn of 1903 I said :

" It is necessary for me to get a wider experience of life. I am thirty-two years of age, and unless I am prepared to live in London, go through the mill, and risk everything for my idea of being a novelist, I shall never be a master."

After careful deliberation, I decided that I would go to London when the new year came. I would save as much as I could for this purpose.

My brother Matt wrote to me from London saying that he was short of twenty pounds for an important plan which he wanted to carry out. I had saved twenty pounds to pay for food and shelter when I should go to London. I sent Matt the money.

That delayed my journey for two months after the new year had come in. In February I had fifteen pounds saved. I explained to my chief that I was going to give up commercial life for ever.

He reminded me that I had already made one mistake in going away from the office. He was kind enough to say, also :

" As long as you pay expenses here—never mind about profits—I want you to stay with us."

My decision was taken. I had fifteen pounds. I gave up my comfortable and well-paid job, and in February 1904, I took the morning mail for London.

CHAPTER XVII

London, the university of universities : The jungle of civiliza-
tion : Breathing cooked onions : My attic in Torrington Square :
I write for a magazine : An editor's money-making instinct :
I begin to " go through the mill."

WHY did I go to London ? It was the centre of
every interest. It had houses where books were
published, theatres where plays were staged, a
Parliament where laws were framed, a Royal Court
where titles were made, a Stock Exchange where
commerce was made, and a Grub Street where authors
were made. I remembered that Goldsmith, Johnson,
Defoe, Dickens, Smollet, Meredith, Stevenson, Fielding and Shakespeare, despite their natural genius,
had had to dig among the roots of humanity there, in
order to learn how to be masters of life. To me,
London was the university of universities, through
which I would have to pass if I wished to complete
my education as a novelist.

It should not be thought that I regarded London as
being in any way superior to a provincial town. I
believed that human nature in any city was just the
same as in any village. But I knew that the simple
fact of two people dwelling together brought into their
lives influences which could not exist in the case of
one lonely being, and that according to the increasing
size of communities, new influences came into play.

Destiny had made London the headquarters of Great Britain, and life there must have the complexities not only of one city but of all our provinces. Yet a knowledge of London alone was not enough. Ignorance of the life outside had made Thackeray write Cockney absurdities at which I had laughed when he had meant to be serious ; and I believed that a Londoner should know the provinces, and a provincial know London, before they could really be sure of what they wished to say. I had looked at life from the provinces, but felt that, to get nearer to the universal standpoint, I would have to study the world from its largest and most complex centre.

Apart from that point of view, I had no respect for London. Two or three previous visits there had given me a definite distaste for it.

I liked mountains when sunshine gleamed on their beautiful summer dress of green, red, brown, and gold ; or on their vast, spotless, white coat of winter. I liked strong breezes blowing across hill-tops, into my eyes and lungs, making my heart pour blood that seemed to be fine wine sparkling and bubbling in my veins. I liked wooded valleys, wide, twisting, glittering rivers, and the vision, from a high peak, of mountain summits resembling green waves on a purple sea stretching away everywhere to a boundless horizon. Great space, the room of earth and sky, lit up by sun, moon, or stars, and decorated by trees, fields and flowers, I preferred for my dwelling-place.

On that February day in 1904, when I emerged from the gloom of Paddington Station, climbed on a horse omnibus with my bags, and, in a midnight noon, was jolted along endless dark, dirty, ugly streets, where the only noticeable things were houses, noise, lights and advertisements, with streams of people struggling to and fro on every pavement and at every corner, as if they were lost souls, and did not know or care which direction they took, London seemed to me to be the jungle of civilization. I felt that the natures of men and women must have developed an animal hardihood, to be able to live in such a wilderness of bricks and mortar, the air of which made me think that I was breathing the unpleasing emanations of cooked onions.

The most miserable person in London, on the day I arrived there, was myself. I was well aware that I had gone there to suffer ; and, although this step had been deliberately taken in the spirit of a martyr, I was still too much of a human being to like what I knew I disliked.

My brother Matt had been in London a few years. He lived in a boarding-house in Torrington Square. I went to live with him. He had a large room on the second floor. I engaged the front attic, at a rental of eight shillings a week.

In my garret with a sloping roof I could not stand upright, except at well-defined spots. The jingle of bells from hansom cabs and the clatter of horses' hoofs on the asphalt, night and day, bothered the life out of me.

My fixed plan was to work hard, and live sparingly, say, at the rate of fifteen shillings a week, so that my fifteen pounds should last five months, by the end of which time the sale of some stories, articles, or a novel, might bring me in a little more money to keep me going.

In my first week, however, I did no work at all, and spent five pounds. At this rate, I should be able to keep alive for three weeks.

The explanation of this discrepancy between my theory and my practice lay in the fact that, although I could measure to a minute how long a sovereign of mine ought to remain in my pocket, any one of a thousand accidents might place me in financial difficulties, without my being aware of how they had come about.

A peculiar gift is needed for the mastership of money. Only a man with the money-maker's instinct, a special mysterious, inexplicable thing, differing from all other elements in nature or character, can hope to become rich. Some men cannot make money, and others cannot keep it when they have made it. I could never make nor keep it.

The inconveniences of living in a Torrington Square boarding establishment made it a pleasure to be out of the house. One morning I strolled down to the office of a literary agency, from the manager of which had come the letters offering me, on behalf of a magazine, three pounds each for my short stories. I had addressed the stories to the magazine editor, and I was curious to know how the agency had become interested in my work. A lift took me up to the third floor. In the office I asked for the manager.

" Wot nyme ? " inquired a boy from behind the counter.

I translated the strange sound into a request for my name.

" Joseph Keating," I answered.

A man, wearing a big fur coat, was leaning over the counter. He had a short, ragged, brown-grey beard, and an angular, sallow face, with little marks in his cheeks suggesting pock-holes. At the sound of my name he raised himself, and turned towards me.

" Joseph Keating," he repeated, in a drawling tone. " You're the man I've been looking for. My name is —— ." I gasped at the mention of it. Not only I but a wide world, also, knew that name. For many years I had read his work and the magazine edited by him.

This situation was so much like one from fiction that it pleased the story-teller in me. My principle of novel-building was that the source of all romance lay in reality itself, and that the finest romancer was one whose large knowledge of actual life enabled him to be a true realist. My own experience in every way bore out the soundness of that great principle. Here was I—and, after all, who was I ?—seeking my fortune in London, and the first time my name was spoken, a famous editor introduced himself to me and told me that I was the man he had been seeking.

He asked me to lunch with him at the Savage Club, and I accepted his invitation. We sat in a crowded, interesting room overlooking Adelphi Terrace. He introduced me to several famous men, whose names I forget. Then we went to his magazine offices, in Henrietta Street. He had published two or three of my stories, and he praised them greatly.

Now, he suggested that I, using various pen-names to disguise my identity, should write two short stories, one character-sketch of some well-known individual, and one review of a book every month, at three pounds for each item. I said definitely that I should be very glad to do so, but would prefer to work in the country and send my " copy " to him by post.

The fact was, my sensitiveness to noises made the idea of living permanently in London painful.

He objected to my proposal, so I accepted his.

Four things of mine, under different names, appeared in each monthly number of his magazine. One of the names I used was my mother's maiden name, Hurley. I began by interviewing and writing character-sketches of Mr. T. P. O'Connor and Mr. Max Beerbohm. I spent an hour in T.P.'s Chelsea house. He was a most interesting study. I admired him as a great Irish Nationalist, and his journalistic work had fascinated me. I took no visible note of any kind, and scarcely spoke a word.

My editor said that the sketch gave T.P.'s character not as I saw it, but as T.P. himself saw it.

Mr. Max Beerbohm lived on a top floor in Upper Berkeley Street. He chatted with me in a pleasant room, which was full of books, dusty and disordered ; and we had tea on a centre table loaded with loose drawing sheets. He seemed to have a poor opinion of my methods. I sat, and said nothing, and used no notebook. He was less of a student than I was. I did not interest him. He gave me a clear understanding of the limitations of a one-sided experience. He thought that his own work was more important than mine.

My editor was so delighted with my Max Beerbohm article that he wrote me a letter of wild praise. He said it was the best character-sketch that had ever been written.

He took me down to the Devonshire Club to listen to Mr. George R. Sims, so that I might write an article about him. Mr. John Davidson, the poet, who was a short, handsome man, with a little black moustache and an eye-glass, and Mr. John Lane, the publisher, were in our group.

" Don't ever get married, Mr. Keating," said John Lane to me. " It will spoil your writing."

We five spent some time in the Club together until at last to my regret the publisher broke up our merry little party by being compelled to hurry away to keep an important appointment ; and John Davidson, screwing in his monocle, immediately rose from his comfortable chair, and went with him.

One good thing said by Mr. Sims that afternoon was :

" France and England are old enemies, but the English will always love a Frenchman. England and Germany are new friends, but the English will never like the Germans."

That was in 1904. Ten years later France and England were comrades, and Germany was at war with them. And in that war the natural barbarity of the Germans broke every rule of fair fighting. They poisoned wells, butchered innocent women and children, murdered unarmed British soldiers, sank defenceless sailing-ships, and in all ways justified the instinctive dislike which Sims had so shrewdly perceived in the English attitude towards Germans.

To be settled so surely in work which brought me in three pounds every week, when I had fully expected that many months, perhaps years, of privation must be endured, seemed such a surprising thing that during my Easter visit home, I said to my father :

" My good luck is too good to last."

My editor wished me to write a sketch of an eminent Member of Parliament. I called at the member's fine house in Mayfair. A footman led me up to his master's study on the top floor. There the great man talked to me for nearly an hour. I went away again. Nothing about him had interested me, and nothing could I write. The editor pressed me again and again for the article. I sat for many hours with pen and paper ready. Not a line would come. He accused me of keeping the character-sketch for some secret purpose of my own. But the fact was that I had seen no character in the eminent politician. I explained my difficulty. My editor swore at me, and I swore at my editor.

Just at this crisis the literary agency manager sent me a note asking me to call at his office. I went down to him. A stranger—a fair-faced, straw-haired little man—was with the manager. They told me that all stories and articles appearing in the magazine for which I was writing passed through their hands, and asked me if I knew that my editor was selling my work in America at four times the price he was paying me for it.

" Mr. Keating," said the straw-haired man, in a

drawling tone. " I've sold sixty-nine pounds' worth of your stories in America this month. That ought to be your money."

America had not come into my thoughts at all, and I had been quite unaware of the existence of the place as a market for my work. I did not know why those agents, who were supposed to be acting in the interests of our magazine, should have given me such valuable information behind the editor's back, except that they wished to be my friends.

While I felt greatly complimented by the surprising demand for my work, the idea of its being sold with no intention of letting me have any benefit out of the sale annoyed me.

It seemed to me that my employer had wished to get more value out of my services than I had agreed to give.

I was aware that the principle of commerce was the absence of principle, and that any means by which a business man could increase his profits, without openly breaking the law against robbery, was supposed to be fair dealing ; but this was my first experience of commercial chicanery and I felt that it was quite unfair to me. I could see no honesty at all in it. " Business honesty " there might have been in it. Personally, I had more than " business honesty." I would rather have starved to death than have taken a wretched penny that morally belonged to some one else.

Supposing the positions between my employer and myself had been reversed. I should have said to the man with whom I was dealing :

" Your stories and articles are worth three pounds each to my magazine. They might be of more value to other journals, but that is not my affair. I offer you only what I can afford to give. On the other hand, if I am mistaken in my view, and they should prove to be worth more than three pounds, I will give you all the profit they may make above that amount, because to you, and to you alone, that extra profit belongs, seeing that I am getting my full value by publishing them once in my magazine."

Instead of taking this straightforward stand, my employer, it seemed to me, had tried to turn my inexperience into a personal benefit for himself. He had not only used my work at his own price, but had re-sold it to other people at more than he had given for it.

At that time I did not know of the practice of editors who bought stories and articles for one special journal, and afterwards re-used the work in several other magazines and newspapers under their control, without letting the author know of it, or giving him any extra fee. In such cases, the defence put forward was that the copyright had been purchased. In one instance out of a million that defence might be true, in all other instances the author had sold his manuscripts under the belief that they would appear only in the journal named. But in his inexperience he was often doomed to find himself mistaken.

I went to my editor at the Henrietta Street office. Sunshine brightened the pleasant room. He sat at his desk, making cigarettes, with the aid of a little machine in his hands. The sun glittered on the bright metal of his instrument.   It was pay day, and he stopped making cigarettes, for a moment, to hand me my week's cheque for three pounds.

Said I :

" The literary agents tell me that you have sold sixty-nine pounds' worth of my work in America."

" Well ? "

" I want the money for that," I declared.

" You're not entitled to it."

" Why not ? "

" All that you write for my magazine is my property," he explained, " because you are working on a salary of three pounds a week, which makes me the owner of the copyright."

" I did not agree to work on a salary," I said, very distinctly.   " I agreed to accept three pounds for each article."

" Well, isn't that the same thing ?   Look at my letters accepting your stuff.   You will see that you sold me the copyright."

" I want the money for what you have sold of my stories and articles in America," said I, more distinctly.

" You won't get it."   He said other things ; but the words were too profane for repetition.

" I will get it," I replied.   " It's like your miserable cheek to think of keeping it.   You are better off than I am.   You live in a pretty little country cottage, and I live in an ugly London boarding-house, yet you try to deprive me of a few pounds.   You use my stuff in your magazine, and then sell it for four times what you give me for it, without telling me a word about it, or intending to give me a penny of the profits. It's a mean trick whichever way you look at it, salary or no salary."

" If I hadn't given you a job, you'd be starving," he said, swearing vigorously. " Authors have no gratitude in their souls ! You talk mightily now that you've got my cheque in your pocket."

His three-pound cheque was the only money I had, but it at once came out of my pocket, was torn in half, and flung into the waste-paper basket near his desk ; and I walked out of his office.

Before I had returned to Torrington Square, a messenger was there with a note from my late editor saying that he had decided to waive all claim to the sixty-nine pounds. He also enclosed another cheque for the three pounds due to me, explaining that he did so because he had the greatest sympathy for damned fools, but that he would never print another line of mine in his magazine.

My prophecy, unlike most prophecies, had come true. My luck had been too good to last. My process of " going through the mill " had begun.

CHAPTER XVIII

My disapproval of London : I rent a cottage in Potters Bar :
Choosing a housekeeper : My house-warming : My writing-
table : A butcher's loss of faith in me : My loneliness : My
flight from Potters Bar : I meet Patterson on the British
Museum steps : My novel " Maurice " : I am robbed of my
all.

THE literary agents informed me that although they
had sold my stories in America they had not yet
received the money. I believed them.

They offered to advance me fifty shillings a week
on what was due to me, if I would allow them to sell
all other work of mine in America, at twenty per cent.
commission. I agreed to this, accepting their word
that one-fifth of an author's earnings was a fair and
ordinary share for an agent.

With the idea of getting well away from town
noises, and yet being within convenient reach of
my agents, I ransacked Kent, Surrey, and Middlesex
for a suitable home.

There could be no doubt that I disapproved of
London. The instinct of home-life, the most human
and civilized of instincts, was very strong in me.
London seemed to me to be the most homeless city on
earth. No one there had a home at all. People
sheltered in parts of houses, flats, hotels, or tenement-
mansions of so many rooms that they reminded me
of rabbit-holes in a mountain side. The inmates lived

the life of rabbits, coming out to hunt for food or amusement, and rushing back to their hutches for sleep. Around those tenement entrances children played like little rabbits that dared not run too far away from the openings to their parental burrows, fearing a million enemies, and, above all, dreading the danger of not being able to find their way back again.

I wished to see healthy, cheerful faces around me. The painted, sickly cheeks, and unhappy smiles of women who were always prowling about Torrington Square offended and saddened me. I longed for the wholesome breezes of hills and valleys, purified by the green of trees and grass, and sweetened with the perfume of flowers. In London, the outside air was poisoned by ceaseless horse-traffic ; while indoors I breathed the stewy atmosphere of a boarding-house. I liked open country, space and freedom. The narrow streets with high buildings at each side shutting out the sky were prisons to me.

Walking through the Metropolis always made me feel as if I were a penal servitude convict, taking exercise inside jail walls. Heaven above was only a blue pencil line.

Altogether, I regarded London as an utter monstrosity, the biggest blunder in the world. The earth was buried. It could not breathe under so many houses, which were as closely packed as tombstones in an old cemetery. Only death could live in a grave-yard. I would have hanged, without any trial, all the titled robbers who, for the sake of grabbing the ground-rent, had stifled the land under a hideous heap of bricks and mortar. I wanted to cut avenues a mile wide through the heap, in all directions, so as to let in God's light and man's liberty.

Though I searched carefully everywhere around the outside of London for shelter, the best I could find to suit my means was a two-storey, red-bricked shelter described as a cottage, in Potters Bar, a mile from the nearest railway station.

The name of my house was "Hawthorn Cottage." It was furnished, and the rent was eighteen shillings a week, for which sum I should be held responsible during a term of six months.

A housekeeper had to be found before I could live in the cottage. I went to an agency for servants, in Tottenham Court Road, and paid three shillings and sixpence for telling the manageress that I wanted to engage an old woman. Nothing else came of my three-and-six. The agency seemed to have no purpose in view but that of taking money for nothing. Friends of mine heard of my trouble about getting an ancient domestic, and a worse difficulty arose. No less than three young women of my acquaintance offered themselves, separately, to do my housekeeping. I would have no young woman, however amiable or good-looking, for the position.

My landlord found the ideal housekeeper for me— a small, elderly widow, with seven children. She arranged to come each morning at seven o'clock, stay till tea-time, and sleep at her own home. The wages she asked were her food, and seven or eight shillings a week. After rent and wages were paid, I should have twenty-five shillings a week left out of my allowance of fifty shillings from the agents, to pay for her food, my own, and my other household and personal expenses. This seemed to be a reasonable arrangement.

To celebrate my entry under a roof of my own, I invited my two best friends from Wales to spend a few weeks' holiday with me in Potters Bar. About twelve o'clock on Saturday night we took train at King's Cross.

Two points disturbed me. First, as I had not yet slept at my future residence, or even seen it for a few days, I was not sure that we should be able to find it. Second, I had asked my housekeeper (who at this hour of night would be asleep in her own home) to store food of some kind for us, and I was not sure that she had obeyed my instructions.

Whether we should discover the place we were going to, and, if found, would there be anything to eat in the house, were the two questions troubling me, though I did not mention them to my companions.

Frank Southwood had grown stout, and disliked walking, and I had wired for a cab to meet us at Potters Bar. We arrived at the station there towards one o'clock, and found the cab waiting for us. We got in and I told the driver to take us to Hawthorn Cottage, secretly hoping that he knew where it was, because I could not describe its situation, and I did not want my friends to know of my difficulty.

The cab, a shaky four-wheeler, took the three of us away through the dark country, and we laughed and chatted in the best of humours.

Frank was so big that he took up all the front seat. When he struck a match to light his pipe the flame illumined his laughing, fair, handsome face, and his remarkable hair, which was so thick and delicately fine that women envied and admired it. In fact there were few women whom Frank did not fascinate at first sight, and he was always in some tangle or other in consequence of this. He was often jealous of me when, by chance, a girl he happened to like showed a preference for me.

He was the young man with whom I had played fiddle duets, fourteen years previously, at midnight, up at his mother's house on the hill in Pontypridd. Ever since those old days he had been a genuine friend to me.

He had extraordinary gifts. He never practised the fiddle, yet he could play it marvellously. His fat, well-shaped fingers seemed to be part of the instrument ; and he had merely to draw the bow across the strings to bring out, with no effort, the true fiddle-tone, so beautiful in quality that young ladies who were listening fell frantically in love with him. Yet he could not be bothered taking his genius seriously. He preferred the gamble of commerce. His masterful personality in dealing with men brought him great success in business.

It was Frank who, about ten years before, had introduced me to Percie Smith, now sitting by my side in the cab. Percie was dark and slim, and had a charming manner. He was happily married and had several lovely children. Frank had asked me to play at a charity concert in Pontypridd. I went up from Cardiff for the purpose. Percie was the conductor of the orchestra. One of the items on the programme was Mozart's " Magic Flute." I was leading the second fiddles, forgot to note the all-silent bar in the middle, and made the whole band laugh by playing a solo in the tacit.

After that concert, we three had spent many week-ends together in Percie's or Frank's house when we had played trios from Saturday afternoon till Monday morning. Percie was a good pianist, a superb con-ductor, and an all-round musician. During a holiday in a motor-car, the previous year, we three had called at our friend Bruerton's place in the Midlands, and at four o'clock in the morning Frank had challenged Percie to play the Goltermann Duo for piano and viola. Percie accepted the challenge, and they took off their coats for the heavy work. Despite its being the hour of dawn, with the household in bed, their performance of the fine duo was brilliant.

As soon as our cab landed us at Hawthorn Cottage, which was in a small street, near the Great North Road, with a police station on the corner, my first action was to light a candle and search the pantry. Bottles of beer and bread and cheese were on the shelves.

While we were feasting, I explained to my friends that, until a moment ago, I was not sure whether we were in the right house, or should find anything in it to save us from starvation. They were merry over my hazardous hospitality.

Our misfortunes began next day. Frank believed he was ill, and insisted on going home by the first available train. This was a bad omen for my future in Hawthorn Cottage.

My housekeeper came at seven and went away at five. In the nights, after Percie had gone, I was alone. My house was clean, the furniture comfortable, and my landlord, himself an artist, had put in a new, big, strong table, made specially for my writing. It was a magnificent work-bench, snow-white, unsoiled by paint or varnish, with massive, square legs that never trembled, even when my pen was at its wildest moments. The mere look of my table made me want to write. We placed it upstairs in a back room, the window of which looked out on pleasant fields; and in the first month I wrote six or seven short stories, which my agents sold to American and British magazines for one hundred pounds.

The agency never sent me more than the agreed fifty shillings a week, and I was not surprised to find that this amount was not enough. One day my housekeeper explained that there was no meat in the house, because the butcher's faith in my genius had been assailed by doubt. I borrowed a shilling from her, took train to London and induced my agents to advance me an extra small cheque. As soon as I got home, I returned her shilling, and gave her enough money to pay the butcher, with instructions that, under pain of death, she should never go into his shop again.

One week, I was entirely without cigarettes. I had taken to a pipe a few years before, but had not been able to master it. None of our family—I suppose, no one in any generation of our tribe—had been a pipe-smoker. But cigarettes had become a necessity for me, and I could do no work that week without them. A cheque came on the following Sunday morning, and as no tobacconist opened in Potters Bar that day, I walked ten miles through the country to buy a stock of my favourites. My craving for a smoke was as terrible as the craving of a starving man for food. As soon as I lit the first cigarette, I was eager for work again.

No doubt, if cigarettes were not to be got, I should, in time, become quite indifferent as to whether I had them or not. But without them, I had not been able to work for an entire week. Supposing, by a foolish revolution, drink was suddenly abolished. We should, very likely, see the work of nearly a whole nation thrown out of gear for seven days. And, in the midst of such a disaster, another revolution would, within the week, abolish teetotalism, to save the country from being utterly ruined.

When advocates of non-smoking and non-drinking talk wildly of cutting off all supplies of alcohol and tobacco, I remember that there is more danger in breaking off a habit violently than in indulging it. A habit grows slowly, and can only be got rid of slowly. Then the question of whether a habit is a good or a bad one is so hard to settle. People who do not like drink or tobacco acquire a bad habit if they devote their lives to preventing other persons from drinking or smoking. There is no harm in being good, but a great deal of harm in being too good. Excess of virtue is a vice, in just the same way as too much eating, drinking, or money-making is vicious. There is no poison in alcohol or nicotine any more than there is in strychnine or morphia. A scientific use of morphia and strychnine is admittedly beneficial. Danger lies only in an improper use of them. The same law applies to all things. Alcohol, nicotine, money, food and passion are innocent and good in themselves. Sin, vice, and poison are only found in the abuse of good things. We should try to do away with drunkenness, not drink—gluttony, not food—immorality, not passion—money-making, not money.

Here I must confess being unable to practise what I preach. I am wicked enough to feel that I would hang all money-makers. Their bad habits I would break violently at the end of a rope, because I would remember only that they had kept the bodies and souls of thousands of poor men, women, and children, wriggling in agony for generations. Undoubtedly, money-making is the vice of vices. For one money-maker to feel joy, millions of poor people must feel misery. No other vice has the far-reaching effects, or is so inhuman in its poisonous cruelty, as the sin of the money-maker. Hang him, and every vice in the world would die with the last kick of his cloven foot.

Potters Bar began to displease me in the second month. Not one human being did I know personally in the place. I was not a cosmopolitan, and disliked making new acquaintances. There was company in the public-houses, but I did not like public-houses. Tramps and pedlars came to my door at evening time, after my housekeeper had gone home, and I found some relief in talking to these nomads ; but they usually took advantage of my friendliness and wanted to make my house their lodgings for the night. I was not Christian enough to permit this.

The village was one rambling street of uneven buildings, with fields and woods behind, at each side, with the Great North Road running between, along which motor cars and motor cycles were continually rattling and hooting. I liked the place itself. There was a green grass border to the road-sides.

When I could not work in the day, I walked to St. Albans or Hatfield. These historic places did not interest me. I went to them merely for exercise, and they served a valuable purpose if I returned from them tired out at night, with a desire for sleep.

Going into my silent and lonely house, in the darkness, saddened me. I knew that I ought to have been married. I knew that my life would be happier if I were met by a smiling wife and cheerfully noisy children, instead of being greeted by ghostly shadows that seemed to be moving towards me from the dark and silent rooms as I opened the street door and went in.

One cause only had kept me single. I had not met a girl with whom I could live. Many girls I had loved, but not one that I would marry. It might be objected that my love had not been love at all. The objection would be quite wrong. My feeling had been the true adoration that did not ask if the girl was worthy of me or I worthy of the girl. I was happy as long as she was with me, until the idea of marriage arose. Then I had to begin to think about her, and ask questions as to whether or no I could be satisfied with her companionship for ever. When love begins to ask questions, it is on its deathbed, and its thoughts about the future are like the fears of a passing soul, wondering if it will be allowed to enter Heaven. If I had met the desired girl, I should have married her first, and thought about her afterwards. But she had not appeared, and I was doomed to live like a monk in a gloomy, cheerless cell.

My lonely nights began to trouble me. The horrors of sleeplessness put thorns in my bed, and the darkness terrified me. When day came, I could not write. No ideas of any sort at all inspired my pen. I wasted hours sitting at my magnificent writing table, trying to work. I wasted further hours roaming the fields in the July sunshine, hoping to recover my power to write. With no one to talk to, except to answer my housekeeper's question as to what she should get for lunch, I spent days without, in the true sense, speaking at all.

An intolerable night came when the desire to converse like a human being prompted me to get out of bed, go to the police-station at the corner, and sit there till morning, talking to any constable who might be on duty. I did not act upon this impulse. For the first time in three years, I risked taking a sleeping draught.

That gave me two hours' sleep.

At seven o'clock, my housekeeper came, as usual.

" I am going away," I said to her. " I will let you know where to send my things, as soon as I have found an address."

She gasped. My tenancy was for six months. Only two months had passed. The rent for four

months more at eighteen shillings a week would
have to be paid. I would pay it for nothing rather
than stay in Potters Bar. I did not care what
became of all my belongings. I took the first train
out that morning. I could not stand the loneliness
another hour.

I did not stop until I reached my home in Wales.

A few hours with my own people and old friends
changed the entire world for me, and I was able to
make a happy August holiday out of my terrors.

It was, I think, during this month that I walked
over the hills from Mountain Ash to Percie's house
in the Big Rhondda, to play the fiddle for him in an
orchestra which he was taking to the Welsh National
Eisteddfod to compete for an important prize. We
were to take train at four o'clock next morning to
some town in North Wales, a few hundred miles away.
Percie was anxious that his orchestra should vanquish
a local rival. If he failed to appear, he would seem
to have feared the result. The humiliation would be
felt by all his orchestra.

Destiny willed that there should be a serious
difficulty in our way. A new life was expected at his
house. He and I sat up all night together, in a room
below ; and, in great anxiety, sent hot cups of coffee
to the chamber above. If the new life did not arrive
in time, Percie could not go to the Eisteddfod, and all
chance of our winning the National prize would be
forfeited. Destiny had no time-table, and our train
would leave punctually at four o'clock. Dawn came,
and the sun shone over the eastern hill-range. We
fancied we could hear the train whistling through the

valley below us.   We perspired.   Then we heard the cry of the new life above.

Our train was steaming out when we rushed into the station.   We and our fiddles were flung into a tail-end coach.   Percie's masterly conducting that day—I think we played Schubert's Unfinished, in B Minor—won the great Eisteddfod prize, and our rivals were vanquished.

In September I went back to London, paid off my Potters Bar debts, and tried to settle down in Torrington Square.   My writing room, now, was the British Museum Reading Room.   There I began my novel " Maurice."   My agents took the three first chapters to a publisher who agreed to pay me a small sum on delivery of the completed book.

Mounting the museum steps one morning, I was astounded to see my friend, J. E. Patterson, seated on one of the outside benches.   Several years had passed since we had last met.   He looked pale.   He told me he had been ill.   His struggle for fame in London was at its hardest about this time.   Only one novel had he been able to get accepted, and the foolish publishers had insisted on deleting many pages of fine literature from the manuscript, so as to reduce the cost of printing.   He was nearly broken-hearted, but as determined as ever to win recognition as a poet and novelist.

We wrote together many days in the British Museum.   He warned me that I was breaking all the rules of the Reading Room by using it as a writing room, and that I was endangering my chance of being admitted.   I had no other place for my writing, and

I thought it would be a wrong and unjust thing for any official to interfere with me. I noticed that the attendants kept an unduly watchful eye on me. One, certainly, did approach me to ask what books I was waiting for. After that, I ordered dozens of volumes every day and never opened one of them.

The humour of the situation did not make me laugh, I regret to say. No other place in London was quiet ; and quiet was not merely desirable for me, but painfully necessary. I had a garret, but could not work in it owing to the rattle of traffic outside, night and day. If I took lodgings where night, at least, could be peaceful, I was afraid to risk writing at night. That had already come near destroying me. I must either write in the daytime, or not at all. The Reading Room had its disadvantages. Nearly all the readers there spent most of their time coughing, or clearing their throats, or turning over leaves of big volumes, and making swishing, irritating noises. Besides, I had never before seen such a collection of eccentricities as were there. The real curiosities of the British Museum were not the silent, lifeless antiques on pedestals, but those dead things that walked about the Reading Room.

How this new novel of mine, " Maurice," came to be started, I could never tell. One day I began writing it. That is all I remember. It was all about deep mines and high mountains—a vision of my boyhood. I could not help feeling the romance of our hills and the mystery of the pits. I had seen the old pastoral life of our village being slowly changed into a hideous industrial existence. The tragedy of that change might have

crept into my story.   Perhaps my own life had been
influenced by the tragedy.   Industrialism destroyed
all beauty, and recognized nothing but the task of
keeping alive.

That was what I was trying to describe, because it
was part of me.   Out of what I had seen, thought,
and felt all my books were made.   A conception of
a phase of life came to me from Heaven knew where
and insisted upon being expressed.   My own existence
had been to me a more fascinating romance than I
had ever read.   Every day was like turning over a
fresh page of an irresistible story in which I never
knew what would come next—whether it would be
sudden death by violence or slow death by starvation.

In the middle of my novel, payments from the
agents ceased.   I had no money, but hoped that
plenty would come to me as soon as my new book
appeared.   To finish it, I went home, and, by the
end of June 1905, reached the last page.

Fourteen pounds, said my agents, was the balance
due to me after deducting advances.   As I had been
living at my mother's expense since Easter, I gave
her the fourteen pounds.   After that I was without
any money for the rest of the year.   I had not even a
few coppers to buy cigarettes, because I would not
ask my mother for what she could not afford.   It was
bad enough for me to be eating and sleeping at her
expense, without attempting to borrow.

A very charming girl in our valley pitied me, and
gave me a two-shilling piece, so that I might get
cigarettes.   I advised her not to think about me at
all, but to think of getting married and settling down.

Of all that I said to her in our walks about the mountains, this was the only thing which she refused to heed.

A new priest had come to our parish and, out of kindness and compassion for me, seeing me idle, asked my mother if he should use his influence with the colliery authorities to get me a job.

To Mountain Ash, I was a rodney who would not work for his living.   My humiliation was painful.   I had thoughts of walking back to London, and would have done so, but that I hoped the publication of " Maurice " would bring me in enough to allow me to write another novel.

The book came out in October.   "The Pall Mall Gazette" said that the story was "a combination of imaginative power and minute realism resulting in impressions that must endure."   But no additional cheque came from the publishers.

The novel came to the notice of Mr. D. Lloyd George, who shortly afterwards was made President of the Board of Trade, and he sent me a most kind letter of praise, which all the newspapers printed. Still no cheque came from the publishers.

In November my literary agents informed me that they had sold a short story of mine in America for twelve pounds.   Their note showed that they had taken six pounds of this amount as their commission. I wrote asking why they were taking half my earnings. The answer was that I had agreed to their doing so. I had never agreed to anything of the kind.   In-vestigation proved that they had been robbing me from beginning to end.   I had trusted them in all simplicity, but their apparent friendliness towards me had been sheer deceit. They were money-makers. I threatened to put them in the criminal dock. One of them died suddenly. The others declared themselves bankrupt. They owed me two hundred pounds, and I never received a penny of it. The Authors' Society tried to do what it could to protect my interests, but its efforts were of no value. I was left penniless.

The humiliation of living at my mother's expense was more than I could bear. In February 1906, I asked my brother Matt, then living in Bloomsbury Square, to pay my train fare to London. Luck was against himself, at the time ; but he scraped up a couple of pounds, somehow, and sent them to me.

My return to London in February 1906, was a forlorn and wild venture. All that I had earned had been stolen from me by dishonest agents. My novel, which was to have made me famous, had left me as obscure and unwanted as I had been at the start, ten years before. My journey cost fourteen shillings, and I had twenty-six shillings left. I had no other money, or hopes of getting any. Yet back I went, ill, disappointed, and almost broken-hearted, but bent on fighting. I said :

" I shall succeed before I die, or die before I succeed—I do not care which. It's a gold watch, or a wooden leg ! "

CHAPTER XIX

FROM my train window, the approach to Paddington
showed me nothing but reasons for wishing that I
was going hundreds of miles away from it, instead of
rushing towards it. I was passing through a valley
of unlovely and unclean backs of tall houses, sad
London dwellings, each giving shelter to many and
home to none. Their windows were dusty and
broken, the sills used as clothes-lines. Red, blue,
and cream-hued shirts, chemises, petticoats, sheets
and quilts, all torn or patched, hung out to dry,
fluttering in gloom, like banners of poverty.

Never had I entered London but in pain and
misery. To me it had always seemed to be an over-
populated desert island.

Shadow and noise, fog, steam, shrieking of engine-
whistles, cab-whistles, clank of coach-buffers, and
rattle of cart-wheels on cobble-stones, made Paddington Station seem to be a junction in the infernal
regions where, midway between hell and heaven,
unfortunate passengers from the Seat of Judgment
were running and screaming, up and down the plat-
forms, for cabs to take them away as quickly as

possible to their own private furnaces, in order to begin the purging of their sins without delay. My only consoling thought was a vague hope that London might, indeed, be my purgatory, and that my body was taking all the suffering which my sins had destined for my soul after death.

Though I believed that I was one of the most distinguished of that crowd under a black ban of exile and punishment for, perhaps, a million years, all I could afford was a two-penny horse-omnibus to convey me and my two brown-leather bags and fiddle to my torture-chamber, a Bloomsbury boarding-establishment.

I waited for the vehicle, outside a corner public-house, called " The Load of Hay," a delightful phrase, striking the imagination with wonderful visions of bright, green fields, just mown, laden with delicious perfumes, and surrounded by fine trees, and hedges and bushes sparkling with wild flowers and blossoms—of women and children, their heads in sun-bonnets, and swinging rakes in their hands, making hay—and, a rickety gambo, wobbling under its high load, and drawn by a fat, slow-moving, glossy-coated, brown horse across the trackless green, towards an un-finished hayrick near a white-washed and red-roofed farmhouse half hidden by trees at the far edge of the grass.

The one-time rustic hostelry had become drab rubbish. Yet inside that metamorphosed tavern, happy miners from our hills spent a holiday in London.

They came out of the Paddington train, after an

all-night journey, and went into " The Load of Hay."
When night and hour of departure arrived, they came
out of " The Load of Hay," and went into the train
again, declaring, all the way home, that their visit
to London had been a memorable joy.

With my bags and fiddle, I struggled to a seat on
the omnibus roof, and we were hauled and jolted down
Praed Street, a disheartening thoroughfare formed by
two ragged rows of dirty bricks with windows.

There is no spectacle of humour and pathos com-
parable to that of a poor and unknown author's entry
into London. No one is expecting him, and no one
wants him. There is no pæan of welcome for a grain
of dust blown from the gutter by the wind. He
awakens less interest than the dust, for the crowd will
shade their eyes from it, and make an effort to avoid
it. Him they do not notice, though he is sitting in
their midst. No lips smile for him, no warm pressure
of a friendly hand greets him, no eye brightens as it
looks upon him. Indifference, titanic, inhuman, and
unconquerable, is the salutation he receives. He
thinks he ought to be riding on a chariot of flame, and
finds that he is riding upon an omnibus. Within him
is the pride that makes him compete for fame with
men whose names are reverenced, whose books are
worshipped as holy things, whose lightest words,
movements, likes and dislikes are chronicled in awe.
With his pride of power, he has the weakness of
vanity : a cruel sensitiveness to every rude, unmean-
ing touch, as if it were an intended insult. He
believes himself to be the equal of the great, and he
sees himself regarded as less than the small. Around

him are memories and symbols of immortals who, on this earth, suffered as he is suffering. Some of them died before their agonies were over. He is not sure that his destiny is to be less terrible than theirs.

My brother Matt had asked me to stay with him at his lodgings in Bloomsbury Square till I had earned some money. A room at the top of the house was allotted to me for sleep. But little sleep could I get in it, owing to the click of hoofs on the asphalt. The chief residents of our boarding-house were a German silk merchant, who committed suicide by flinging his naked body out of a top window, and a Jew who was a German spy.

Every morning at nine o'clock I went to the British Museum Reading Room to write. I called the place my factory. I wrote much that was utterly worthless. My manuscript was full of crossed-out lines. Between them was a network of corrections, also crossed out and rewritten. My pages resembled my mind. Thoughts, without meaning, chased one another, scribbling out one another, crushing one another, until I did not know what to think, or how to write, and my face and forehead were as full of lines as one of my pages.

Frank and Percie came to London for a holiday. With them was Dai Harris who played the 'cello for our quartets. We had dinner at Frascati's, and Dai, falling in love with the colour of benedictine, drank a whole bottle of it. Next morning, Percie drew Frank's attention to my face.

Frank said : " For God's sake, Joe, come away with me, or you'll fall to pieces." He had arranged to work at Bournemouth for a few months. His extra-ordinary regard for me made him insist on my going with him. A novel had come into my mind, and I was glad to get a chance of peace for writing.

He rented a lovely, lop-sided, thatched cottage at Wick, four miles beyond Bournemouth, on the bank of an amber river that had as many fishes in it as there were people in London, and a ferry-boat for crossing, with Christchurch Abbey behind the marshes at the other side, and the sea itself within a mile. At sunset, tranquillity and the red on Christchurch towers, the marsh, and the river were, for me, the face of Heaven, painted by the greatest master. The picture was framed by our front window.

On the first morning after our arrival, Frank went out on his business. I stayed at home, and began to write my novel, " Queen of Swords."

Our landlady was an amiable, young woman, who had brought her husband, a Scotsman, from London to Wick for his health, and supported him and their two little girls by her industry. She took the greatest care of her new tenants.

We lived simply and well on our breakfasts of coffee, bacon, and eggs, a chop or steak for lunch, and strawberry jam for tea. At evening-time we hired a boat, and rowed or fished on the river till dark. At four o'clock each morning I was pleasantly awakened by a blackbird's song from a tree under my bedroom window. Never before had I noticed the song of a blackbird, the most melodious, refined, and delightful of singers, soft and low-toned, with no hint of the hardness which I had sometimes found in the shrill trill of a thrush. My blackbird seemed to be less of a singer than a talker with a wonderfully musical voice. The notes were so varied and changeful in pitch that they had a human sound, as if their owner were holding an interesting conversation with another blackbird in a tree, with the river between them. My bird began by giving out a few notes which sounded like :

" Don't you think it's a fine morning ? "

Then followed a slight pause, after which, from the opposite bank, came an amiable reply.

" I don't think I ever saw such a fine morning."

" I'm of the opinion that we shall be even happier to-day than we were yesterday."

" Personally, I have not the slightest doubt about it."

" Isn't it a charming world, altogether ? "

" Really, I am abound to agree with you. It would be quite impossible to better it."

" Did you sleep well last night ? "

" Beautifully, thanks. And you ? "

" Splendidly."

" Suppose we go out and get breakfast, and arrange how we shall enjoy ourselves for the rest of the day ? "

" What an excellent suggestion ! How did you think of it ? Just a moment. I'm coming across the river to you."

" Oh, please don't trouble. I'm coming over to you."

My bird flew away. In the evenings I saw it again, perched on the highest twig, right at the tree-top, exchanging views with its neighbour about what a glorious day they had had, as if they were two people of charming manners and cultivated voices, who had been to a play and, now at home, were sitting at their open, drawing-room windows, telling each other across intervening fields how much they had enjoyed themselves. The sight of my bird's shining, black coat, and bright, yellow beak, amidst the green leaves, made me feel unusually good-natured. Its melody awakened supreme tenderness, and nothing else, as if the blackbird sang always right in tune with the human heart.

A mounted policeman ambled down the long, tree-shaded, and pleasant lane connecting the high road with our riverside cottage. We lived opposite the ferry-boat crossing. That morning I had received a solicitor's letter, readdressed from several quarters, threatening me with courts and prisons for having evaded payment of a tailor's bill of ten pounds, a relic of my dandy days which, though less than three years past, seemed ages old. I feared that the mounted policeman, the first I had seen anywhere near our retreat, had found out where I was hiding and was going to arrest me.

My debt had been incurred in Cardiff when money was coming in to me regularly, and I had fully intended settling it at the proper time, but disaster had come upon me abruptly. This tailor's bill was the only tradesman's liability I had been unable to pay. It had troubled my conscience for nearly three years. And now, the sight of the mounted constable, coming so sharply on the solicitor's threatening letter, which had been following me from place to place, really alarmed me. I was out on the river-bank, in the sunshine, watching the stout, red-faced ferryman punting and piloting his little boat and its occasional passengers of women and children to and fro across the brown, gleaming water. I ran back into our cottage.

Frank was at home that morning. He was stretched out on a couch, smoking a big pipe, and reading "The Daily Mail." I told him of my difficulty. He advised me to remain out of sight, near the back door, in case it would be necessary for me to make a dash for liberty while he harangued the policeman.

Frank dropped his paper, lifted his huge body from the couch, went out, and sat on the low wall in front of our window, filling his pipe lazily. I heard him hail the horseman with a cheerful, friendly greeting, and holding him in amiable talk. In reality, he was trying to find out upon what secret mission the invader was bent. I knew that Frank would have lied largely and effectively (he was a most skilful diplomatist) if any question of my whereabouts arose. No hint on that point came out ; and the officer, parting on the best of terms with Frank, jogged away towards the coast.

Percie joined us at Easter, which fell late that year, and in unusually fine weather ; and we three had hilarious hours under sun, moon, and stars, rowing and fishing, on river and sea, with intervals of playing trios for piano, fiddle, and viola in our thatched cottage.

Our landlady, before we had come to her, had

agreed to let the place to other people for June.
Frank found a house that would suit us, at Parkstone,
on the edge of a pine wood, with the sea behind. The
tall, straight trees delighted me at first ; and each
time I walked amidst them I quoted Shelley's lines :

> *We wandered through the pine forest*
> *That skirts the ocean foam.*

Gradually a violent dislike of the monotonous
accuracy of line in the high trunks and their mop-
like heads, came over me. I hated the sight of pine-
trees. In order to keep my back turned towards
them, I would walk miles out of my way to reach the
sea.

Thunder and sheet-lightning of an extraordinary
kind one night terrified Frank, though he tried to
hide this by gibing at me for being frightened. That
was his way. If ever a superfluous taste of alcohol
took him one degree within the circle of intoxication,
he tried to hide it by saying :

" Joe, you're drunk ! "

Our housekeeper's bills became so excessive that
Frank believed he was supporting the entire community. He fretted, too, about his business. The
pine wood, which was only just outside our door,
bothered me a great deal, and Frank and I quarrelled.

Throughout our long friendship, we had frequently
sworn at each other, and forgotten all about it in an
hour.

This time a sore, and exasperating barrier was left
behind. On Whit Monday we took a sailing-boat
out, in Poole harbour, and pretended we had made

up our difference. But our boat got stuck on a lee
shore, and we could do nothing except sit and scowl
at each other all day, while we ate our ham sandwiches and drank our bottles of beer in our helpless
craft.

At home, he found it difficult to stay in the house
with me. When he was out, I found it hard to write
my novel, because I knew that he thought my conduct
captious and irritating. I do not know which of us
was to blame. I know now, and knew then, that all
the trouble was no more than a surface trifle in reality.
I was living on his good-nature. Such a fact might
have made other people more gentle than it made
me. It humiliated me to feel that I was troubling
him ; and, though I knew quite well how hurt he
would be if he realized what I was feeling, my attitude
towards him was more exacting than it had ever
been before.

The sullen, silent conflict interfered with my
writing ; but " Queen of Swords " was finished, in
spite of unfavourable conditions, towards the end
of June. That same day I went out with it to the
post. On the gravel path outside our door I found
sixpence, which I picked up as a good omen.

" My novel has found money already," I thought.

A literary agent had been recommended to me.
He had sold some short stories of mine. Now I sent
him my new book, with a letter saying that I wanted
a hundred guineas advance on royalties for it, within
a month, or he was to return it.

What chance there was of my getting such a sum
I did not know. I felt that the story was good, and

that the privilege of publishing it was worth a hundred guineas.

When Frank came home that evening, I told him I was going away. His first question was how could I live without money ? I explained that I had more than a sovereign. He next asked me not to be an idiot, and would I allow him to send me two pounds a week, wherever I was, till my luck turned ?

That was Frank all over his big person. He could do the finest of things, yet not abate one jot of his grievance against me ; for, next morning, after I had packed up, he came down with me to the station, and as we shook hands at the coach window, with the train moving out, he said :

" Joe, I wouldn't live in the same house with you again—not for a thousand pounds a day."

The train took me to London. I hired a garret in Mecklenburg Square, close to the Foundling Hospital ; and next day called at the literary agent's office to hear what his views were about selling " Queen of Swords." He told me that a publisher had already offered to advance something less than the amount I had asked for the right of publishing it. I accepted the offer, sent five pounds to Frank, another five to my mother, and engaged a Chancery Lane typist for a week, at two guineas, and dictated to her a complete dramatic version of my novel. With the few pounds left out of my " advance," I went to our Welsh hills for a holiday.

CHAPTER XX

A 1906 wonder—of serious importance, in my view
—was the election of a Labour Party to the House of
Commons. I could not help being interested in
working people, because I was born in their midst,
and in every way was one of them.

Wherever I had been, at Mountain Ash, Pontypridd,
Barry, Cardiff, or Swansea, I had been saddened by
the sight of pale, hollow cheeks, telling of bad nourishment, and staring, unintelligent eyes betraying lack
of education. Those two evils were always seen
together in the pale faces of work-people's children.
In large towns like Paris and London I had seen still
deeper marks of hunger and ignorance in childish
features—especially in the east and centre of London,
where houses were crowded together over so many
square miles that not even wholesome air could
reach the youngsters, and they played in foul holes
of streets and alleys instead of in fields and woods.
I knew the simple cause of such painful conditions.
The fathers and brothers of those little boys and girls
were not allowed to receive enough money to enable
them to live as pleasantly as their employers did.

Children of employers, and of the men who owned

the land upon which too many dwellings were built, lived in splendid houses surrounded by lovely trees, lawns, flowers, and good air. To my mind there was no reason why workers should be forced to live in worse surroundings than their employers, except that laws had arranged this unjust and sinful condition ; and I was glad to see, by the labour elections, some sign that the government of the country would be taken away from earth-stealers, called landowners, slave-drivers called employers, and legal bravoes called government lawyers. This unholy trinity had, I believed, always ruled in Parliament, and ruled badly. Each section had a separate, evil mission. The mission of the first gang was to steal fields, woods, rivers, mountains, and air from the workers ; and that of the second gang was to steal the workers' earnings. The third gang, the lawyers, were hired to draw up the best plans for carrying out the villainies of the other two gangs, strictly according to law. In the name of the law any crime could be committed with impunity. By law, Parliament, originally created as a shrine of liberty and justice, had become a temple of the money-maker.

A money-maker is any satanic sinner who tries to gain riches by rack-rent land or houses, or paying bad wages, or buying cheaply and selling dearly.

The instinct of a money-maker is the instinct of a beast in the jungle. The wild animal uses its cunning and strength to track, strike down, and remorselessly tear out the entrails of a prey, and drink its blood. Poor children and their mothers are the prey of the money-maker. We do not see the money-maker tearing out the entrails of women and children, and drinking their blood; but that is how money is made.

This explains what Christ meant when He said that it would be difficult for Him to permit a rich person to get into Heaven amongst all the victims of that rich person's crimes. Imagine Herod in Heaven—the bloodstained king who tried to murder God, and slaughtered so many innocents, merely to protect a crown of gold. Employers and landowners, I saw, were economic Herods. They were money-makers who cared not at all how many babes were massacred, if golden crowns were saved by the slaughter. In every yellow sovereign they coined there was a red drop of human blood. Their piles of gold in banks were mountains of slain mothers and infants. I no longer wondered why the money-changers in the Temple were the only sinners that Christ whipped.

Out of this new influence came the idea of my novel " The Great Appeal."

While I was thinking about the plot, my fine friend, my former chief at " The Western Mail "—(I was staying at my sister's, in Cardiff, at the time)—asked me if I would care to publish a book of my mining stories. I had written altogether about a hundred of them, and they had appeared in American and English magazines. " The Daily Mail " printed nearly a score of the shorter ones. I was glad of the offer and at once arranged a volume entitled " Adventures in the Dark." Some enthusiast on the staff of a Swansea newspaper, called " The South Wales Daily Post," wrote a two-column review of this collection, declaring that " if outsiders could only realize the atmosphere of the book, these mining stories would be famous all over the world."

When " Queen of Swords " came out that autumn. " The Daily Telegraph " said I was a disciple of Stevenson. As I had been compared with Æschylus, Zola, and Shakespeare, in my other books, this addition of Stevenson labelled me with one quality, at least : variety.

During the winter I wrote more short stories, and went on a valley tour, lecturing about the characteristics of Welsh miners. My first lecture was given at a hall belonging to the Young Men's Christian Association. I had put on an evening suit. Just as I was ready to go out of our house, a man knocked at the door. I opened it. He said :

" Are you Joseph Keating ? "

" I am."

He put a county court summons in my hand.

The tailor to whom I owed ten pounds had seen the posters announcing that I would be in Cardiff for one night, at least, and had tracked me down. I was greatly upset. This county court summons was the first I had ever had, and I felt ashamed. But I stuck the paper in the pocket of my tail-coat, went on the stage, and delivered my lecture.

While my audience laughed at my humorous delineations of mining characters, I was thinking sorrowfully of the county court summons in my tail-pocket.

A small society of Welsh undergraduates at Cambridge University invited me to speak on my subject there. The experiment was a success in one sense only : it gave me an impression of university students listening to a lecture that did not interest them.

Short stories in " The Strand " and other magazines had brought me a few pounds to pay for food and shelter. By the summer of 1907, I had enough to be certain of being able to live for three months ; and, with this advantage behind me, I began my novel, " The Great Appeal." I had been thinking about the book all the winter, so all that I had to do was to write it.

To get quiet for this I walked three miles out from Cardiff, every dry morning, Sundays included, to the Kibbwr country. To my right were fields and a river, forming the boundary-line between Wales and England. To my left were more fields, with a stile over which I climbed and went into a little wood, a hundred yards, or so, from the dusty road.

My chair was a fallen tree beside a clear brook in which small, beautifully shaped trout could be seen. They vanished each time I came, but I was so silent that they soon returned, and resumed their own style of fishing. When they looked up at me, they seemed to think that I was only an old, harmless stump. My writing desk was my knee.

Birds and blossoms decorated my studio. Squirrels with proud tails came along my fallen trunk, up to my knee, read what I was writing, found no interest in it, and went away again, up the nearest tree, nutting. I could see them sitting amongst the branches, and hear them cracking nuts. The nuts were unripe ; but the squirrels seemed to be as little capable as human beings of judging from appearances ; for they could not tell whether they would find a kernel inside a shell or not until their teeth had made a hole in it.

A glance at my wood gave a false impression of stillness. The earth was alive with strange, minute crawling forms. I had no knowledge of their names.

Each tree and bush held as many workers on its stems, branches, leaves, and buds, as could be found in the busiest factory. Not stillness, but activity, was in every inch of my little forest. I was as busy as the others, with my fountain pen and paper. Yet through all this industry the silence was so deep that every falling leaf could be heard as it broke from its twig and fluttered down. A huge wild cat, green-eyed, striped brown and yellow, and grown out of all domestic proportions, with a tail as long as a tiger's, came out of some mysterious hole, stared at me for a whole minute, as if trying to recall where it had seen something like me in bygone ages, then walked slowly, wearily, and sadly past me into the unknown from which it had come. I confess that the sight of it, while it stared so solemnly at me, made me shudder.

The shallow, running brook at my feet curved widely where I sat, and flowed brokenly over smooth, round stones. After three days I discovered that it was not an ordinary stream. I was quiet. Dry, yellow sand silenced any restless movement of my feet, and my pen merely whispered my thoughts.

Keats once asked for a golden pen, in days when

such a request was regarded as the extravagance of an unbridled imagination :

> *Give me a golden pen, and let me lean*
> *On heaped-up flowers in regions clear and far.*
> *Bring me a tablet whiter than a star*
> *Or hand of hymning Angel. . . .*

Mine was that golden pen. No matter what insignificant notion I asked it to scribble, no ill-bred scratch from it broke the spell that hung over my little wood, or made discord with the music of my running brook. And in the enchanted silence, I heard singing on the stream—always after I had sat quietly for a few minutes. The sound was faint, yet strangely clear and full. Many voices and instruments were singing and playing in harmony, with the breaking water rippling through as a distinct melody. And when I looked amidst the smooth, yellow stones, where the water broke and gleamed most brightly in the sun, I saw the tiniest and most beautiful forms, womanly in outline, but shining and intangible, dancing on the brown stream, with filmy, rainbow-coloured ribbons flying gaily from their shoulders, waists, and every part of their loose, crystalline, almost invisible robes. The orchestra from which their music came, I never saw. But the singers and dancers I saw every day. When I arrived of a morning, they were not there. They always appeared a little while after I had seated myself, and they remained while I wrote. When I rose from my tree to go home, they vanished.

In the warm summer evenings, I trudged along the

dusty road with waistcoat open, my jacket slung over my shoulder, like the farm labourers going to and from their work in the fields. One night, on my return to my sister's house, my little niece, Eileen, said :

" Uncle, why do you never bring flowers home when you go to the woods ? Everybody else who goes to them brings flowers home ; because the woods *are* for flowers."

I took the day's writing from my pocket, and said that my flowers were there ; but my answer appeared to be unsatisfactory.

" The Great Appeal " was finished in September. My friend Dai Edwardes read the manuscript, gave his opinion that the story was colossal, pointed out its weak parts, which we put right, together ; and he said that the book would make me famous. It was sent to London.

The year passed.

Nowhere could my novel find a publisher.

My microscopic store of money had been exhausted while I was writing " The Great Appeal," and none of my other books was bringing in anything. I did not relish the idea of staying at my sister's, without being able to pay for my keep, because her means were little enough for her family ; and the thought of becoming a tramp, sleeping anywhere on the roadside at night, and doing odd jobs for food in the day, suggested itself to me as the only way out of my serious difficulty.

Why, in the face of such persistent discouragement, would I not give up writing, go back to the mines, or to the pleasant routine of an office, and be content with a certainty of eating and sleeping in comfort, like an ordinary human being ?

Mere existence, such as thinking of how I might secure enough to eat and wear, that is, mere living, did not interest me. Getting a living was not life. Doing some fine thing was life. I was challenging the whole world in my desire to make it clear that the lowest of the low was as good, on this earth, as the highest of the high.

I had the most complete disrespect for all idiotic symbols of superiority. Kings, queens, dukes, money-makers, or flunkeys of any kind, had no value at all in my view. I had come from a family of working people, and I believed that a child of the workers might be born with as much intellectuality, spirituality, and manhood as the child of any other sort of people. Wealth, titles, or even education, I thought, could not give anyone what Heaven had refused, but could only help to train what nature had planted in an individual.

I felt in no way superior to kings, queens, dukes, financiers, and so on ; nor, indeed, better than any human creature ; but felt, in a worldly sense, that I was inferior to nobody. Humble I never was. Outside religion, I could not understand the meaning of humility. My only virtue was vanity.

Some people spend their lives chasing phantoms. Whether I, in following my ideal, was one of those people or not I neither knew nor cared. As for my supposed failure, better writers than I had been treated worse. What I actually felt was that a man was not beaten until he gave up fighting. Giants fought fate. Only dwarfs gave in.

CHAPTER XXI

My mysterious visitor : My voyage to Rouen on a coal boat :
Telepathy : Stage carpentry : The passing of youth : Hamp-
stead : I write a comedy : My mother's death : No. 13 gives
me a mysterious illness : My unacted play : "The Great
Appeal" finds a publisher : I am accused of high treason :
The great failure and the greater hope.

My sister Molly said that she would never forgive
herself if she turned me out in my poverty. So,
instead of going on tramp, I wrote more short stories,
sent them out, and, fortunately, sold them to various
London magazines ; but had to wait many months
for publication and payment.

Early in 1908, a stranger called at my sister's house
and asked for Joseph Keating, the author.

This was mysterious. I was discovered.

I was writing in a dark, back room, and the visitor
was brought in to me.

He was very short and small. He wore a light,
loose, tweed suit, had white hair—youthful white,
not aged white, for he was young—and a face as white
as his hair. He introduced himself as " Mr. Joseph
Nelson." We shook hands and sat down at my
table. He explained that he had wished to meet the
writer of the mining sketches published in " The
Daily Mail."

He said :

" I expected to find an old man who had, by a

thousand years of suffering, mastered all the art of making drama out of an everyday nothing."

I did not deny my age.

" Are you getting the money value of your work ? " he inquired.

" I get what I can," said I.

" Are you making, at least, five hundred a year ? "

" No."

" Well, I am. I get it easy. I'll show you how to get the same or more."

This stranger, whom I had never seen or heard of before, spent two days teaching me how to make five hundred pounds a year by my writing. He had nothing to gain. He had no interest of any kind to serve, except mine. What he did, he did out of the purest and most exalted generosity.

He wished me to know how stories, called serials, which appeared in daily and weekly instalments in all papers, were constructed. The principle of the stories was drama without characterization. The talent required was ingenuity. The material was love, murder, and money. Each person in a story obeyed only one primal instinct, with the exception of the evil genius who, besides murdering everybody who interfered with his wishes, was allowed to love the heroine, as well as rob her of her fortune. The writing itself had to be arranged so that all of it could be understood by people who were nearly illiterate. The whole was story, and only story.

A modern novel, with its analysis of motive, its creation of atmosphere, its morality or immorality, and its relation to actual phases of life, is a develop-

ment based on the ancient art of telling a mere story.
The old form was new to me, and I was deeply anxious
to master it. I sent my new friend four plots. He
rejected them all, as not being sufficiently ingenious
to hold a reader's interest over a period of two or
three months. At the same time, he suggested that
the fourth plot might be sent to a certain editor,
whose address he gave me, for a final decision. I acted
on this hint, and the editor offered me seventy pounds
for the completed story.

This was more than all my novels put together had
made.

In August I went to Rouen on a coal boat, with my
friend, Ifor Hughes, whose poetic nature and grey
hair made him resemble a fading flower that would
retain all its beauty and fragrance until the last petal
had withered on its stem. We admired old Rouen,
noted the life of low cafés, and gazed reverently on
the spot where Joan of Arc was burnt to death. In
the Café Royal, a peculiar instinct in me by which I
could nearly always tell when some disaster or good-
fortune was coming to me, asserted itself, and I said
to Ifor :

" Mark the date—August 27, 1908. There is good
luck coming towards me to-day."

At that moment we were some hundreds of miles
from home. When we returned to our house, nearly
a week later, there were two unexpected letters
bearing the date on which I had spoken, inviting me
to write stories and offering payment enough to keep
me in food and lodging for twelve months. That
was, certainly, the best luck I had had as an author.

During our voyage home, however, there had been a sickly swell on the sea, which had laid me flat upon my back, on deck, all the way from off Cherbourg to Cardiff Docks.

Following an inclination that seemed to have always been in me, I began to learn how to write a play. My instructor was Jim, the Theatre Royal carpenter ; and under the stage at night, while actors were declaiming in the limelight overhead, I studied the principles of dramatic construction, and wrote two plays.

In that summer of 1908, I had fallen in love. She had very dark hair, red cheeks, and brown eyes. In the glass I saw why she could not give me a thought. She was young. Writing had given me a wrinkled face that looked a million years old. I thought a great deal of her, and suffered.

A little earlier in the summer, the fact that I was becoming fossilized had first appeared. I had gone with a party of a few hundred young men and women to a far-off Eisteddfod. Our all-night journey home had begun at twelve o'clock. At dawn all in the train, except myself, were as lively as the birds. In the careless, pleasant fashion of such parties every girl became some young man's sweetheart for the train journey. I found myself alone in a compartment, a neglected old man, with only the sunrise for a companion. Three laughing Welsh girls passed down the corridor. They looked in at me, sitting in the corner ; and, still laughing, the three came in and put their arms around me affectionately, as if they pitied my loneliness.

Feeling the need of still adding to my experience, so that whatever views of human nature I held might be tested by as wide and varied a knowledge of actual life as it was possible for me to gain, I returned to London in October.

Bruerton—who, of all my friends, had the most highly developed mind—had become the landlord of a public-house in a side street near Oxford Circus. I called to see him.

" Here am I," he said, shaking hands with me across the bar, " Captain of a sinful London pub."

He advised me to take lodgings in Hampstead, which, he said, was a tolerably quiet place with real air. I settled down at Holly Bush Hill, next door to George Romney's old studio where Lady Hamilton had often visited the painter.

Hampstead pleased me, because it was not like London, but had a character. The reason Hampstead had an individuality was because its big Heath was natural. The charming, ramshackle old streets there were tenanted by distinguished ghosts. Keats had lived in Hampstead. On the Heath were trees and grass, and I could breathe. Above all, the hilly ground pleased me, probably because I had been born amongst the mountains. I disliked flat country. As soon as I felt my feet climbing the steep hill to Hampstead Heath I was happy.

All day I wrote stories, and every evening I went into the centre of London so as to continue my studies of new phases of life.

At Christmas time . I went home. Not once in

thirty-seven years had I been absent from home for our Christmas dinner.

By New Year's Day, 1909, I was back in Hampstead, writing a comedy. I had arranged, at the same time, to write a long, serial story, suited to the interests of almost illiterate readers. In the serial I dared not put any character or life. The comedy required all the character, wit, and life I could give it, for the development of its plot. My brain had to divide itself. In the morning I wrote an instalment of the serial for bread and butter. In the afternoons I wrote a page or so of my comedy for fame.

When Easter came, a letter from my mother told me that she was not in the best of health. I had no notion that her illness might be grave, because she said she was not laid up ; and I thought that if I spent the holiday at our house the extra work this would entail might be too much trouble for her. So I decided to wait till Whitsun for my home visit.

Bruerton invited me to spend Easter with him and his people in the Midlands ; and, as my comedy was finished, he asked me to bring it so that he might read it in the train on our way to his place. When the train left Euston, he lit a cigarette and began reading the first act, which did not please him. For the second act he lit another cigarette, but never smoked it, because he was laughing so much ; and at the end of that act he slapped his knee, and said :

" Wonderful ! How, in Heaven's name, did you do it ? "

This enthusiastic outburst made my holiday the happiest I had ever had. Bruerton's mother, I discovered, was a delightful cynic. Satirizing the jealousies of local church-goers, she said: " It's a poor bazaar that doesn't upset the whole parish."

When I returned to Hampstead, a startling telegram from my sister—she was in Mountain Ash—told me to go home at once. My mother was dying. Never had a holiday ended so sadly for me. An accusing thought was on my conscience that I ought to have spent Easter with her. My visit might have cheered her loneliness. I took the first train to Wales.

Our home for the last seventeen years or so had been in Cresselly Row, a low, small terrace of grey-stone dwellings, with a few blades of grass and some bits of evergreen trees in front, facing the valley highway, a railway, a river, and a colliery. The Cresselly Inn, after which the Row had been christened, stood at the top end.

When I arrived, rain was filling the valley. A melancholy mist hid the mountains.

The doctor had ordered my mother to be nursed in an upper room, at the back of the house, which, owing to our kitchen fire being underneath, was warmer than any other part. But the first thing she asked of me was to carry her to the front room where she had always slept, and put her in her own bed, an old-fashioned, mahogany four-poster. Many years before, she had bought it as a bargain at some auction sale, and we had all admired the carved and curving pillars and legs. Though I was a child at the time, I had a clear memory of the pride with which she had brought home this ancient four-poster. Now her pride was to die in it.

" Thank you," she said, very humbly, when she was laid in it. She asked for nothing else.

Not one of her sons or daughters, seven in all, had she had as a companion during the past nine years. One daughter was dead, another and a son were in America. The remaining four children were seeking their fortunes in different parts of the United Kingdom. And I know that my mother's proud and affectionate nature had felt the cruelty of a lonely house, with her family scattered by death and destiny.

" After all me sorrow and trouble in rearing ye," she would say, " here am I, at the latter end of me days, living as lonely as if I never had chick nor child."

Her three sons and daughter, brought home by sad telegrams, were around her death-bed.

" I have nothing to live for," she said, smiling ; and I felt almost heart-broken to hear her say such a thing. I remembered when she would have all her young boys and girls, Kate, Annie, Matt, Maurice and myself, around her of a winter's night, while she tuned an old Irish jig for us to dance to it, down in our big kitchen, with a blazing, red fire in the grate, the lighted lamp on the table, the sanded flags trembling under our lively feet, and she laughing at us, and almost as much out of breath from her tuning as we from our dancing. Those were her happiest days—the days she was always recalling. She would recall them no more. With the last breath going from her body, her shoulders raised themselves from the bed with a mighty heave, then sank again, and she died.

She had, by some mystery of careful management, saved enough to buy a house of her own, and had been looking forward to a convenient day when she could go and live in it. Her new house—God rest her !— was her grave on the hillside, under the stone that covered her youngest child, my sister Annie.

Though I disliked changing my address, one of the many trifling troubles of being in lodgings forced me to seek residence in another part of Hampstead, and at my new place I woke one morning with an extraordinary pain in my left side. I could scarcely rise. The acuteness with which I had felt my mother's death was, I thought, responsible for this strange attack.

The doctor whom I consulted made me toe a line and close my eyes. I had heard of such tests being applied. If, standing with my eyes shut, I happened to overbalance, he would decide that I was an idiot. If I could stand properly, he would decide that he did not know what was the matter with me. I felt horribly indignant, paid his fee, and refused to use the medicine he gave me.

My new address was, in fact, No. 13. That was the cause of my mysterious illness. Superstition had nothing to do with my view in this case, because I did not find out the number until I was being nearly torn to pieces with the pain in my side. The house had a name, and all letters came to me addressed to that name. But one day I noticed that the street-numbers ran 1, 2, 3, and so on. Our house stood between 12 and 14, and the people of my lodging had feared to allow its real number to remain on the door.

But it is not enough to remove the appearance of evil. The inner sin remains. My lodging was a hypocrite and ought to have been pulled down. It had given me rheumatism.

Never, in all my life, had any hint of this miserable malady come to me, until I had been deluded into living in a house which stood between 12 and 14. If that did not prove 13 to be unlucky, nothing could. For six months, all that doctors and hospitals could do for me was increase my pain. My left arm was withering, like a decaying branch on a tree that had been struck by lightning.

At my sister's house, to which I had returned in torture, I lay in bed one summer-night, my body twisting like a dying snake, burning agony in my spine, and an inhuman racking in my shoulder, as if four wild horses had been harnessed to my left arm and were trying to pull it out of its socket. I believed that I was to be crippled for life, and, at an unbearable point, I said :

" Very well. Now, you may tear and twist my limbs and body as much as you like. I don't care."

From that moment I began to get well. A real, genuine defiance had helped to conquer even the malicious spirit of rheumatism. My diet was largely cabbage. This purified my blood, apparently ; for within a month I was back in London again, writing as usual, with scarcely a twist or a twinge, except when an east wind purposely and viciously sought me out and bit me. Then I felt as if a passing ghost had breathed on my left shoulder, and I ate more cabbage, as a charm against dead enemies and evil influences.

For the time being, I had taken a dislike to Hampstead, owing to the bad way it had served me, and lived near Baker Street.

My comedy had been sent to various theatres, and returned. I had foreseen a long delay in getting any manager's serious attention ; and, indeed, had told Bruerton that he and I would be five years older when my play reached the stage. He thought that such suitable work as mine was would certainly be accepted before the year was out. He did not know, as I did, of the wholly unnecessary waste of time there was in all dealings with editors, publishers, and theatre people.

Though I was writing, I was not selling. One of the after-effects of the past months was a difficulty in finding what editors regarded as suitable plots for stories. I was working without any prospect of being paid, and much time was lost. Then came a letter from my agent telling me that my novel " The Great Appeal," after having been rejected by fourteen publishers, had been accepted by the fifteenth.

Rejections had never influenced my hopes. Whenever I wrote a novel, I knew that the day of its publication would eventually come and bring me the most brilliant good-fortune.

My idea of the finest form of luck was freedom to do what work I liked. Everything considered, I should, undoubtedly, have put the first use of luck to the pleasant duty of giving myself twelve months' rest. My brain was jaded, and I wished, above all human things, to be able to say that for an entire year I need not make a note or write a line of anything but friendly letters, asking how my friends' children were, where they were going for their holidays, how the new servants were behaving, what about the experiment in pig-keeping, with fattening food so dear, and were the chickens still laying well, now that the price of eggs was so scandalous.

My new novel, which was to be published before Christmas, would, I was sure, as usual, be a magnificent success, would be read all over the country, would crowd the bookstalls and libraries, and would bring me in enough to live where I liked in the happiness of complete freedom.

The book came out. " London Opinion " placarded the Strand with walking posters declaring that I had committed high treason in my novel.

" NOVELIST INSULTS THE KING."

This promised a sensation, and my hopes were higher than ever. Nothing would have pleased me better than being tried for high treason, with a sentence of two years' imprisonment. That would enable me to rest, at least.

No more was heard of " The Great Appeal," which was to have thundered and flamed through the world. The book had dropped like a stone in a pool, and, after the first ripple on the surface, made no stir or sound, but fell deeply to the bottom, and lay there, still and silent.

A few pounds had been sent to me on the day of publication. That was all I seemed likely to receive. My long illness had not only taken what I had earned earlier in the year, but had prevented me from having any other work ready to sell.

Christmas came. I had as much as would pay the train fare home for my Christmas dinner. After that, the likelihood of getting any other dinner was doubtful. " The Great Appeal " was a great failure, and my heart had nearly failed with it.

The longer a hope lives, the longer it takes to die. My hope was nearly fifteen years old. In that period it had fallen from great heights many times, but had never lost its life. If buried deeply under the waves, in the day when the sea gave up its dead my hope would come up alive, smilingly alive, amidst the mournful wreckage. At our Christmas table, my hope sat with me, its face as radiant, gay, and charming as ever. It reminded me that though the fate of my novels had certainly been discouraging, there was my new comedy which was bound to succeed. And, after all, what was a whole library of novels compared with one real little comedy ? It might see the footlights sooner than I had expected. Think of the triumph ! No achievement could equal it in brilliancy. It would pay for the work of a lifetime. If I could make London laugh, I should be its master.

No doubt at all had I that my play would be staged. In that case there would be no name for the glory and

joy that must come to me.   One success in a West
End theatre was three or four fortunes.   There
would be gold galore, which I could fling about
London gutters if I wished.   Once my comedy was
accepted I could make a football of the world for my
amusement.

CHAPTER XXII

Youth grown old : A changed home : Writing in the mountains : My belief in " The Marriage Contract " : Brain-strain :
Back to London : Reading a play in pyjamas : Pickpockets and
burglars : I become a ghost : Hunting in Fleet Street : My
imitation of a city man.

BEFORE New Year's Day, 1910, my plans were made.
I would stay at Mountain Ash with my father, write a
dozen short stories, sell them, and on the proceeds
write the finest novel in the world. The idea and plot
for this book came together into my mind suddenly.
Its title should be " The Marriage Contract." I did
not know, at the time, that Balzac had used the name
for one of his books.

Fourteen short stories I wrote, in the spring, but
could sell only four of them—one to " The Pall Mall
Magazine " and three to " The Red Magazine." Still,
with another ten stories, possibly a hundred pounds'
worth, going round looking for editors, I began my
new novel.

Our ground floor had a front room and a kitchen.
I wrote in the front room, with little green trees
scraping the window outside, and the portraits of our
family decorating the inside. My father lived in the
kitchen. Only he and I were in the house. A young
girl came in to make the beds, and attend to us at
meal times, and my sister Molly came up from Cardiff
periodically to put the place in order. The gap

made by my mother's death was painful. Our home was still our home ; but it was a body without a soul.

My father was extraordinary.   He was approaching eighty, and he read newspapers up to one or two o'clock in the morning regularly.   When he was not reading he was talking of the glories of Ireland and the Catholic Church.   He believed that if the Pope were still the head of temporal governments, all the poverty and hardships of working people would have entirely disappeared.

" Sure, the firrst thing the Churrch would do, Glory be to God," he said, " is see that ivry poor man, wummun an' child, had enough t'ate."

My father's chief complaint against me was that when he went out, I forgot to keep up the kitchen fire.   Some time after midnight he would make tea for himself, then go to bed, and sleep so soundly that his snoring shook the mountains.   His taste in tea was a standing rebuke to all health-faddists.   For breakfast he preferred tea that had been brewing all night.   Tea that had been kept hot in the pot for thirteen or fourteen hours was a delight to him.   His digestion was like a furnace that could melt cast iron. Ailments of any kind he never had, beyond a slight cold.   He broke every known rule of health, and was always well and gay.   Certainly he had been a teetotaler and non-smoker for over forty years ; and, personally, I believe that but for this fact he would have been even healthier than he was.   In every sense, except years, he was younger than his son.

He no longer danced ; but when I played old Irish tunes on my fiddle in the kitchen, he would put down his newspaper, and declare :

" Irish jigs and reels is the grahndist moosic in the whole wide wurrld."

And he would stretch himself on our rickety wooden bench, a " settle," beside the fire, and sing " Johnny from the Glen " in Irish. Music made him reminiscent. Memories of old days filled his mind, and for an hour he would talk, half to himself and half to me, his faded eyes fixed on the lighted kitchen lamp that stood on the table opposite him.

Our lop-sided, old-fashioned house had once been situated in tranquil, idyllic surroundings, on the valley road, at the foot of big hills, with the clear Cynon river in front of us. Now, when I was writing in the front room, I looked out on a railway fence and the black framework of a colliery, with clouds of steam always in the air. The noise of railway-wagons, shunting, often made it impossible for me to work ; and, if the day was fine, I climbed the mountains and wrote up there.

My evening amusements were few. I played the fiddle, or played chess with Ifor Davies, who had become assistant master at the big school to which I had been sent from Newtown. All the fun of old days seemed to have passed away. The Barracks, where so much human joy had been mine, was about to be knocked down in order to make space for an inhuman railway. The quarter might have had its limitations as a training-ground for respectability. But lack of respectability, as I had always been convinced, never did imply lack of inspiration. Two boys who had lived in The Barracks had become mining engineers and were in control of great works and several thousands of men, two other sons of that family had entered the Church and, if ability counted, would develop into bishops, and Matt, my brother, had gone into Parliament.

A generation had not really altered the crowd which I saw in the streets at home. Habits, manners and tastes were much the same as when I had been a boy. The hats and dresses of women and girls, however, had lost all local character, and resembled what might be seen in any town. Years ago the women had been less courageous in adopting new fashions. The young men wore, as formerly, clothes that had neither taste nor grace in cut. But men and youths were as amiable and good-humoured as ever. I felt human in their company.

The place where a man spends the first twenty years of his life remains for ever in the centre of his heart, and is, for him, the centre of the world. That was how I had always felt about Mountain Ash. A curious element was in that fact. I was entirely Irish in every way—in blood, traditions, sympathies, training, and temperament. I regarded Ireland as my country ; and not only as mine, but as God's ; and its people as a race chosen, above all other nationalities, by the Almighty, to establish the ideals of spiritual perfection, moral perfection, and intellectual perfection, " the triple tiara of the Gael," as an enthusiast phrased it.

Now Mountain Ash was Welsh. Yet this bit of

Wales, where I was born and had spent my first twenty years, was so rooted in my Irish heart that I neither would nor could think of any other place on earth as my home. It seemed to me that the feeling of nationality had nothing to do with the land of birth, but was inherited in the blood. Irish children, scattered to the ends of the earth, loved the lands in which they were born, yet still regarded Ireland as their country, though they had never seen it.

During my outdoor hours I looked at Mountain Ash with two eyes, and saw the truth. We had both altered very much in appearance since we were young. Outwardly we had both grown unattractive. I was wrinkled and haggard, and found it hard to laugh ; while the ancient streets were no longer pleasant and picturesque, but grimy with coal-dust and disfigured by hideous extra storeys, here and there, that looked like carbuncles growing high on the heads of the poor old shops. A young hat on an old woman does not look so tragic as does a new storey on an old house. Hundreds of new streets, long, straight and ugly, and terrible hills of pit refuse, filled the fields in which I had played. The Cynon river was nothing but flowing mud, so black that it seemed to be in mourning for itself. All semblance of its former silvery winding was gone. The only gleam in the valley came from the white surface of railway metals.

In many parts the mountains and farms themselves were being buried under pit rubbish. Black industrialism would not stop until it had utterly destroyed the old pastoral life. The valley was filled with endless strings of trucks loaded with coal.

Mountain Ash had been beautiful, and I had seen it in one generation, transformed by mines and railways, much as if an evil spirit, for some wicked purpose, had changed a lovely child into a coal-scuttle.

Yet seeing all the faults of my home did not alter my affection for it. The contrast between the romantic hills and the sordid pit-works in the valley gave me the vision of true sympathy for the lacerated heart of the place.   On the mountains, gorgeous with coloured foliage, birds still sang merrily.   Underneath those brilliant slopes, a mile down from the sunlight, men and boys were in danger.   One little flame of a lamp, a spark from steel on stone, could send a thousand souls flying through the great, solid hills above, to the highest mountain summit, where the throne of judgment stands.   Birds singing in the sunlight, and human beings toiling below were seeking the same end : merely to live.

With the summer sun shining on my pen and paper, in the most beautiful nook amidst the mountains, the hollow of Raven's Crag, I finished my novel.

Dai read it, and said it was the wisest and wittiest of books.

In a letter from me to my brother Matt at the time, I said that I did not care if I never wrote another line. I had written " The Marriage Contract," and my comedy " The Perfect Wife," and believed that those two phases of the same theme, the love-relationship between a man and wife, were literature, and would be read for ever.

No publisher would accept " The Marriage Contract." My distress at seeing the year pass without any sign of this novel being brought out was the most terrible I had ever known. The strain of getting the book ready for the autumn publishing season had been great, and I could not do any more writing of any kind for the time being. A brain creating an idea is like a woman giving birth to a child.

My ten short stories remained unsold. No money was coming in to me from any source. How was I to continue to exist ? Moreover, how was I to live in the future if I could not live in the present ?

By the Easter of 1911 my poverty had reached its cruellest stage, and I wondered whether it was worth while trying to exist at all. For nearly ten years I had been writing, always writing, and always against time, in order to buy food and shelter, and that frightful task seemed to have stunned my inspiration. I felt as if, for ten years, a steam-roller had been passing and repassing over my brain, flattening out its ideas in the same way as the stones of a road were crushed to a smooth surface.

No plot of a marketable kind would come to me. My attempts at writing to please the public were failures. Formerly, I had been able to hit on dramatic moments in stories which pleased me in the writing as well as interested editors. That happy combination of influences had been lost. I was more than ever inclined to write only what pleased myself ; but that sort of amusement failed now to make me smile.

To be interesting to other people—that was the only source of a beggar's existence. He might be spiritual, or he might be satanic, but to get attention his ideals or his vices would have to be interesting.

Art, and even religion itself, required that quality. Without it, art could not civilize the body, and religion could not save the soul. I saw in the Eisteddfod crowd that Easter, at Mountain Ash, a preacher to whom not one of the thirty thousand people there would listen. I wondered at that, because a Welsh crowd was so religious in its tendencies.

The preacher stood on a wooden chair at the corner of a little side street, below the Taff station. Thousands of men and women, youths and girls, slowly passed and repassed him, but the preacher remained isolated. He held a small Bible in his left hand, and gesticulated with his right. The throng turned its eyes towards the lonely man, then walked by without stopping.

I went up the street.

When I came back the preacher had moved his kitchen-chair pulpit nearer to the fringe of the main thoroughfare, in order, I supposed, to insist on getting attention. But none was given to him.

Trying to understand the cause of this indifference and neglect, I listened to him. The preacher's voice was flat and cracked. He seemed to have ruined his vocal chords in competition with the terrible brass band of a Salvation Army corps near by. He had broken his voice in shouting the Gospel, and the people would not heed him. He had no gift of eloquence. His phrases were as flat as his voice. He had nothing fresh to say—worse still, he had nothing stale to say in fresh form. I could not doubt his piety, but I saw that he had failed to make it interesting. The crowd would not listen to the Word of God because that Word was not spoken in a desirable fashion. That preacher illustrated my case, I thought. Disciples of imagination and the Gospel would have to be interesting, or the world would do without art and God.

My father was of opinion that I ought to look for some sort of job about the colliery works; but I borrowed thirty shillings from him, and took the morning train for London.

I had no plans and no hopes.

The capacity for writing seemed to have left me for ever; but I had reason to be a great believer in the value of change in my surroundings and way of living as a cure for a sick brain.

On my arrival, I called at " The Fountain " to see Bruerton. He appeared to be very pleased at my visit, and said, laughingly, that he supposed I had made my fortune since he had last seen me. Never was I so near crying over my misfortunes as at that moment. But all I said was that I did not feel well and had come back to London for the sake of my health. He told me that his wife was away and that he would be very glad if I would stay with him for company. His kindness was remarkable.

My bedroom was on the top floor. A dairy shop opposite woke me every morning with a milk-can concerto.

Among our hotel residents were an actor, a singer, an aviator, a motor-car maker, a painter, a dentist, and an advance agent for a musical comedy company, who received long love-letters from some girl, and answered them after three months with " Yours, in haste, Jack."

At supper we had French bread and gorgonzola cheese, which I ate with zest, while Monsieur Canard, a teacher of French, with a womanly, white face and a black beard, talked volubly, though I could not understand a word of what he was saying. His English was limited to :

"Top o' de morning."

He said this at all times of the day. He sang grand opera in French in the middle of the night. He said that he understood the words he was singing, and explained that this was a French gift—not an English one. At dawn, he would be sitting on his bed, studying the "Grand Course" as he called it, from London newspapers, under the heading, "Racing intelligence." At tea time he would tell me radiantly :

"J'ai gagné deux shelling."

Sometimes he was mournful at tea.

"J'ai perdu—'alf-crrrown," he would explain.

Our housekeeper, the bar-manager's wife, also backed horses.

"I mike a regl'r study of 'The Dily Mirrer', I do," she said. "I puts fythe in it. I puts a shillin' on. Me 'usban' was losin' money. So I said, 'I'll mike a bit, old dear.'"

When she was not sober I had to listen to her telling me of her past glories when she owned "The Ironmonger's Arms" in Mile End, East.

One of the bar-tenders had been a journalist on the staff of a pigeon fancier's paper. He disliked the housekeeper so bitterly that he was always trying to get her husband, the bar-manager, into trouble by playing tricks with the cellar pipes so that the beer should come up " muddy."

Extraordinary characters drank at that London public-house—painters, sculptors, journalists, actors, musicians, society entertainers, pickpockets, card-sharpers, and burglars.

My acquaintance with burglars gave me a great respect for their courage and skill. As they explained to me, going into a dark and silent house, not knowing at what moment a poker or a clenched fist might knock them senseless, was no joke. And, even when they had entered safely, there might be nothing in the place worth taking away. Again, in a well-ordered house, by the time they had collected all the valuables they wanted, it often happened that a police-whistle would be heard. Then the only chance of escape was to climb up to the roof and crawl along the tiles, with no light to guide them, and two or three policemen crawling after them. Sometimes the unfortunate burglars were compelled to leap across an opening from one roof to another. A running jump would have made the passage an easy one. But on sloping tiles there was no footing for such a thing. Missing the edge of the next roof by an inch meant a head-long fall through the darkness, from a height of four or five storeys ; and the end would be a dead and mangled body on the pavement below. I noticed long absences on the part of some of our customers. They were hiding from the police, or were peacefully in jail.

The burglars were mostly English, but one was an Irish Cockney, a short, quiet, amiable fellow,

whose pride was his young son whom he had sent
to a convent school, the high fees for which were
difficult to find, and whose one anxiety was to
have his boy brought up as a good Irishman and
a devout Catholic.

The most interesting of all who appeared at the
bar of our pubic-house was Troubadour Din. He
composed for the most popular music-hall singers.
"Scales" he laughingly called the classics. He
wrote his music at a beer-table, in the midst of all
the noises made by men and women drinking and
quarrelling. His genius was beyond all question, and
he threw away his gift as contemptuously as the barmen tossed the dregs of beer into a sink. One morning,
at the bar, I saw his head twice its natural size. The
night previously one of his associates had tried to
murder him with an iron bar. Red wounds and black
eyes made his face appalling to see. His neck was
swollen to the thickness of a ship's beam. His ears
were like sails, and his cheeks like two balloons.

Bruerton's admiration for my comedy was so great
that he wanted his resident guests to hear it read ; and
at six o'clock on a Sunday morning, in my bedroom,
with the sun shining on the script, and tea brought up
to us, I read the play, sitting in my pyjamas, with
Bruerton and the others—the actor, dentist, motor-car
dealer, musical comedy advance agent, all laughing,
gibing, criticising, applauding, in various states of
nudity, around me. Horace, the actor, said there
was a fortune in the comedy, and suggested some
points which were valuable owing to his stage training.
Bruerton's views bore more on the art of expression ;

and his help in improving the lines and strengthening the plot had been so boundless, that I said to my audience.

" It is Bruerton's comedy. I only wrote it."

All were sure that I had a brilliant success waiting me. My friends swore picturesquely at the idiocy of theatre managers who had refused to produce the work. This was encouraging. Indeed, my one hope now was my comedy.

For a week or two I waited to see if, amidst this enjoyable variety in companions, my power to write stories which might please editors would come back to me.

At evening time, when lamps were glittering in the mirrors around the bar of " The Fountain " I stood at the door, merely looking out at the lights of Oxford Street shining on the wet road and pavement.

The postman handed my comedy to all the theatre managers. Once I registered the parcel, addressed to Mr. Charles Hawtrey, and hearing some time later that he was going to America immediately, I called down at his manager's office in the Haymarket to find out what had become of my play. The manager picked it out of a pile of other packages. My big, registered envelope had not been opened at all, and probably would never have been opened if I had not thought it necessary to take out the script and send it to some other theatre manager.

It became clear to me that I should not, for some months, be able to invent and write stories which could be sold. I decided to look for a post as secretary in order to pay for my board and lodging. My shorthand had not been used for many years, but I had not forgotten it, and believed that a day's speed-practice would bring back its value for taking down letters from dictation. An acquaintance suggested that a certain popular novelist wanted a secretary.

The name of that popular novelist I promised not to tell to anyone.

My letter to him pointed out that as I had written much fiction I might be of use to him as a temporary secretary. He invited me to call and see him. He said he did not need a secretary, but would be glad to put work in my hands.

From the files of a woman's weekly journal he brought out an old-fashioned serial, and asked me if I could alter and modernize the story for publication as a present-day novel, with his name on the title-page as the author.

As I had learned to do all kinds of writing, short stories, articles, essays, novels, newspaper serials, and plays—everything, except poetry, which I regarded as sacred, and beyond me—I at once undertook to turn the old rubbish into new rubbish.

A curious thing in the writing revealed itself. My battered brain could not invent for itself in that period of exhaustion, but could reconstruct other people's inventions with ease. Within a week I had re-written three chapters. I took them to him. Then the rate of my pay had to be settled. I had become a pedlar in words. I suggested that the work was worth the ordinary price for serial writing, one guinea for a thousand words. He said he could not afford that amount. I would not work for less. We agreed on what should be paid to me for the chapters done, and parted.

A short time afterwards, I saw the novel in libraries and on bookstalls, with the first three chapters as I had reconstructed them, the remainder done by some other pen, and the popular author's name on the title-page as the creator. Dozens of novels bore his name. I do not know if all his books were created out of ancient crumbling files, and written by ghostly hands.

In Fleet Street I tramped from office to office of the evening papers, day after day, looking for report-ing or article-writing jobs. The " Westminster Gazette," one afternoon, sent me out to interview a French actor who had arrived in London. He could not understand my English and I could not understand his French ; but I made a special article out of the interview, and was paid fifteen shillings for it.

Through a newspaper advertisement, I found a post as secretary to an accountant who was compiling a book on company law. His office was in Walbrook, in the shadow of the Mansion House. Every day I went into the City on a penny 'bus, wrote shorthand and transcribed it on a typewriter, and in that way earned one shilling an hour. At " The Fountain " breakfast table, each morning, I gave an imitation of a City man leaving hurriedly, putting on his hat, and completing his toilet as he rushed away to get to his office in time. The other guests laughed, and ap-plauded my imitation.

CHAPTER XXIII

Lunch at " The Fountain ": Mystery of a vanished genius :
Publishers fear that " The Marriage Contract " is indecent :
My captaincy of " The Fountain " : Vicious characters : " The
Marriage Contract " accepted : My pocket is picked : My
strange experience in Ireland : Return to sheer disaster : My
supper of two postage-stamps : Crucifixion, as it is practised
to-day.

LUNCH-TIME at " The Fountain " was a variety entertainment. Clerks, warehousemen, drapers' assistants, and all kinds of slaves of commerce crowded
the dining-room, where a cut from the joint and two
vegetables could be had for sixpence.

The lift serving between the kitchen above and the
eating-place below rattled up and down like the cage
of a colliery winding coal at high pressure. Steaming,
full dishes came down, and cold, empty ones went
up.

" Above ! " shouted barmen and waitress, up
through the shaft, to cook and kitchen. " Shepherd's
pie an' two vege."

" On the lift ! " meant that a load of soiled plates
were to be hauled up for washing.

An automatic piano played popular " rags " (as
American negro tunes were called) for coppers dropped
into a slot, and the plutocrat who could afford a
penny benefited the entire assembly by serving music
with the feast.

At our table sat a young Welshman, very voluble, with a big, white face and large blue eyes. He talked folklore and nationalism while he ate and drank ; and, after finishing one lunch, he generally ordered a second, and went on talking learnedly. He called me a devil-worshipper because I insisted on working for my living. He afterwards found a profitable Government job, which gave him a living without working.

On my right was, I regret to say, an outcast Catholic bishop, whose diocese had been in a far-off, uncivilized island of sunshine. He had a grey beard and a benevolent, dignified, pale face, and sad grey eyes that told a tragic tale. What his sin had been I never asked, or wished to know. It was painful enough to see his wounds, without probing them. He was learned and gifted and unhappy. He lived by doing research work for ecclesiastical lawyers. The bishop borrowed a half-crown from me, and I was delighted at being able to lend it. When funds to spare came to him a few months later, his lordship travelled six miles to pay me back my half-crown.

In front of me, at the opposite side of our lunch-table, sat young Gay. Gay was a friend of many well-known literary men who frequently called in at " The Fountain."

He had many friends here, and into their circle had introduced the Welshman and the bishop.

Gay was a tall youth, with a face as white and well-shaped as the features of a Greek statue, with smiling lips, fair, shining hair, and cold, grey eyes

in which there was the steely light of an alert
and subtle mind. Smiling, he was for ever on the
watch to use anybody's argument against the
speaker.

He talked more cleverly than any man I ever met ;
yet he was scarcely out of his teens. He did not
seem to have studied much, but took what was said
on any subject, twisted the point of view expressed,
and showed by the actual words uttered that the
speaker was hopelessly and entirely wrong.

Young Gay was undoubtedly an intellectual genius,
learned without being a student, and witty without
being wise. We spent many summer evenings
together, strolling along Oxford Street, to Hyde Park
Corner and back, eating two-penny worth of cherries
from paper bags in our hands, I listening delightedly
to his keen and lively comments on art, religion,
sociology, human nature, and the beasts of the field.
In his contempt for the public statuary which
obstructed London streets and stifled open spaces,
he said that Londoners were still in that low stage
of development when they shared the possession of
Europe with the mammoth, the cave-bear, the woolly-
haired rhinoceros, and other extinct animals, and that
the essence of British character was a palæolithic
paganism which expressed its worship of kings and
fools by making large sacrifices of stone to their
honour and glory.

One day, during lunch-time at " The Fountain,"
young Gay waved his hand to me as he went out,
smiling. Never again did I see him. No one could
tell what had happened to him.

That astonishing boy had vanished in mystery.

A call which I made on my literary agent upset me. He told me that some of the publishers to whom he had sent my novel, " The Marriage Contract," had expressed a fear that the book was indecent.

This view I regarded as piling crime on crime. Not only were they refusing to publish my work, but they were libelling the author.

My sister Molly had read the manuscript before it was sent to my agent, and she approved of it. That was enough for me. My friend Dai Edwardes, whose literary instinct was of the highest and truest kind, had declared the novel to be a masterpiece, intellectually, humanly, and morally.

I said to my agent :

" The book is fiercely moral."

He agreed with my view, and added :

" Curiously enough, a publisher who read ' The Marriage Contract ' some time ago, and refused it, only yesterday asked me to let him have another look at it."

My agent thought the result would be a sale.

I hoped that the publisher would accept my novel. Publication would be profitable, I felt sure, and would relieve me of many anxieties. I was not paying for my board and lodging, because Bruerton had flatly refused to allow me to pay a penny, though he had little to spare himself. He was a real friend.

All my life I had found true friends. No matter what had been my troubles, when things were at their worst with me my friends were always at their

best with me.   Life, in my case, had not been a
perfumed rose.   But my experiences had taken away
all false notions of human nature.   In the truest
sense I had no illusions.   I had discovered that there
was a genuine soul somewhere in the world, and I
could never feel bitter.

Quite unusually, I felt tired and sleepy one night
and went to bed at half-past ten.   By half-past
eleven, the barmaid was knocking at my bedroom
door.

Some catastrophe had happened below in the
bar, and she implored me to go down.   Bruerton
was away in the Midlands with his wife, at their
country home, as about this time their first child was
born.

Downstairs I went.   Lamp-globes and mirrors
were cracked, and, under the lights, bits of smashed
drinking-glasses were glittering on the floor.   A
crowd in the bar was noisy.   The bar-manager had
got drunk during his master's absence, and had been
squabbling with the clients.   The clients had floored
the bar-manager and he was being attended to in the
grill-room, his head cut, and the blood reddening
his shirt.   I sent him to bed and took charge of the
cash—an important charge, because the next thing
our customers might do was leap over the bar and
take away the till.

The man—a clumsy swindler and general " crook "
—who had struck the bar-manager, was pointed out
to me.   I rebuked him.   He answered :

" I was bound to hit him in the jaw, Mr. Keating,
or I should have lost prestige with my colleagues."

In the morning, having to go to my office, in my capacity as an imitation of a city man, I arranged affairs as best I could, and sent a telegram to Bruerton, advising him to return. I knew that the bar-manager, having got drunk once, could not be relied on again to keep sober. He had tasted blood, as it were, and had lost his self-control.

My diagnosis was accurate. He was drunk by the time I got back from the office, at half-past one. A wire from Bruerton was waiting me, saying that his wife's illness prevented him from returning, and requesting me to safeguard his interests. I ordered the drunken manager out of the bar, took control, and spent the afternoon seeing to beer-barrels, accounts, and clients, as manager of " The Fountain."

Saturday night and Sunday night were quiet periods.

On Monday night there was havoc. With all the lights up, and glasses clinking, the crowd in the bar— women of the streets, and their men-protectors, who were also thieves, burglars, swindlers, forgers and card-sharpers, broke loose into an all-round fight. A beautiful, young woman, who had been educated in a convent, had her white, perfect, front teeth shattered by a blow from the fist of her so-called husband, a coward and bully. The others joined in the quarrel, and there was a hail of chairs, tables, jugs, bottles, and glasses sweeping through the bar.

It would have been wrong of me to call in the police, because the authorities might have taken away the licence, by way of a penalty for serving such bad characters, and my friend Bruerton would have been ruined.

The law was always unjust.

A publican could not tell what kind of people his customers were from their appearances, but the police prosecuted him, and the magistrates endorsed his licence—that is, put a stain on his character— if any trouble arose through the bad behaviour of his visitors.

Personally, I had never been so deceived as I was by some of the frequenters of " The Fountain." The young men seemed to be just ordinary persons, and the women harmless creatures with a weakness.

In reality, a certain section of those young men and women were guilty of the most filthy and horrible crimes and vices known to perverted human nature.

Some of the girls had the innocence of children in their faces, and the fury of devils in their tempers.

The young men would steal the penny from a dead man's eye ; and, when they were fighting, would kick their fallen opponents in the face, stab them with pocket-knives, and bite off their noses.

After learning such facts of characterization, I decided that I could never judge human beings from their outsides.

One young woman there, the mistress of a titled Member of Parliament, and dressed in the costliest and most charming fashion, with a gold rim and gold chain to her hand-bag, which was studded with diamonds, had to be watched for three hours to prevent her from smashing all the mirrors in the bar. The piano was played to her, her friends chatted amiably with her, and every kind of attention was showered upon her ; and all the time she stood sullenly swearing, and drinking absinthe and green chartreuse, breaking out suddenly, now and again, with a water-jug raised in her hands to fling at the shining sheets of glass around the walls.

The one man upon whom we depended to keep uncertain tempers in order was Dan, an Irish book-maker, who had such an extraordinary personality that all those desperate and lawless men and women feared to cause a row of any kind when he was in their midst. Dan feared nothing and nobody. He would fight ten ruffians at a time and beat them. His notion of honour was the most marvellous thing. Any harm, either by pocket-picking, cheating, or otherwise, done to a friend was done to Dan, and the perpetrator had to suffer. He had taken a strong liking to Bruerton, and no one dared cause any trouble in the bar while Dan was present, or there would be more trouble than the offender desired.

Unfortunately for me, Dan was absent during the Monday night that I was in charge.

Order was restored somehow, about midnight ; and the next day I sent a long dispatch by wire to Bruerton explaining that my captaincy of " The Fountain " was a failure, and that he had better return at once, or he might lose all he possessed. Happily he was able to announce, the same day, that the birth of his child and the excellent health of its mother would allow him to resume control of his duties immediately.

My literary agent sent me a note saying that the publisher he had mentioned would accept " The Marriage Contract " if I would make a few corrections in the text. Though I saw no reason in the request, I agreed to meet it ; and, once more early on a Sunday morning in my bedroom, and pyjamas, with Horace, the actor, Bruerton, and all his guests laughing and chatting around, and taking a before-breakfast cup of tea in their sleeping-suits, I corrected my manuscript. One drawback about the publisher's offer was that he would pay no advance on royalties till the book was out ; but I was sure that " The Marriage Contract " would be a success, and the prospect of its publication made me happy.

Percie, from his home in Pentre, South Wales, wrote suggesting that he and I should spend an August holiday in my father's county in Ireland. With the thoughts of my novel coming out, I at once agreed. I had saved up three pounds ten in gold. That would pay my fare to Ireland, and I could arrange for settling the other expenses with Percie, at a future date.

In the same letter he asked me to meet, at Liverpool Street Station on the following Saturday morning, his two young daughters, Muriel and Dorothy, who were coming home for the summer vacation from their Convent School, at St. Trond, in Belgium. I rose at seven o'clock, too late to admit of walking to Liverpool Street from Oxford Circus. So I hired a hansom, the only cab in sight at such an early hour. At half-past seven the girls' train arrived, and I was there to meet them, see to their boxes and trunks, and transport them to Paddington for home.

At nine o'clock I went to my city office as usual. Accidentally, I put my hand to my hip-pocket where the small leather purse which held my three sovereigns and a half was kept. There was a terrifying absence of the purse. My pocket had been picked at Liverpool Street Station, possibly while I was bending amidst all the luggage, searching for the girls' boxes.

The only money I had possessed was stolen.

It had taken me a long time to save three pounds ten. A holiday in Ireland had been villainously picked from my pocket.

When I went home, Percie insisted on carrying out the arrangement. Expenses could be divided, and I could pay my share when my novel was published.

We crossed to Ireland from Fishguard and landed at Rosslare. As soon as my feet touched Ireland, I knelt down and made the sign of the Cross on myself.

We passed through Cahirciveen, where my father was born. All along the countryside I found relatives of our family, down as far as Darrynane, where we stayed for a week. The sea and hills of Darrynane were the loveliest in all the world ; but I was so melancholy that one night I went down in the darkness, all alone, to the water's edge, and cried. No explanation could I find for that sadness.

When I returned to London the greatest personal

disaster—at least, it seemed so—happened to me and, in fact, nearly killed me.

A letter from my agent informed me that the publisher had changed his mind, and now refused to publish " The Marriage Contract."

The news almost blinded me. It explained the terrible sadness I had felt in Ireland, for the letter was an old one dated within the period of my stay at Darrynane, when I had wept to myself in the darkness at the edge of the sea ; and my mysterious instinct for feeling a joy or sorrow that was coming to me had influenced me, though I had not dreamed of such a letter, believing that everything had been entirely settled with the publisher.

Before leaving London for my holiday, I had taken a room at 32 Langham Street. It was to this new address that I had returned. The rent would be eight shillings a week. My feeling had been that in the privacy which this plan would give me, I might be able to study and write again. The man for whom I had been acting as secretary, in Walbrook, had asked me to let him know when I got back to London, so that the work he was doing could be continued. The salary of one shilling an hour which he paid me was all that I could now hope to get for some time. I wrote him saying I was ready to recommence work.

He replied by return, telling me that other business prevented him from going on with his book about company law, and he had no need of my services.

His letter, on top of my agent's, was like the last stab from the dagger of Brutus, under which Cæsar fell.

In the sunshine of that September morning, I

walked out of my dark room in Langham Street, and down Great Portland Street, amidst the hooting and clatter of motor-omnibuses, taxicabs, and railway vans, feeling that the end of the world had come for me at last. I had no money at all and no hope of getting any ; and to be without money in London was to be without everything.

Only one thing could be got for nothing in London— starvation.

I could not go back to my friends, and say :

" Give me food."

That night I was hungry.

I had eaten nothing since breakfast, which my landlord had served in the ordinary way, believing that I could pay for it at the end of the week. I had been expecting to be at work that day, and could have got a small sum in advance of pay-day.

As the night went on, my increasing hunger reminded me that I had two penny stamps in my pocket. I turned into a public-house and asked the barman if he would give me some bread and cheese for the two stamps. He was obliging, and I ate my supper of bread and cheese in the street.

I blamed no one for what had happened. I did not even blame myself. There were millions like me, passing me in the noisy, glittering thoroughfares, or living from hand to mouth in the wider circles of the world.

Indeed, my undesirable position, as a craftsman starving amidst plenty, fairly illustrated the drawbacks of being an employee and not an employer, or a tenant and not a landowner. I had seen the landowner and the employer in their pleasant country houses surrounded by trees and lawns, and I had seen their tenants and employees in their stable-like dwellings, slums, and tenements, surrounded by dust-bins, machinery yards, and sewers. I had seen miners crushed to death under falls of roof, but had never seen a mine-owner in that unhappy plight. I had seen the miner's children starving, and barefoot, and shivering, in winter, because their father's earnings could not feed, clothe, and warm his family. In London, I had seen ragged and hungry boys and girls ; and found that they belonged to working people, who dwelt in slums.

I had not seen the children of employers and landowners crying for food and fire.

In the West End that night I saw landowners and employers flushed with too much wine and feasting, and with diamonds gleaming in their crumpled shirt-fronts, being taken in beautiful motor-cars—lolling and swaying in them as comfortably as if an obliging sea were obeying their drunken wishes—to their spacious, well-lighted, healthy homes ; while their tenants and employees crawled, unfed and miserable, into dark and narrow streets, and crowded with their families into rooms where human breathing poisoned the air. I had seen, among my own people, stables and cellars used as houses ; while the lord of the manor and the mine-owner were never huddled into any inconvenient shelters of that kind.

We were poor. There was nothing else the matter with us. We were poor and they were rich. That was the only difference between us.

I saw that landowners, employers, and all rich men and women were social criminals. They were like the High Priests of the Jews, and were every day occupied in the crucifixion of the poor.

The poor lay down railways, lift bridges, excavate huge docks, fashion ships, engines and machinery, forge guns of destruction and erect hospitals of mercy, sink mines into darkness and raise cathedrals to the light. All the wonderful works of the world are testimony to the energy and suffering of the poor. Every stone upon stone of the magnificent structures which awaken our admiration is cemented with the blood of the poor. They make vast cities, and fructify commerce as Heaven fructifies the earth. Their industry is the soil of commerce. Imperial revenues and banks are gorged with the wealth of their productiveness. The poor make swift motor-cars in which they shall never ride, construct splendid ocean yachts in which they shall never sail, grow fine fruits which they shall never taste, dig tons of gold which they must not spend, polish pearls, sapphires and diamonds which they must not wear, stitch brilliant dresses—and are attired in rags. They build palaces for their enemies, and hovels for themselves. There is something Christ-like in the poor : obeying an inscrutable Will they humbly bear their cross of cruelty, permit, in effect, their bleeding hands and feet to be nailed to it, and, though in numbers and strength possessing power to destroy the world, do not murder their crucifiers.

CHAPTER XXIV

I am a City clerk : My budget : I discharge my employers :
The Fleet Street hunt again : I am an expert in finance : The
1912 Coal Strike : My harvest : Writing at the bottom of a well :
I am the gloomy Ghost of Truth : A plan for getting a comedy
produced : "The Perfect Wife" : "The Marriage Contract"
accepted at last : Interview with a publisher : My comedy
accepted : A brilliant climax.

By next morning I had analysed and grasped my
problem.

For a week, at least, I should be able to keep a roof
over my head, on credit. My landlord would not
ask for his rent until the following Monday. All
that remained for me to do was to stave off hunger
until I could find a means of earning money.

Trying to keep hunger away till money came had
been the death of a good many whose experience had
not made them so resourceful as mine had made me.
I pawned my overcoat for ten shillings, went into the
City, and found, by hard seeking, a post as shorthand
clerk and typist, at one pound a week, in a Moorgate
Street office. This success struck me with the notion
that all persons could find work, if they had the tools
for it and knew how to use them.

My references would have to be tested, and a delay
of a few days must be endured patiently. After
the settling of that point, another week must pass
before I could draw any pay.

My rent and appetite would not wait.

Willie Cule, a friend of long-standing, had become an editor at the Baptist Missionary publishing offices. He had begun as a story writer, but had found editing a more reliable calling. I called upon him at his office, and explained that my financial arrangements required one half-sovereign for the perfection of my plans. He offered me more than the amount mentioned, but I did not need it and would not take it.

On Monday morning, at nine o'clock, to Moorgate I went, took down letters in shorthand and transcribed them on the typewriter, till six in the evening.

Towards the fourth day I began to doubt whether my enterprise was profitable. I had to rise at eight, and could not return to my lodgings before seven. Practically, I was giving eleven hours a day for three shillings and fourpence.

My day's expenses exceeded that sum :

My day's wages, 3s. 4d.

	£	s.	d.
Rent at 8s. a week (Sunday's proportion included)	0	1	5
Breakfast	0	0	6
Lunch	0	0	9
Tea	0	0	4
'Bus fares to city and back	0	0	2
Washing	0	0	4
Cigarettes	0	0	4
Beer	0	0	0
Amusements	0	0	0
Supper	0	0	0
	£0	3	10

	£	s.	d.
My cost of living per day	0	3	10
My day's earnings	0	3	4
My losses per day	£0	0	6

In reality, instead of my employers paying me, I was paying them 6d. a day.

In addition, I was doing without any supper, in order to finance their concern, as a reward to them for letting me work eleven hours a day for nothing.

With a balance of 6d. on the wrong side every day, I could not continue to live.   The sixpences would go on increasing until they exceeded the amount coming to me at the end of a week, and I should have to work without any food at all.

I at once decided what was to be done.

On the first Saturday, when the cashier handed me my sovereign, I explained that I could not afford to employ the firm any longer, and that I was not coming to their offices any more.

My employers were indignant at my way of putting the point, and complained that by leaving so suddenly I was inconveniencing them.   I replied that they were inconveniencing me by starving me.

Once more I hunted for food and fuel in Fleet Street, and found an editor who bought a short story from me and gave me three guineas for it on the spot. Now I was in funds.   My prompt action in the City had already brought me two hundred per cent. profit.

An introduction from my brother, to the editor of " The Financial Review of Reviews "—I had studied finance among other subjects—brought me fifteen guineas for an article on investments.

That article concluded with a paragraph the humour of which was only seen by me.

" Capital," I wrote, " should never depend on the welfare of any one community, but should be spread over the earth's main divisions ; so that if one invest-ment should fail, the others might be ready to snatch the certain rise in some other part of the investment world. A patriotic investor might hesitate to finance the operations of foreigners. But the first meaning of capital is that it should bring in the highest income to its owner. Money knows no country, no politics, no party. Its function is to increase and multiply, and by so doing benefit the entire universe."

Trouble in the coal-mining world was threatening, and " The London Magazine " asked me for a twelve-guinea article, describing underground workings and conditions.

Guineas fifteen and twelve made me feel that fate was expressing its approval of my sudden break with the City of Starvation. Just at this time, too, an editor asked me to write a special article about Mr. J. E. Patterson's early struggles. This request was the strongest proof that Patterson's work had won fame. I knew that he possessed extraordinary gifts, and I was delighted at the chance of saying so to the wide world.

The looming general coal strike of 1912 interested me both from the large social issues involved and the small personal view. I remembered that I had written two novels with mining scenes in them, " Son of Judith " and " Maurice."

Early in 1912, I sent " Son of Judith " to the offices of George Newnes. The publishers offered me twenty pounds for the rights of a cheap edition. I never would sell my " rights." I preferred to accept a few pounds as advance royalties.

" Maurice " was sent to several houses. Dent, the publishers, made me an offer of twenty pounds in advance on a two-penny royalty if I would allow them to include " Maurice " in *Everyman's Library.* The idea of seeing my book in that famous collection appealed to me strongly. I regarded the suggestion as an offer of immortality. Hutchinson offered to publish the novel in a sixpenny edition, and I, desiring it to be read by the ordinary public, agreed.

At the same time I wrote many mining sketches which appeared in " The Daily News," " Daily Chronicle," " Daily Mail " and " Reynolds's News-paper." Other stories and articles were bought by Cassell and Company's press agents, who asked me to write a mining serial story for sixty pounds. I agreed. I was busy.

My indignation with the City seemed to have re-awakened my gift of invention. I felt able to write any mortal thing, except poetry—which is immortal.

All my writing was done in my den of a bedroom on the first floor of 32 Langham Street. An Austrian boy brought up my breakfast to me in bed. To no one in the house (every floor of which was tenanted by foreigners) did I speak, except to the boy, during the twelve months of my stay there.

My bed was small, but it almost filled my room. A chair, a flower-table which I used for writing, and a mirrored mantel-piece which I used for shaving, were my furniture.

The darkness of my room was lessened to some extent by a window.

Outside the window were the conveniences of a

dress-making shop, and young women were continually running up and down stairs ; while over the roofs came the hooting and scratching of motor-'buses, the weight of which as they passed made our house tremble.

Down at my home there was a huge, Eisteddfod pavilion, erected to hold thirty thousand people. I longed to have such a building for my study. My idea of a writing-room was a great, spacious palace, with a lofty dome, and all inner rooms taken away. There should be no street, industrial, or domestic noises near me to frighten away ideas ; because ideas are as shy as fairies who will only play and dance to the music of pastoral silence. Nor should there be any ornaments or pictures on the walls ; because decorations are as disturbing to the imagination as noises are to thought. But I would have countless windows all around me, letting in sunshine, with high mountains seen everywhere, and a brook running through the middle of the vast hall, close to my writing-table, and a blackbird singing on the topmost twig of a tall tree beside me.

Destiny decreed that I should write in a dark hole, with the dirty backs of high buildings all around me, shutting me in as completely as if I were scribbling at the bottom of a well, like the gloomy ghost of truth.

My day began at eight, finished at eight, the size of my den in feet was eight by eight, and my rent in shillings was eight. Troubadour, the music magician, said that I lived in the figure eight.

As soon as the manuscript of my serial story was delivered to Cassell's, they asked me to let them have another. I agreed, and, feeling the need of change, transported myself and my papers and pens, to 27 Downshire Hill, Hampstead. I did not wish to leave London at the time, as I had joined the Ancient Order of Hibernians, and found a great deal of pleasure in going round the suburbs speaking at meetings for the organization.

When the second serial was ready, Cassell's asked for yet another.

But I, having fifty pounds clear, with all debts paid, had decided to carry out an idea of my own. I declined to write the third story.

With my fifty pounds I began on a daring plan, the object of which was to secure attention for my comedy. In that play all my hopes were rooted. I still most firmly believed that the script was my fame and fortune lying idle, rejected and neglected.

After much deep thinking, I said :

" I will get this comedy produced at a West End theatre. How ? Out of the play I will make a novel, and get a publisher for it. The novel shall be a success, shall draw attention to the stage value of the situations, and some manager shall be influenced to such an extent that he will produce my comedy."

With only my own view to bear out the right or wrong of such a conclusion, and taking all the risk of using up my fifty pounds on a notion that might be utterly false in reasoning, I wrote, during the autumn of 1912, " The Perfect Wife," and the first publisher to whom I sent the manuscript accepted it.

In the interval between acceptance and publication, all my funds melted.

Sad news came to me from Percie. His wife had died suddenly. I went down to Wales to her funeral. She was one of the finest-natured women I had ever known. She had always loved to see her house full of her husband's friends.

At my new address in Hampstead I finished " The Marriage Contract," sent it round, and a publisher asked me to call and talk about terms. He made me an offer. I accepted it, signed the contract, and received a cheque for fifty guineas there and then. " The Marriage Contract " which, during four years, had been rejected by every publisher in London had found a home after all. I was pleased.

" The Perfect Wife " came out during the autumn of 1913. Bruerton, who had disapproved of my plan, opened the volume carelessly, scoffing at it and me. He began it in the middle and read backwards to the first page. Then he read it from the first page to the last. That night I was playing cards at the top of his house with Horace (the actor), Willie (the motor-car dealer), and Bob (the melodramatic play-writer's secretary). Bruerton came running up to us with " The Perfect Wife " in his hand, and said, pointing at me :

" Look at that damned Keating ! Do you know, you fellows, that you're playing cards with a great man ? He's written ' The Perfect Wife.' "

No book of mine had been so well reviewed as " The Perfect Wife " was. Many reviewers who, apparently, had never heard of me or my expectations, laid stress on the stage qualities of my dialogue and scenes ; and, following a big and good-natured review in

" Reynolds's Newspaper " written by a man who did not know me, a letter reached me, through the publishers, from a prominent agent for plays, saying that he had read " The Perfect Wife," and was of opinion that it could be turned into a stage comedy. He ended by asking if I would allow the book to be dramatized ?

Such a letter I had expected. The novel had drawn attention to the play. More letters of the same kind came to me by every other post. But the first note had appealed to me strongly.

The original stage version on which my novel had been based, was put into the agent's hands. In a few days, he informed me that Messrs. Vedrenne and Eadie of the Royalty Theatre wished to know if I would adapt certain scenes to suit Miss Gladys Cooper ; and, if so, they would produce the play almost immediately, with that popular actress in the cast.

Frankly, I did not think that the part assigned to Miss Gladys Cooper would suit her. The agent asked me to go and see her acting in the play then running at The Royalty. I paid a half-crown for a place in the pit, and stood against a pillar, analysing her performance. I informed the agent that her temperament and talent would not do for my comedy. He said : " For Heaven's sake, don't tell Vedrenne that ! "

An interview with Mr. Vedrenne and Mr. Eadie had been arranged. Mr. Eadie was enthusiastic about the play. Mr. Vedrenne took it for granted that I would make the suggested changes in the script, under the guidance of a dramatist, who was said to be a master in stage-craft.

My opinion was that the proposed alterations would weaken the play. They argued that they had had a wider experience than I in such things.

Many factors had to be seriously weighed by me. Here was the chance of a lifetime, perhaps ; and I ought not to cavil at details. The object of all negotiations is achievement. I wanted the negotiations in this case to achieve the production of my comedy.

Mr. Vedrenne's terms seemed to me to be generous. He offered me two hundred pounds on signing the contract and a royalty rising from five per cent. to twelve and a half per cent. I signed the contract, and attended rehearsals.

The name of my heroine was a source of great trouble to everybody but me. Her real name was Julie. But one wanted it to be Nancy, another wanted it to be Norah, and Miss Cooper wanted it to be Peggy. Her request was final. My heroine was rechristened Peggy.

Next came fretting about the title. Mr. Vedrenne had a superstition that the word " Perfect " in a title was unlucky. After weeks of searching, Mr. Eadie suggested " Peggy and Her Husband." So from being " The Perfect Wife " my play became " Peggy and Her Husband."

For me the great mountain of achievement towered gloriously above all such small anxieties. The date and year fixed for production was February 28, 1914. I had finished the comedy in April 1909, and had given five years as the period within which my work would be staged.

Again, I had begun to learn how to write novels in 1895, and had allowed five years as my testing time. My first novel, " Son of Judith " was accepted in 1900.

In both cases, play and novel, my judgment and patience had been rewarded.

Mr. Vedrenne told me privately that he believed my comedy would be a brilliant success, reminded me that my first chance had come from him, and asked me to give him the option of accepting my next play. I was only too pleased to do as he requested, because I felt that he had been just and splendid in his dealings with me.

He was an important manager who had produced Bernard Shaw, Arnold Bennett, Granville Barker, and Continental authors of high distinction. He had paid Shaw, and some of the others, five thousand pounds a year each, in royalties. He advised me not to allow myself to be led into evil ways by the surfeiting wealth which would now be at my disposal.

I grew afraid. Five thousand pounds a year seemed to be a lot of money at that time. As most persons would have done in my circumstances, I had already planned out a worthy life, when riches should come to me. I needed very little, and believed that the rest should be given away. But I was disturbed because I had observed that while people cannot change stones into sovereigns, gold almost always changes human hearts into stones.

A week before my play appeared, London streets and railway stations were placarded with posters bearing my name in huge red letters. About the same time, "The Marriage Contract" was published, and this book, despised for nearly five years, reached a second edition within five weeks.

But my comedy filled my thoughts. Whether it ran for a year and a day, or only a day without the year, nothing could deprive me of the achievement itself. Whatever might happen, my chance of success, at least, had been given to me.

Could anything more clearly prove that in the world of imagination all were welcome if they could establish a claim to be heard ? No privilege, no caste, no bribe had I as a key to the door of the charmed circle. I was an utter stranger yet I was admitted. The humblest and poorest scribe could have got in as I did. Then let my tribute be large and generous to the glory and reality of the Republic of Letters. Without friends, money, or influence of any kind beyond that which had been won by my books, a play of mine had reached the most difficult point on the modern road to fame and fortune : the stage of a popular West End theatre. Thousands of dramatists, men and women, were offering their souls for such a prize.

For the night of production, I asked my best and kindest friends to sit with me in the author's box— Percie, and Bruerton and his wife (Frank Southwood had gone to Australia). Countless other friends and acquaintances of mine were among the fine throng that crowded to the theatre doors. When my companions and I arrived, numbers of gleaming motorcars were rushing to the Royalty steps, with well-known men, and fashionable women in exquisite dresses, passing into stalls and boxes.   My surprising career had suddenly leaped up to a brilliant climax.

A rain of gold might pour down upon me from that night forward. I hoped that the yellow showers would not fall for me alone, but would nourish the root of charity in my heart.   For myself I asked only enough to allow me to do my best work in tranquillity. Fame might come to me.   That likelihood did not greatly interest me.   Candidly, I had come to regard fame as nothing more than being a somebody among the nobodies.

To me, the prize I had gained appeared to be only distinction for its own sake—the justification of my belief that a nobody might be a somebody.   My success would, I hoped, make the world believe what I believed, that there was no such thing as superiority in the possession of wealth, titles, social advantages, or education, and no inferiority in poverty, social disadvantages, or ignorance ; that the notion of class was false and foolish ; and that not only death, but life also, made one human being just as good as another.

INDEX

SIMPKIN, MARSHALL, HAMILTON, KENT AND CO., LTD.